ON LIBERTY AND
ITS ENEMIES

ON
LIBERTY
AND ITS
ENEMIES

✦

ESSAYS OF
KENNETH MINOGUE

Edited by Timothy Fuller

ENCOUNTER CLASSICS
ENCOUNTER BOOKS
NEW YORK · LONDON

First American edition published in 2017 by Encounter Books,
an activity of Encounter for Culture and Education, Inc.,
a nonprofit, tax-exempt corporation.
Encounter Books website address: www.encounterbooks.com

Manufactured in the United States and printed on
acid-free paper. The paper used in this publication meets
the minimum requirements of ANSI/NISO Z39.48-1992
(R 1997) (*Permanence of Paper*).

FIRST AMERICAN EDITION

LIBRARY OF CONGRESS CATALOGING-IN-PUBLICATION DATA

Names: Minogue, Kenneth R., 1930–2013, author. | Fuller, Timothy, 1940–
  editor.
Title: On liberty and its enemies : essays of Kenneth Minogue / edited by
  Timothy Fuller.
Description: New York : Encounter Books, 2017. | Includes bibliographical
  references and index.
Identifiers: LCCN 2016040428 (print) | LCCN 2017006451 (ebook) | ISBN
  9781594039133 (hardcover : alk. paper) | ISBN 9781594039140 (Ebook)
Subjects: LCSH: Liberty. | Individuality. | Political correctness. |
  Education, Higher—Aims and objectives.
Classification: LCC JC585 .M7796 2017 (print) | LCC JC585 (ebook) | DDC
  320.01/1–dc23
LC record available at https://lccn.loc.gov/2016040428

PRODUCED BY WILSTED & TAYLOR PUBLISHING SERVICES

CONTENTS

Kenneth Minogue

(1930–2013)

Professor Timothy Fuller

Kenneth Robert Minogue was born September 11, 1930, in New Zealand and died June 28, 2013, as he was returning from a meeting of the Mont Pelerin Society in the Galápagos Islands. His family moved to Australia, where he attended the University of Sydney without completing his degree. He resumed his studies in England, earning a BSc in economics with first-class honors at the London School of Economics (LSE). After a brief period lecturing at Exeter, he was invited by Michael Oakeshott back to LSE, where he taught for forty years until his retirement in 1995. Minogue was a man of multiple talents and a prolific writer. He wrote or edited many books and a vast array of articles and reviews, and he developed a six-part television program in 1986. At his death, he was president of the Mont Pelerin Society. A Euro-skeptic and a leader of the Bruges Group, he was also a trustee of Civitas and active in the Centre for Policy Studies. He was the first president of the Michael Oakeshott Association (2001–2003). He received the Centenary Medal from the Australian government. And as I mentioned, he was a distinguished teacher and scholar at the London School of Economics.

Ken was my friend and colleague for thirty-four years. His colleague and fellow New Zealander Robert Orr introduced us in

April 1979. We pretty quickly discovered an intellectual affinity and, when I was an academic visitor in the Department of Government at LSE starting in the fall of 1979, we became devoted friends. I regularly stayed with him on my semiannual trips to London. He visited Colorado College a number of times until heart problems in 2006 precluded his coming to Colorado Springs (at 6,200 feet above sea level), though our meeting at lower altitudes both in the United States and Europe continued. For three years (2003–2005) we co-taught a summer course on British politics, based at LSE, for Colorado College students.

Ken was notably a friend and colleague of Michael Oakeshott at the LSE. A passage in Oakeshott's *On Human Conduct* describes Ken's approach to life:

> Hidden in human character, there are two powerful and contrary dispositions, neither strong enough to defeat or to put to flight the other. The one is a disposition to be "self-employed" in which a man recognizes himself and all others in terms of self-determination; that is, in terms of wants rather than slippery satisfactions and of adventures rather than uncertain outcomes. This is a disposition to prefer the road to the inn, ambulatory conversation to deliberation about means for achieving ends, the rules of the road to directions about how to reach a destination, and to recognize that
>
> > The road runs always to the sea
> > 'Twixt duty and delight.
>
> . . . The other is a disposition to identify oneself as a partner with others in a common enterprise and as a sharer in a common stock of resources and a common stock of talents with which to exploit it . . . outcomes are preferred to adventures and satisfactions to wants . . . preferring . . . security to the insecurity of seeking to satisfy chosen wants.[1]

Ken exemplified Oakeshott's self-employed man who understands himself as self-determining and self-regulating, who welcomes adventures rather than depending on outcomes, who prefers the road to the inn and ambulatory conversation to deliberation over means for achieving utilitarian ends; he subscribed to the rules of the road, but his destinations were his own business.

Ken's last book is called *The Servile Mind* (2010). It is the pessimistic sequel to his 1963 book, *The Liberal Mind*. Both *The Liberal Mind* and *The Servile Mind* describe and dissect the ideal type of the security seeker in contrast to the friends of liberty, but they also show an evolution in Ken's thinking about the fate of liberty and individualism.

Ken was writing a preface to the new Liberty Fund edition of *The Liberal Mind* when we were scholars in residence together at Liberty Fund in Indianapolis in 1999. We discussed the conditions for the flourishing of liberty, and the threats to liberty, more than thirty years after the book's first appearance, though this was not our only occasion to do so. Ken's friends knew him as a cheerful and endlessly amusing conversationalist whose severe criticism of human foibles did not induce in him gloomy melancholy. But he was a realist about the human condition in the tradition of the Greeks and the Bible, and the occasional break from cheerfulness would occur. Consider this excerpt from his modern preface to *The Liberal Mind*:

> To revisit *The Liberal Mind* turns out to be something that provokes me to pessimism. In those optimistic days of yore I had confidence in the broad commonsense of my world. I wrote that the ideas of the liberal mind could never really dominate the thinking of any society, because "such institutions as armed services, universities, churches and cultural academies . . . have nonetheless a powerful impulse to generate non-liberal ways of thought." So far as the armed services are concerned, it has been said, not entirely face-

tiously, that we shall soon need wheelchair access to tanks. In universities, the fact that academic life requires active ability in students has been strongly qualified by a concern for irrelevancies such as sex or race. It is no longer just a matter of being intelligent. And the churches have largely given up any decent dogma in favor of finding a new role counseling and communalizing their diminished flocks. What future then for saints, soldiers, and scholars? They have all been boiled down into the soup of "generic man."

Ken's style was punchy and direct. Not only did he display no anxiety about his political incorrectness, he often emphasized it when the surrounding sentimentalism began to drown common sense. He was frequently active in politics, yet politics never fully absorbed him. Even when engaged *by* politics, he was never quite *of* politics. Here is his opening gambit in *The Liberal Mind*:

> The story of liberalism, as liberals tell it, is rather like the legend of St. George and the dragon. After many centuries of hopelessness and superstition, St. George, in the guise of Rationality, appeared in the world somewhere about the sixteenth century. The first dragons upon whom he turned his lance were those of despotic kingship and religious intolerance. These battles won, he rested a time, until such questions as slavery, or prison conditions, or the state of the poor, began to command his attention. During the nineteenth century, his lance was never still, prodding this way and that against the inert scaliness of privilege, vested interest, or patrician insolence. But, unlike St. George, he did not know when to retire. The more he succeeded, the more he became bewitched with the thought of a world free of dragons, and the less capable he became of ever returning to private life. He *needed* his dragons. He could only live by

fighting for causes—the people, the poor, the exploited, the colonially oppressed, the underprivileged and the under-developed. As an ageing warrior, he grew breathless in his pursuit of smaller and smaller dragons—for the big dragons were now harder to come by. (p. 1, italics in original)

In his essays, he sometimes speculated that the era of classic liberalism was an interim between the old monarchical orders and the emergence of a new, threatening age of minute bureaucratic regulation. Here is his opening observation in the foreword to *Politics: A Very Short Introduction* (1995), which generalizes his indictment to nearly all of the intellectual elite:

In politics things are real, and propositions are (more or less) true or false. People bleed and die. Politics, with difficulty, sustains the common world in which we may talk to each other, and philosophers who dissolve experience into perspectives, horizons, sensa, values, dominations, cultures, and the rest will destroy that common world. Politics is the activity by which the framework of human life is sustained; it is not life itself. The sceptical philosopher, the moral relativist, the rancorous academic social critic, the religious visionary, and the artistic seer have their place in our civilization, but their intrusion into politics has not been happy, especially during the last two centuries.

I have referred already to Ken's critical analysis of the modern intellectual mentality. Above all, Ken was a man of the university, a teacher and a scholar. He was passionate about protecting the integrity of the university as an independent center for pursuing the life of the mind. His skepticism about politics was at the same time his recognition that politics too has an independent character. He opposed the common tendency to disregard the features which distinguish these undertakings from each other and to mix them together in what he called "category mistakes." In *The Concept of a University* (1973), he summarizes the fundamental distinction:

> One of the primary distinctions between the academic and the practical worlds rests upon the simplest and most luminous of facts: that in a university, no one has to come to a conclusion upon which a decision must be based. A don can afford the luxury of allowing the evidence to dictate quite precisely what conclusion he will come to, and dons do, in fact, spend a great deal of their time explaining the reasons why nothing very substantial in the way of conclusions is possible. . . . In the academic world, conclusions simmer together with the evidence, and there is no point at which they can ever be detached from it. In the practical world, on the other hand, conclusions often outlive the evidence for them. Decisions have to be taken and minds made up . . . on what are, in academic terms, inadequate grounds. There is about the taking of decisions in the practical world an irredeemable element of improvisation which renders it necessarily, not contingently, subject to error. And it is the vast achievement of establishing universities as institutions to have created conditions of life in which this constant practical pressure towards the botched or best available conclusion has been neutralized. (86)

Ken knew, with T.S. Eliot, that there is no such thing as a lost cause because there is no such thing as a gained cause; we fight to keep something alive because it is worth keeping alive, not because we expect final victory. At the conclusion of his reflections on the university, Ken distinguishes the academic life from the life of the intellectual: although intellectuals are natural allies of the university, usually having been formed in them, their immersion in the practical world makes them dangerous allies. Intellectuals "are the source of those passionate ideas which periodically seize the imagination of the masses, sometimes even capturing governments, and then demand to be declaimed from the lecture rostrum as final truths" (222).

What then are we to do? "The only thing that universities ought to do is the only thing they can do: sustain the academic world." Ken meant that we must continually cleanse our conception of the university as it is attacked and invaded by alien powers. We need the peculiar experience of transcendence which the university offers, transcendence of "the most elusive and parochial of all provincialisms: that of the present moment" (223).

In the twenty essays selected here—written across more than fifty years—one will find a sustained commitment to the task of transcending the passions of the moment, allied with an indefatigable defense of liberty and individualism. Ken was engaged with politics but always with that detachment which reflected his profound awareness of the contingency, the transitory and self-contradictory character, of our opinions and our aspirations. He lived willingly and courageously in the tension between what we hope for and the unavoidable limitations of our temporal, historical context.

Ken was a friend of liberty and the liberal tradition in its classic sense, and an eloquent exponent and defender of what it means to be free. He was also an acute diagnostician of the ever-present threats to the practice of liberty. He exposed the perennial hostility to the demands of self-dependence and individual responsibility that dogs the commitment to liberty, hostility to the point of redefining what it means to be free as the opposite of individualism, redefining liberty as "liberation." These are in fact plans to be freed from being free, the graveyards of the unique achievement of the Western tradition. His analysis is reminiscent of such works as Erich Fromm's *Escape from Freedom* and Eric Hoffer's *The True Believer*. But he had a profounder idea than they of what freedom truly means. If politics is the activity at the intersection of our ideals and aspirations with historical contingency, to be free means to live in that tension and to resist those who claim to offer an escape route from that tension, who falsely promise a harmony which actually is the enemy of humanity. His 1984 essay, "The Conditions of Freedom and the Condition of Freedom," is a good place to start in order to gain a picture of the themes running through all of his writings. On the one hand, suitable historical conditions—the rule of law and impartial adjudication, property rights, limited government, the transformation of relations of command and obedience into relations of authority and subscription based on recognition—are needed for individual liberty to flourish; but the conditions of liberty do not guarantee the healthy "condition" of liberty for that "depends upon a morality of integrity rather than a morality of survival. . . . Europe has always contained people characterized by the courage to sustain it. It has also contained an underworld of professional survivors—the equivalents of Falstaff and Good Soldier Schweik."

These essays consistently criticize "servility," "ideology," and "salvationism." The "servile mind" desires to be taken care of, to be regulated by a state bureaucracy and a welfare system which relieves one of responsibility for oneself but which demands in return the sacrifice of independent judgment and personal choice. Ideologies are abstract visions of perfected order, the appeal of which depends on refusing to attend to actual experience; ideologies present an "alternative reality" which is seductive until one suffers the destruction consequent on their attempted implementation. "Salvationism" is the belief, stemming from the radical enlightenment of the eighteenth-century, that there are no insuperable limits to the perfection of the human condition: wars to end all wars, making poverty history, eradicating "bourgeois" property rights and inequality, the withering away of the state, and so on. The premise of these movements is that the traditions of Greek philosophy, Christianity, and the rule of law—that complex emergence of the conditions under which responsible freedom became possible—stand in the way of entering the various versions of the putative promised land at the end of history. Once those obstacles are dismantled (de-constructed), so it is alleged, the way will be open to putting the struggles of humanity to rest.

The consistent theme of Ken's work, then, was to lay out clearly the historical conditions under which freedom became possible in Europe and its offspring, and to identify the threats to that unique achievement with which we are now confronted. These essays ex-emplify Ken's steadfast and courageous defense of liberty against its enemies.

NOTE

1. Michael Oakeshott, *On Human Conduct* (Oxford: Clarendon Press, 1975), 323–325.

ON LIBERTY AND
ITS ENEMIES

A Fable of Time and Class

SPRING 1961

There have been times when men drew their values from Tradition, or from God, or from the State, or from some transcendental realm beyond the reach of experience. While all these sources of valuation remain, they are now overshadowed by a comparatively recent innovation: The Future. The present is merely subsidiary to this, the only unchallengeable absolute of the century.

As a result, the typical man of the twentieth century is a diagnostician. He is a man with his finger on the pulse of his society. The instrument he uses for his diagnoses is not the stethoscope but the theory, and the theory provides him with trends. This intellectual diagnostician is looking for the diseases which sociologists, in particular, have discovered: conspicuous consumption, other-directedness, power-elitism, organization manhood and so on. Such an intellectual can be extremely subtle, and does not even hesitate when confronted with the paradoxical diagnosis of an Alexander Herzen: "We are not the doctors, we are the disease." Flanks may be turned, but never the corner to understanding.

Kenneth Minogue, "A Fable of Time and Class." This article is reprinted with permission from the publisher of *American Scholar* 30, no. 2 (Spring 1961): 203–210. Published by the Phi Beta Kappa Society, www.jstor.org.

Only those who take their analogies from history will *not* find this strange. To them it is clear that civilizations go through various phases of a cycle, from youthful freshness to mature development, and finally on to a stage of dissolution characterized by morbid self-consciousness.

Yet it is strange, and has raised the question: Why has European civilization suffered such a signal lack of confidence precisely at the moment when its powers have enormously expanded? Is this a genuine illness, or a form of hypochondria? A wealth of literature has concentrated upon the related phenomena of totalitarianism and two big wars as demonstrating that something is obviously wrong. No one can dismiss this kind of answer; yet even here it is not impossible that we have been somewhat overimpressed by mere bigness. The twentieth century has no monopoly of nastiness; but its nastiness is certainly more efficient.

The theologian also has a particular explanation. Our increased power over nature and each other has alienated us from knowledge of God, and from the humility that is essential to a sane and balanced life. Anxiety is no substitute for humility. This is a voluntarist explanation, offering us an escape route if we renounce our errors. Theologically-minded historians like Toynbee can combine explanations, resting upon the vital (and false) premise that decadence is something that characterizes not merely some activities within a society, but the whole society itself. The study of past civilizations permits the generalization that technological vitality and political expansion are signs that the last phase in the cycle of civilization is upon us. Since decadence is to us what impotence is to an aging rake, we worry about it.

There is one further diagnosis of the century that needs to be cited here because of its logical interest: the view that the main characteristic of the present epoch is that of change and transition, or in other words that it has *no* distinctive character. We are moving from a past we know to a future that will be stable, but we are simply in motion. This thesis is clearly the product of living in the future (which is much the same thing as creating fantasies), but it is popular, particularly among those who wish to persuade us into something.

The genesis of this kind of Futurism may be indicated in the form of an intellectual fable.

Once upon a time, when essences were as secure as kings on their thrones, there were three classes: an aristocracy, a proletariat and a bourgeoisie. They were distinguished by their conception of time. The aristocracy lived in the past, for the simple reason that it was the class of tradition and had nothing to hope for. The proletariat lived in the present because it knew little and cared less about the past and was too depressed to have much hope of the future. If a member of the proletariat acquired some money, he had a good time while it lasted and returned to poverty when it was spent. This characteristic made most lovers, and some artists, spiritual members of the proletariat at various stages of their lives, no matter what their class of origin. And, lastly, there was the bourgeoisie, and it was the class of the future. Since it was moving up in the world, it wished to repudiate its inglorious past. But even the present seemed inconsiderable compared with what the bourgeoisie expected to achieve. It believed in working now for pleasure later, and its slogans were thrift and industry. As time went on, it became the rich and prosperous member of this family of classes.

But two things eluded the bourgeoisie. One was fulfillment, and the other was prestige. Fulfillment eluded it because of the elementary fact that the future never turns into the present. Just as, in evolutionary terms, creatures are presumed to have lost organs that they failed to utilize, so it was with time. Those who lived in the future ended by losing the present. Like the poor, the future is always with us, but it is usually a generation away. The bourgeoisie found that no matter how much time passed, it was still working for the future. And even the success that attended the efforts of the bourgeoisie (and it was a dazzling, if never completely satisfying, success) simply reminded it that one can look to the future not only with hope, but also with fear.

Prestige also eluded the bourgeoisie. Its young were rebellious and impatient for fulfillment; they took a long time to settle down to working for the future, of which each generation had a rather different conception. Prestige went to the heroic, the beautiful or the pious, and the bourgeoisie were none of these things.

In spite of these failures, the bourgeoisie grew and grew, and, perhaps in revenge, it turned cannibal and ate up its rivals. Only scraps remained of the proletariat and the aristocracy. This development was not unexpected, since while no one could imagine a society in which everyone was aristocratic or everyone proletarian, it was quite possible to imagine an almost exclusively bourgeois society. The bourgeoisie was the only class which claimed that its moral code was suitable for everyone. So everyone lived in the future, and in proportion as their hopes increased, so also did their fears.

In an agony of masochism, they invented new instruments of self-torture, such as the social sciences and statistics. The social sciences invented new things to fear and statistics showed precisely the rate at which bad things would get worse. Given the central obsession of change, to which everything directed attention, people began to suffer the sensations of an inexpert rider astride a runaway horse. All they could do was to reason that the horse must have stood still sometime, in order to grow, and that it would have to stop sometime, else it would drop dead.

Some such fable as this lies behind many serious cultural histories whose main intent is to explain our present situation. What limited plausibility the fable has derives from the fact that ways of life (distinguishable in terms of time conceptions) were once approximately co-extensive with social and economic class. The relation held good in spite of inevitable modifications due to such factors as age, temperament and mood. It no longer holds good because, however we may define classes, they have ceased in any sense to be related to time conceptions.

Those who are sensitive to change cannot resist attempting to predict its direction. By emphasizing the virtue of foresightedness and attacking the vice of complacency they may further impose this sensitivity on everyone else. The fact of change is then common ground, and political struggles are argued out in terms of persuasive predictions. What always accompanies such a development is a conviction of the novelty of the situation. Men have never before had to face so imponderable a future.

But that, of course, is largely illusion. Some element of change is endemic in human life, and there have been many other periods when men have feared decadence and have been bewildered by their conviction of instability. Not infrequently this very conviction itself became the agent of further change, leading to further bewilderment, and so on cumulatively. It is indeed very difficult to shake off the feeling that the past really was as fixed as it looks in historical narrative.

Conversely, it may be doubted whether things do in fact change as much as they sometimes seem to. The evidence for the stability of human affairs is just as easily at hand. Even where change is most dramatic, there is always an undertow. The tide looks as though it will engulf everything, as science at one point looked as though it might engulf religion, but there is always the ebb. In social affairs, one might even propound a weaker version of the second law of thermodynamics: To every action there is a *nearly* equal and usually opposite reaction. Political traditions, for example, do not easily change simply because men wish it so. Whether we see the stability or the flux depends, to a large extent, on us.

Why then are we so sensitive to symptoms of change? To some extent the fable gives an indication of where we must look for an answer—namely, in the diffusion of attitudes that were once to be found primarily in one social class. An important vehicle of this diffusion was the historicist social theory, of which the best ex-

amples are Marxism and a belief in Progress. It makes little difference that few people now subscribe to such theories, their defects
having been fully exposed, for what haunts us now is not so much
the doctrines as the disposition to see events as symptoms. Old
theories never die, and they take a long time even to fade away. The
reason is simple. They become superstitions. Seeing the future as
more important than the present, because it will be the fulfillment
of what we do now, is the kind of superstition that drains reality
away from experience. The superiority of the future implies, for
example, that the ethics of the future will be superior, and this is
explicitly affirmed in Marxism. A living sense of the future cannot
help but spur us on. If it holds success, we will be encouraged to
hasten it; if it is thought to hold disaster, then we shall bend all our
efforts to avoid it. But the future is like the carrot in front of the
donkey. It is suspended from our own backs, and all we will ever
get is the exertion, not the carrot.

The vision of success in the future comes from successful control of environment in the past. This too is a trend: our control of
the world will continue to increase as it has done in the past. Perhaps, indeed, it will. But the rub lies in the simple word "our." It
is possible to argue that the first person plural pronoun is the most
dangerous word in our political vocabulary: who, in other words,
is Us? And who controls the controller? The Liberal solution to
this question is simple but wrong: namely that "we," by controlling
our own desires, will become increasingly rational and then our
control will become beneficent. But this is merely the pious hope
that everybody will become a liberal.

The Puritans, in a sense, began it all. How did they face the
prospect of disaster? Their usual procedure was to cleanse their
souls, purify their thoughts, and resolve to merit divine grace in the
future. We have followed them in this. Just as the anxious individual has his New Year Resolutions, so nations have their resolutions.
(June, July, and October are the months that spring to mind.) Every revolution proclaims that things are going to be different in the

future. This illusion may be termed the myth of the New Start, and it has given a new and dangerous significance to daydreaming. The sort of New Start that has absorbed most people over the past two centuries has been political. The history of France, especially, has been a long series of New Starts, interspersed with periods of panic, ever since 1789. Indeed the French have set out so often to reject the bad traditions of the past that the difficulty has been to find something new to reject. But rejection—starting anew with a purified spirit—is itself a tradition, namely puritanism.

Fear of future disaster usually turns into fear of present decadence. It is a pretty dim social philosopher who is unable to make out a case for the decadence of his own time. Trends are an invaluable help, and every event can be seen as a symptom. The defect of what might otherwise be an amusing intellectual pastime is that desperate fears suggest desperate remedies. The most important progeny of the modern obsession with decadence has been fascism: fear of decadence leads to the worship of will power. If we are falling short, then we must gird our loins for the big effort that will hurry us past the dangers in our path. Those who do not join in the effort are traitors to the cause; they must be coerced. Under the shadow of this kind of anxiety, the exercise of ordinary liberties begins to look like feckless complacency, and those who wish only to be left alone get accused of selfishness and indifference to the national interest. These more or less totalitarian strands in western thinking (always present in some form) now appear under the guise of sermons about our moral fiber, materialist inclination or economic weaknesses.

There used to be a vogue for displaying in shops and houses printed cards bearing the legend: "Don't worry. It may never happen." And so much of hope, fear and illusion goes into our conception of the future that it might even be safe to commit oneself to the proposition that the future never happens. But this line of thought can be refined even further. We can observe that the future is a quite mythical place, and that it is logically impossible to prefer anything in the present. *All* our choices are present choices. The archetypal form of the illusion that they are not is to be found in the practice of saving—whether one saves one's money, virginity, energy or anything else does not affect the situation. Saving is a form of voluntary deprivation that moralists have always recommended. Among the inducements they claimed for this form of behavior was a belief that the satisfactions surrendered in the present could ultimately be drawn out of the bank swelled with interest. We have already noted that, as a matter of experience, the Future never comes; we may now add to this discovery that it never was there in the first place. All that we can ever do is prefer one present policy (for example, thrift or chastity) to another present policy (for example, indulgence). We may have prudent reasons for our choice, but the choice is not one between present and future.

Any attempt to diagnose one's own time is doomed to futility, but it is an irresistible temptation. The myth of the Future is now, if not in decline, at least being threatened. The evidence of this is to be found most strikingly in the strength of conservative political forces at the present time. Some time in the seventeenth century, one class of European men suddenly awoke to the fact that the future was not necessarily like the past. They elaborated their notions of what it could (or must) be like and started rolling along in pursuit of their conceptions. Some time around now, people are beginning to feel that the future will be, in essentials, roughly like the past. Essentials are, after all, only what people choose to make them, and fashions in technology need not qualitatively change human life. Of course, all possible varieties of these opinions will long continue to co-exist, and the move toward conservatism, although it may be symptomatic of a desire for some sort of stable present, will not save us from worry over the melodramatic prophecies each year will undoubtedly bring forth. It is difficult, if not impossible, to distinguish irrational anxieties from rational prudence.

Yet politics, particularly, have been greatly modified. Democratic politics have always contained a large element of Futurism.

Political leaders have been rather like Lincoln Steffens, arriving perpetually from some new Moscow to announce: "I have seen the future, and it works." Only a very few years of prosperity have been needed to create a more influential kind of pronouncement: "I can keep the present going along nicely, thank you."

How to Make Trends
and Influence People

SUMMER 1961

A free society has often been seen as the social system that provides
the best conditions for education and the pursuit of truth. There is
much to be said for this view; but a free society can also be seen as
an excellent breeding ground for gullibility, along with such consequences as ignorance, panic and hysteria.

In traditional societies, custom determines most lines of behavior. Where it breaks down, coercion is used to unify a state. But in
democracy coercion is a sign of failure, and the result is the opening up of a great new frontier for the man whose technical skill is
persuading individuals to act in a required manner.

In modern democracies intellectuals like to divide up society
into the educated few and the uneducated masses. The uneducated
masses cause them a great deal of anxiety. Television, advertising,
horror comics—all of these furrow the intellectual brow as it con-
templates their evil effects upon a populace too uncritical to see
what is being imposed upon it. The modern intellectual is a man
who sees himself, upon rather scanty evidence, as the child in the

Kenneth Minogue, "How to Make Trends and Influence People." Sections of this
article are reprinted with permission from the publisher of *American Scholar* 30, no. 3
(Summer 1961): 323–331. Published by the Phi Beta Kappa Society, www.jstor.org.

fairy story who cried: "The Emperor hasn't any clothes on." But those who see the nakedness of others ought to be prepared to undress themselves once in a while. For the truth is that while an advanced education protects us against some crude forms of propaganda, it lowers our defences against others.

All propaganda conforms to one of two logical patterns which, in ethical terms, we may call the deontological and the teleological. The simplest form of deontological propaganda would be: "God commands you to do X." In a devout community, this form of persuasion is uniquely effective and there is no doubt that all modern propagandists look back wistfully to times when they imagined persuasion was so simple a matter. In the present time, however, divine injunctions about the Maidenform bra or the brand name on one's breakfast cereals would be regarded as out of place. In any case, "God wishes you to do X" obviously will cut no ice in a community of atheists, nor, indeed, in a community where different views of God exist. This emphasizes the defect of deontological forms of persuasion. They lose effectiveness from the moment that the skeptical rot has set in. In various forms—often where an abstract entity such as the State has been substituted for God—they sometimes reappear. The highest ingenuity recorded in the deontological tradition was that of Kant, who created command persuasion without a commander. The effect of a command without a commander is to make the persuasion less vulnerable to skeptics of one kind or another; but the result is so formal that its use is severely limited.

The main effect of democracy has been to put a high premium upon teleological persuasion. This technique starts from the undeniable premise that we all want things. Our wants establish hopes and fears upon which the persuader can play his tune. The logical form of this kind of persuasion is: "We all want X (which is some highly abstract entity like happiness or security), but we will get it only if we do Y." The persuader is here telling us how we can get more efficiently what we happen to want independently of his persuasion. In this formula, persuasion comes to look like expert guidance, and thus conforms to the first rule of all good persuasion: it should not look like persuasion at all. This is the technique used almost exclusively in the largest single branch of the persuasion movement, which is commercial advertising. So long as the device convincingly begins with what people want, it can make even the partial and subjective look like the impartial and objective.

The current intellectual version of this general technique is founded upon the trend. The trend here is simply a statement of any series of events forming a pattern amidst the flux of life. When projected into the future, the trend becomes a prediction. The number of possible trends is infinite, but the number that the persuader can use is more limited—he is looking for trends that can be connected with our hopes and fears. He offers us both fulfillment and salvation. He must show us desirable things to be gained and disasters to be averted. Both the desirable things and the disasters lie in the future, so he must predict them. The way to make his predictions convincing is to discover trends that seem to lead to them. Thus the technique of trend persuasion soon becomes the construction of a certain kind of future, which is both enticing and menacing.

Time is very important in the intellectual world that results. There are the mistakes of the past, from which we may learn; there is the crisis in the present, which forces us to act; and there is the question of survival and fulfillment in the future, which we must face. The persuader thus appears as someone more prudent and more longsighted than we are, and since he is purporting to describe an objective situation, his vested interest is not at all obvious. Indeed, there seldom is anything that might vulgarly be considered a vested interest. In the elevated sphere we are describing, vested interests are usually emotional, rather than material or financial.

This kind of persuader is generally an idealist. And he may move further away from the embarrassing logic of persuasion by seeing himself as a protagonist of a drama. Rather than a man with a policy to recommend, he may see himself a man of active virtue battling against a vice, to which he generally gives some such name as complacency or apathy. (The behavior described as "complacency" or "apathy" is an alternative policy, but its status is lowered if it is seen in negative terms.) If the persuader does take up this role, he may begin to outline a moral psychology in which the conception of will power plays an important part. The mistakes of the past, he is likely to say, resulted from no one "finding the will" to put them right; people preferred to drift. But now things have reached a crisis point, and therefore our survival is at stake.

The pronoun "we" is an outstanding feature of trend persuasion. By means of it, the reader or listener is beguiled into an implicit alliance with the persuader, and there are many general theories that can be called on to substantiate this alliance. "Any man's death diminishes me," wrote John Donne, and much political thinking has gone into elaboration of this view. Thus the theory of the common good has the effect of showing that no individual can retreat from his community. Or, to take a more extravagant example, the theory that "society is really the criminal" opens up many possibilities for the persuader (especially the more moralistic one) by asserting that crime cannot be eliminated until we "reform" ourselves. The effect of all such theories is to bring into the persuader's net the widest possible audience, and to infect it with a sense of duty and responsibility. The harassed citizen can no longer ward off these Ancient Mariners with an irritable: "It's none of my business." The eye of the persuader is righteous, as well as hypnotic.

Entrenched thus, the persuader can safely use his two key terms, "crisis" and "survival," as absolutes affecting everybody. They are, so to speak, the ultimate persuaders. If one asks: "Crisis for whom?" the instant reply is "for you." If one demands: "Whose survival is at stake?" then the answer is always "yours." Problems also acquire a curious kind of objectivity; they are always simply problems, or perhaps social problems, and they are equally everybody's business. In this way, the persuader has a moral claim upon the attention of everyone, and the inattention has become a sin. He can now present his trends—the increase of world population, the growth of delinquency, the incursions of communism, the new brazenness of homosexuals, et cetera—in the confidence of having a receptive audience.

The emotion that the persuader first hopes to arouse is that of urgency in the face of his problems. The ideal situation, in a sense, is therefore war, when such questions as survival are more plausible than in peacetime. When not using a problem-solution type of logic, the persuader is happiest when employing military metaphors. It is thus that we find ourselves now waging the cold war against communism, the war against want, the battle against crime, and even the persuader's battle par excellence, the fight against apathy. The contemporary importance of war has no doubt greatly affected the technique of trend-persuasion. War is habit-forming, and peace is confusing to many people who cannot deal with conflicting standards and feelings of guilt. Besides, war has demonstrated what immense things can be achieved "if we really set our minds to it." Thus the trend-persuader with an ambitious policy to recommend is offering us something far better than war, which, even with its incidental advantages, is a nasty and destructive business: he is offering us a war substitute, a despotic goal in terms of which life can be organized.

The trend in question here is voluntaristic; it contrasts a picture of what we can achieve with another picture of what will happen if we do not rouse ourselves. This kind of trend is now dominant. There was a time when the determinist trend, which sees the future as a wave in which we either swim or drown, was more striking, and threw up such classic instances of the genre as the *Communist Manifesto*. But the determinist trend has been weakened at all levels. Intellectually, it crumbled along with its close relation, historicism. And as a vehicle of popular support, generating fanaticism, it was most successful when it was virtually without rivals.

But when the market place was full of persuaders, peddling equally inevitable but rather different trends, the populace became bored and skeptical, and when the ebbing passions of a generation were no more, the determinist trend disappeared from the scene. It may return, but not for some time.

The result has been to make the voluntarist trend the more convincing, since the intellectual attack on historicism was an attack on inevitability. If nothing was inevitable, then we might be aroused to do anything. Many dangers remained. Furthermore, persuaders using the voluntarist trend could co-operate in a way not open to those favoring determinism. They could join in attacking complacency. They could infiltrate the democratic conscience with a conception of the good citizen as a man who understood the Great Issues of Our Time, giving their own content to this promising slogan. Perhaps their greatest achievement in this direction was to suggest that one battle could be won by sending people to fight another. Thus enterprising social investigators discovered that few young people read such authors as Kierkegaard and most adored Elvis Presley. This was obviously a problem. Its solution lay in getting the youth interested in the Great Issues of Our Time, and in convincing them that it was somehow adult, responsible and mature to sit around and chat about the problem of nuclear energy or of the world food supply.

Now one might well imagine that most people react to this by shrugging their shoulders and going about their own business, more or less unaffected. And this, no doubt, is just what most people in fact do. Yet a substantial number are drawn into this persuasive movement, whose symptoms are a feeling of guilt about complacency and strong moral feelings about the duty of responsibility to others. How do we explain this susceptibility?

The reader trained in the social sciences will already have observed that what has been outlined as a technique of persuasion is identical, if certain refinements are neglected, with the operative rules of much social science. It used to be thought desirable to create something called a "value-free social science" in which the trends would simply be identified, measured and related, whilst their "use" was left to "policy framers." Thus the social scientist thought he was concerned with *means* (which trends in the context of a policy can become) whilst others decided what the ends ought to be. One main difficulty of this position was the sheer psychological impossibility of the separation. Trends wouldn't lie down. They became predictions, or justifications, or refutations of something the moment they were detected. Great numbers of social scientists were, in any case, too confused to tell the difference between a practical problem and an intellectual one. Further, trend detection became as habit-forming as taking drugs. Just as the neurotic scrutinizes the faces of his associates for signs of hostility, so those who formed the trend-habit could not help scrutinizing everything they encountered for signs. The discovery of trends even grew into an art form: the sociological best seller, in the tradition of Veblen, spread the habit. As Lionel Trilling has remarked, this form of social diagnosis took over some of the talent and much of the impetus that in other times has gone into the novel. This development flowed along with an obsession with change and insecurity; such a world is paradise for anyone with an inclination toward the voluntarist trend (and most of us do have such an inclination).

All this might mean that we had all become alert, responsible, democratic citizens; or, alternatively, that we had all become rather hysterical babes in a wood, looking for a gleam of light. What it would certainly indicate is a connection between gullibility on the one hand and the orthodox theory of democracy on the other. Somewhere between those responsible for policy in a society, who live in a world of speculations about the future, and those who care for nothing except their immediate and local life, there is a large class whose interest in social and political problems lacks the anchorage of direct responsibility. They are eager to do the right thing, and they have often been taught that their duty is to take an interest in world affairs. Normally they lack experience of these matters, and often their education has not made them discriminating about the printed word. They are, indeed, a valuable section of the community and they are not the least effective of checks on government. Perhaps for this reason, they often have an ingrained suspicion of politicians, yet their own political judgments are wildly erratic. They are decent, sympathetic and idealistic.

Their main fault is that they are prey to intellectual fashions, and fashion is the main guide to the vicarious worries they take upon themselves. A decade ago their primary worry was Communist aggression. More recently, it has been the prospect of total annihilation from Hydrogen Bomb warfare (with such allied worries as genetic effects). More recently still, the gap between arts and science, as related to perennial problems like food shortage and overpopulation, has come back into vogue. It is no doubt true that any man's death diminishes me, but this doctrine can easily be taken to the verge of hysteria. No one would deny that these are important questions opening up explosive political and social possibilities; but for most of the inhabitants of Western countries they are vicarious ones. Short of disrupting his normal life (which he is not prepared to do), the average man can do very little about them. But, feeling a compulsion to act, he chooses substitute acts— passing resolutions, going to meetings, writing letters to papers— and imagines that he is "doing something about it." This sort of mind is found most prevalently, although by no means exclusively, in the political tradition of liberalism.

Trend persuasion is, then, a modern and popularized version of the kind of calculations that politicians have always had to make combined with an extraneous philanthropic moral theory. How should one estimate this development? One consequence is to keep democracies alert and flexible in (to use a persuasion cliché) "a changing world." Yet trend persuasion is also subject to fashion, and therefore likely to distort social and political policies according to the (often misguided) emotions of the moment. A vicious circle operates: the more trends we discover, the more insecure we feel; and the more insecure we feel, the more we go on looking for trends. If the anxiety grows too much for us, we may become easy victims of the charlatan who offers us a panacea. Logically speaking, this road leads on to totalitarianism, the attempt to find a total solution for a bogus problem. But this would be to take trend persuasion as itself a trend.

The problems are always new, the solutions always old. This is the fact that must make us suspicious of persuasion. We imagine that experience presents us with problems. And *then* we start to seek solutions. Whatever the weaknesses of this belief, it yet determines the way in which the persuader presents his case. Historically, however, the solutions always come first. Seldom in the twentieth century have we lacked prophets telling us about the need for competitive industry, the duties of international philanthropy, better distribution of world production, the need for more science in education and the value of the lash as a deterrent. Such policies are part of the air we breathe, and as such rather too familiar to rouse us very much. They are much more striking if they can be presented not as possible policies we might follow, but as *solutions* to problems. The persuader is thus not a man who must find solutions for problems, but one who must construct problems to fit pre-existing solutions.

It remains to consider the possible distortions that persuasion might have on social life. If society be considered as a complex of activities and institutions—religious, artistic, industrial, commercial, academic, et cetera—then the character of the society will emerge out of their relations. But those institutions not only cooperate; they also compete (financially, morally, intellectually, for example) and each tries to carve a larger future for itself. Now if into this context of struggle one introduces ideas of the "great issues of our time," then it is clear that some institutions will be strengthened and some will be weakened. If the great issue of our time is how to prevent malnutrition among Asians and Africans, then the events of scholarship must seem very far from the battle.

Who would elucidate a text of Chaucer when his duty lies out in the monsoon region? How futile experiments in painting technique must look when the survival of the species is in question! Artistic movements are implicitly reduced to the role of entertainment, and a Flaubert torturing himself for a week over the structure of a sentence can only seem absurd. Universities have traditionally followed the trail of truth; but truth is an irrelevance in a world crying out for "science in the service of man." Here is a menace more insidious to religious institutions than any debate about evolution. Industrialization, wrote one recent prophet, is the only hope of the poor—words that echo an evangelical tract, and announce the discovery of a new religious truth.

This idealistic, persuasive movement might be compared to a wind sweeping across a landscape. Without the wind, the air grows fetid and stale. But if the wind blows too violently, and if the fixtures of the landscape lose their anchorage, then the wind becomes destructive. To talk of the "great issues of our time" as fashionable worries no doubt sounds cynical, yet it is important that we recognize the element of fashion their discussion contains, and that we also recognize and retain the large and valuable area of stability our institutions and traditions possess.

The persuader offers us "survival," an abstraction without content haunted only by that theoretical dinosaur known as the "common good." The fact that our plural and diverse Western democracies are still haunted by the ghost of the "common good" testifies to two related things. One is the strength of the trend persuasion movement, and the other is the resulting weakness of political and social studies.

The Modern Liberal's Casebook

SUMMER 1962

The story of Liberalism, as liberals tell it, is rather like the legend of St. George and the dragon. After many centuries of hopelessness and superstition, this new dragon-killer, in the guise of Rationality, appeared somewhere in the world about the sixteenth century. The first dragons upon whom he turned his lance were those of despotic kingship and religious intolerance. These battles won, he rested a time, until such questions as slavery and prison conditions and the state of the poor began to command his attention. During the nineteenth century, his lance was never still, prodding this way and that against the inert scaliness of privilege, vested interest or patrician insolence. But, unlike St. George, he did not know when to retire. The more he succeeded, the more he became bewitched with the thought of a world free of dragons, and the less capable he became of ever returning to private life. He *needed* his dragons. He could only live by fighting for causes—the people, the poor, the exploited, the colonially oppressed, the underprivileged and the underdeveloped. As an aging warrior, he grew breathless in his

Kenneth Minogue, "The Modern Liberal's Casebook." This article is reprinted with permission from the publisher of *American Scholar* 31, no. 3 (Summer 1962): 359–372. Published by the Phi Beta Kappa Society, www.jstor.org.

pursuit of smaller and smaller dragons—for the big dragons were now harder to come by.

What gives liberalism this dragon-killing image is its long series of fights—against despotically inclined monarchs like Charles I and George III, against slave-owning and racial intolerance, against the persecutors of a Dreyfus and a Lattimore, against corruption and intolerance and indifference of suffering. Liberalism as a political movement means this kind of political behavior—struggles lit up at intervals by rhetoric about liberty.

For intellectuals, liberalism is a political theory closely linked these days with such democratic machinery as checks and balances in government, an uncontrolled press, responsible opposition parties and a population that does not live in fear of arbitrary arrest by the government. A liberal state is one where most actions of the government are taken with the consent of at least a majority of the population. A liberal political philosophy is a description of this kind of state, and an attempt to work out the general principles that can best rationalize it.

A good claim could be made for John Locke as the founding father of liberalism, even though the doctrine did not then have its present name. The term "liberalism" was imported from Spain early in the nineteenth century. In the early formulations, liberal philosophers build an edifice of doctrine upon the natural rights of man. Their successors, blooded by idealist criticism and Marxist social theory, admitted that the "individual" was an abstract and implausible hero for a political doctrine. Men, liberals now agreed, were largely molded by the social environment in which they grew, and to talk of "natural rights" bordered on metaphysical dogmatism. Indeed, as time went on, liberals did not merely admit their error; they positively rushed to embrace the corrections that Marxists and Idealists forced upon them—for reasons that should become clear. Out of this intellectual foray emerged modern liberal doctrine, representing political life as the struggle by which men make their society rational, just and capable of affording opportunities for everyone to develop his own potentialities.

But liberalism is not only a political movement and a political philosophy; it is also a moral character. Liberals are tolerant. They dislike recourse to violent solutions. They deplore stern penal methods for keeping a population in order, and they disapprove strongly of the death penalty. They have rejected the stern patriarchal order that Europe has inherited, and they are critical of puritanism in sexual matters. They also deplore the heritage that has organized men into competing gangs called nation states which periodically rupture human brotherhood by savagely falling upon each other in warfare. Liberals are prepared to sacrifice much for a peaceful and cooperative world order, which can only come about by the exercise of great self-control and a talent for compromise. These are moral characteristics recommended to all men. Liberal social theory is frequently an attempt to discover the social arrangements that most encourage this kind of behavior.

We have still not exhausted the content of liberalism. For it is not only the habit of campaigning for reforms, not only a political doctrine and a moral character, it is also a special kind of hope. It not only recommends to us a political system of democratic liberty; it also tells us what will result from such a system. One result will be prosperity, for the energies of the people will be released from the varied oppressions of the past. Another result will be political stability, for one of the reasons why it is wise to permit political opposition is that otherwise discontent, forced underground, will turn nasty and foment rebellion. Parliamentary government based on popular consent will by definition produce what the people want, and people who get what they want are happy. Many of these fruits have indeed been plucked in the centers where liberalism originated—in the English-speaking world and in parts of the continent of Europe. In others, however, liberalism represents both the aspiration and the promise of these things—and one thing

more: that industrialized prosperity and power that have now en-
chanted most of the world.

This side of liberalism can be seen in its keen sensitivity to time,
the character that disposes it to serious use of such political terms
as reactionary and progressive. Even sophisticated liberals, aware
of the crippling arguments against historicism, are nonetheless
prone to believe in progress, because they have domesticated Victorian optimism into a general belief that progress means getting
more of what one wants. Thus for liberals "the present" means not
only everything that is happening now; it also means what *ought* to
be happening now. On the basis of this ambiguity traditional societies like the Yemen are described as "advancing headlong into the
thirteenth century." Time, like everything else in this social world,
is simultaneously a fact and an aspiration.

This, in general outline, is the subject matter with which we
are concerned. Its interest is partly intellectual, partly topical. It
is intellectual because political argument and social inquiry in the
English-speaking world are strongly colored with liberal assumptions and carried on in a liberal manner. It is topical because most
of us today are, in some degree or other, liberal. It is only the very
cynical, the unassailably religious and the atavistically conservative who have remained unaffected. Our concern is simply to inves-
tigate liberalism as a movement. It is neither to praise nor bury it,
but to consider what might be called its intellectual and emotional
dynamics.

What is distinctive of modern liberalism, in which the visionary
and hopeful element has in this century grown stronger, is a new
understanding of politics. Politics in earlier centuries by contrast
involved little more than the maintenance of a traditional structure. Occasionally some blinding vision, such as the recapture of
Jerusalem from the infidel, might captivate rulers and even provoke
widespread enthusiasm. But no ruler could commit his state to any
long-term objective, and the possibilities of social mobilization,

even for war, were severely limited by the independence and varied preoccupations of a most unservile nobility. This older view sees politics as something apart from particular visions, but constantly bombarded by them—pressed by those who envisage a tidy hierarchical system, or by those who dream of a population contentedly obedient to the church; for all important social activities generate visions of a society most suited to their demands.

The general features of medieval society were determined by the relations between the activities of worshipping, fighting and food-producing; within a complex system, poets and craftsmen, shoemakers and beggars all could find some room to work. As time went on, more and more people were drawn into the cities; here they produced goods and exchanged them. Some men became more interested in explaining the physical world, whilst others began thinking independently and heretically about religion and morals. A new range of activities grew up, and this led to different laws and social relations resulting from conflict between activities. One cannot pursue scientific inquiry if one is hampered by a dogmatic theological orthodoxy. One cannot follow a commercial life and grow rich if social life is constantly in ferment because of quarrels between teams of nobles. In this way activities come into conflict with one another, and as some weaken and others grow stronger, so politics change; and as politics change, so also do people.

Liberalism, however, has come more and more to see politics simply as a technical activity like any other. We first decide what it is that we want, how we think our society ought to be organized, and then we seek the means to our end. The politician must be an expert skilled in political means, and his ends must be democratically supplied to him by popular demand. This view of politics introduces a novel inflexibility both into the actual work of politicians and into the hopes we have of it. It means, for example, that all widespread problems turn into political problems, inviting a solution by state activity. It follows logically that peoples commit themselves to long-term planned objectives roughly as individuals commit themselves to New Year Resolutions. But while individuals may break their resolutions if they change their minds, peoples cannot be flexible in this way. Faced with backsliding, governments must coerce. They must control the climate of thought in which people live, and if necessary they must engage in large-scale and protracted repression to keep a populace consistent with what it seemed to want sometime in the past.

These consequences of considering politics as a technical activity are, of course, most fanciful if we consider Britain and America where liberalism is prevalent in all its fullness. But they are fanciful simply because the political traditions of those countries remain stronger than the prescriptions of liberal ideology, and because what the British and Americans declare politically that they want to do represents with some accuracy what they are in fact disposed to do. The consequences of a technical view of politics actually can be seen only in nonliberal countries with a totalitarian system of government. Here only force and propaganda can whip a reluctant or unenthusiastic populace into conforming to what is taken as the popular will.

But the fact that liberal theory does not have such dramatic consequences does not mean that it is without effect.

Liberalism is an ideology. We may define an ideology as a vision that, having a definite social location, interprets both past and present with a characteristic vocabulary, and from time to time generates remedies for what it identifies as defects. Ideologies develop out of common human moods. Most people at one time or another must have regarded social order as a miracle, considered men as being primarily selfish and subscribed to that unlikely cliché that "civilization is merely a thin veneer over our natural barbarism." Such moods are likely to make us conservative, unwilling to tamper with any institution that has worked in the past. But these moods do not develop into ideologies unless there is an important group of people—in the example of conservatism, usually those in established positions—for whom the mood is a justification of their

position. Similarly the kind of mood that makes people liberal—a
general hopefulness for the improvement of social life—no doubt
arises under many social conditions; but its flowering into an ideology appears to depend upon the growth of a large commercial
class. Once developed, of course, the ideology frees itself from the
mood and becomes, as Engels wrote, "occupation with thoughts as
with independent entities, developing independently and subject
only to their own laws." If we connect ideologies with moods, then
it will not be surprising that any objective discussion of them will
reveal both practical inadequacy and intellectual evasion.

   If ideologies picture for us the details of a world seen in a certain mood, they also seek to promote and encourage that mood.
Ideologies therefore are not to be found exclusively or even pre-
dominantly in the writings of political philosophers. We must look
further afield—to political discussion of current issues and to all
forms of narrative art—if we are to understand the emotions that
constitute liberalism and that are no less important than the arguments presented by liberal thinkers. We recognize liberalism in
a discussion of the claims that individuals may legitimately make
against the state; we recognize it just as surely in the cinematic
plot in which an enthusiastic reformer is pitted against a corrupt
and cynical authority. For liberalism is optimistic, constructive
and compassionate. It is optimistic, for example, in believing with
Paine that ignorance, once dispelled, cannot recur. It will recognize progress, but not regress. It is constructive in its constant
search for solutions, although it will not recognize that to some political problems there is nothing that can be called a solution. And
liberalism is compassionate by virtue of its overriding concern with
the happiness and the sufferings of individuals.

   Compassion may seem an odd emotion to attribute to liberalism. It was not conspicuous in the operations of the Whig lords
who largely engineered the 1688 revolution in England, nor in the
early economists who contributed so much to liberal attitudes.
Certainly there is little that is compassionate about the *laissez-faire*

system whose advocacy was long associated with liberalism. Yet even before the end of the nineteenth century liberal politics began to involve the state in welfare programs, converting the state from a threat to freedom into an agent of individual happiness. In the last half century this development has gone far to reunite liberals previously divided over whether political solutions should be individualist or collectivist. The sufferings of any class of individuals is for liberals a *political* problem, and politics is an activity not so much for maximizing happiness as for minimizing suffering.

Yet compassion and a disposition to relieve the sufferings of others can hardly serve to distinguish liberalism, for these emotions may be found among men and women everywhere. There is, however, an important difference between goodwill and compassion in the ordinary concrete situations of everyday life, and these emotions erected into a principle of politics. For liberalism is goodwill turned doctrinaire; it is philanthropy organized to the point of efficiency. If one seeks guarantees against sufferings, then one is ill-advised to look to the spontaneous sympathy of men and women. One must create a mechanism that impartially and comprehensively relieves suffering: a ministry to pay the unemployed, a medical service to care for the sick, and so on. Suffering is a subjective thing depending on individual susceptibility; politically, it can only be standardized. And it has been standardized, over a long period of time, by an intellectual device which we may perhaps call a suffering-situation.

The condition of child labor in nineteenth-century Britain or that of slaves in the United States exemplifies suffering-situations. In the case of child labor a powerful group of employers was ruthlessly using for its own purposes children who could neither understand what was happening to them nor do very much about it. Here was what everyone agrees was a wrong, and one that could only be changed by the disinterested goodwill and active intervention of a third party. Negro slaves were a similarly helpless group of people; although here the criterion of suffering was less conclusive.

It was easy enough to produce vicious cases after the manner of Harriet Beecher Stowe. But it was also possible to produce cases where the slaves were kindly treated and seemed content. The idea of suffering had to be supplemented by arguments about the immorality of allowing people to be born and to grow up dependent upon the arbitrary and unchecked will of a slave owner.

The point of suffering-situations is that they convert politics into a crudely conceived moral battleground. On one side we find oppressors and on the other a class of victims. Once the emotional disposition to see politics in this way is established, then we find people groping around trying to make the evidence fit. Of course people living in slums are miserable about it and want (the only alternative possible in modern societies) a clean well-equipped bourgeois household! Of course colonialism is an evil; look at what King Leopold did to the Congolese; look at all the African parties claiming independence; those who do not claim independence must be puppets of the colonial rulers, for we all know that colonialism is an evil! And so on. Politics proceeds by stereotypes, and intellectually it is a matter of hunting down the victims and the oppressors.

Suffering-situations may be extended even further, in most cases by generalizing from particular instances of suffering to the proposition that the institution is evil and must be reformed. But this line of approach is elastic enough to develop what we can only call the theory of implied suffering. This may be illustrated by the case of parents with delinquent children. Here the fact of delinquent behavior is taken to imply a history of suffering, since delinquency is explained in terms of unstable family circumstances and lack of love. Parents appear as potential oppressors. This use of the suffering-situation makes a number of assumptions we need not discuss here, the most important being the liberal assumption that virtues are natural (since man is spontaneously good) whilst vices are the result of some part of the environment.

Environmentalism is an essential feature of all suffering-situations. Victims are by definition the products of their environment, and they sometimes put to the test the purity of our rational concern by exhibiting unsavory characteristics. This complicates liberal moral reactions, for the ideal suffering-situation is one in which the victims can be painted as virtuous and preferably heroic —noble savages, innocent children, uncorrupted proletarians, freedom-loving struggles for national independence. But where caricatures of this kind break down, as they often have in the past, then environmentalism supplies a means of conserving liberal sympathy for the victims. The delinquency of victims is an index of the extent of their suffering.

Those who fit into the stereotype as oppressors, however, are not seen as the products of their environment for that would incapacitate the indignation that partly fuels the impulse of reform. Parents, for example, are taken as free in a sense in which children are not. Yet a logically consistent environmentalism (as far as that is possible) would invalidate this distinction; either we are all the products of our environment, or we are not. Similarly, the rich are free to mend their ways, whilst the poor are driven by the pressures of the society around them. This kind of illogicality is, of course, typical of ideologies and results from the attempt to explain and to persuade, all in the same breath.

So far we have treated suffering-situations as being composed of the two elements, oppressors and victims. But there is also the third element, those whose interests are not directly involved. Many of these people might agree with a liberal diagnosis of a social evil but remain passive on the ground that it was none of their business. Against this attitude, liberals have been able to assert the duties of democratic participation. This could be, and was, broadened into a general indictment of neutrals on the ground that those who do not help to remedy an abuse must share the responsibility for it. Child labor was not merely the responsibility of avaricious employers; it was a blot upon the whole community, especially those who, knowing about it, did nothing to stop it. This third element, led by the liberals themselves, was taken as entirely free of environmental pressures, and upon it rested the unrelieved burden of choosing to act or not.

Two other features of suffering-situations are worth noting. One is that the liberal attitude is entirely secular. It will not countenance theological arguments that suffering in this life is better passage to heaven than worldly prosperity. The entire game is played out on earth—a feature that is important, although seldom explicit, in discussions of capital punishment. It is partly this feature of liberalism that incurs theological disapproval. The Roman Catholic Church, for example, regards liberalism as a product of "that fatal and deplorable passion for innovation which was aroused in the sixteenth century, first threw the Christian religion into confusion, and then, by natural sequence, passed on to philosophy, and thence pervaded all ranks of society."

This Catholic position must, however, be seen as an attack primarily upon continental liberalism, a more dogmatic version of rationalism than is usually found in English-speaking countries. For Anglo-Saxon liberals theology is simply a different territory, on which they do not really have to pronounce.

Secondly, liberals choose to rely upon peaceful persuasion rather than upon violent means for the reform of the abuses that cause suffering. Liberalism is impossible without the assumption that all men are reasonable and will in the end come to agree upon the best social arrangements. There are, of course, some liberals who become impatient and advocate violent remedies. To this extent, however, they move outside the tradition of liberalism toward more messianic faiths. In general, liberals disapprove of violence, on the ground that it creates more problems than it solves. But their disapproval of the violence of others varies according to who carries it out. All left-wing revolutions are carried out by groups who make out their own credentials as victims, and liberals are likely to dismiss such violence with gentle regret. The violence of a Mao Tse-tung is more acceptable than that of a Chiang Kaishek, that of a Castro more than that of a Batista. The violence of left-wing revolutionaries is excused partly by the past and partly by the fu-ture—the past because violence is taken as an inevitable response to past oppressions, the future because revolutionary violence is conducted under the banner of hope: hope for the end of suffering, and the initiation of a new order.

Interpreting their behavior through the stereotype of the suf-fering-situation, liberals see themselves correctly enough as a mid-dle party. For one thing, they usually come from the middle class, or at least soon take on many middle-class attitudes. For another, they have often found themselves uncomfortably sandwiched be-tween derisively indifferent oppressors, deaf to appeals for reform, and men eager to solve the problem by means of violent revolution. Where political situations have polarized in this way—as they did in Russia up to 1917—then liberals have been reduced to political ineffectiveness. But in more sympathetic surroundings their influ-ence has been enormous, the greater no doubt because they have been able to present the dilemma: either carry out reforms volun-tarily, or be overthrown and lose the opportunity to do so.

Liberals are also a middle group according to their moral inter-pretation of political life; for while most of society has appeared as a complex of groups each struggling for its own interests, liberals alone have been a disinterested force for good, seeking merely to correct what all reasonable men recognized as evils.

Liberalism cannot be understood unless it is seen to possess an emotional unity of this kind. And about this it is extremely hard to maintain objectivity. For it is difficult to analyze the dogmatism and crudity of the stereotype without simultaneously seeming to imply that liberals were misguided in attacking suffering wherever they thought they saw it. Clearly they were not. The same problem recurs if we attempt to discuss the motives that led liberalism in this direction. All human behavior stems from a complex of mo-tives, and it is a simple propagandist device to justify or discredit a movement by pointing to "good" or "bad" motives. Yet we can-not understand either the political role of liberalism or its consequences unless we do consider its motives. For motives in men are movements in society. We cannot therefore simply accept the view that liberalism arises out of an uncomplicated passion for good.

All we need keep in mind at this point is the testimony of foes of liberalism. Its conservative enemies often like to attribute its power to the fact that it organizes the sleeping envy ever-latent in the bottom of the masses. From the Marxist side, the attack on motives takes the form of attributing liberalism to middle-class guilt. Marxists see liberalism as the desperate attempt of the more intelligent among the privileged classes to paper over the gaping contradictions of capitalism in order to preserve that system. Both Marxists and liberals deplore the condition of the proletariat. But while Marxists argue for the complete overthrow of the system that produced proletarian degradation, liberals can only offer steady doses of welfare, insufficient to cure the sickness but enough to discourage the proletariat from drastic remedies.

Neither of these views would affect the intellectual validity of liberal doctrine. But the Marxist view is interesting in explaining some features of the liberal attempt to involve everyone in the campaign for reforms and its insistence that all citizens share responsibility for any evil that exists in the community.

The ideology that we are considering may thus be seen as one concerned both emotionally and intellectually with the problem of suffering. What makes any intellectual structure an ideology is partly the fact that it has a particular appeal to some social group. Can we locate the liberalism in this way? The conventional answer, and the one propounded most assiduously by Marxists, is that liberalism is a bourgeois doctrine. Many historians of thought have correlated its rise with the rise of the commercial classes all over Europe. But whatever use this explanation ever had has long since evaporated in proportion as so-called bourgeois doctrine merely serves to expose the imprecision of class theory generally. In Britain or America one might say as well that conservatism was a middle-class movement.

Answers of this kind are much too crude to explain the social role of liberalism. Indeed, what is most evident about social movements and doctrines is that as circumstances change they fall into different hands. Throughout its long career liberalism has always retained a strong bias against established authorities, a bias that makes it a useful recourse for any group of insurgents. Further, most recent political struggles have involved bringing into politics groups that had previously taken little part in political struggles. It is not surprising therefore that liberal slogans are to be found most fervently upon the lips of the newly enfranchised, those who learn to think of themselves as the victims. Liberalism vies with nationalism for their adherence; but it is the weaker partner in this unequal struggle. For the newly enfranchised are impatient and are liable to turn to less self-disciplined movements than liberalism itself. They have learned a lively appreciation of their own sufferings, and they are looking for quick remedies.

The question of finding a social location for liberalism thus opens up many other questions. It reminds us that in talking of liberalism we are considering an abstraction; and that in treating it as a single movement we may be doing violence to the facts. But we may at least distinguish between those who, like the French intellectuals of the eighteenth century, believed that all men are born free and equal out of a consciousness that *they* were not being freely and equally treated and those modern liberals who adhere to the same belief simply because they consider others are not being so treated. The former group were very likely to change the moment they attained power, and their analogues will be found today in the leaders of various colonial liberation movements. The latter are those who consider themselves morally bound to become involved in any suffering-situation of which they are aware. These people are the most deeply involved in the liberal movement. They are the product of secure societies in which notions like decency and fair play are deeply rooted; in them liberalism takes on something like the heroic stature of a frequently defiant moral integrity.

It is precisely these people who are most clearly aware of what we may call the liberal paradox of freedom. It may be stated thus: Victims are not free, and in a hierarchical social system those at the bottom of the hierarchy will be victimized by those above. The road to freedom therefore lies in the destruction of all hierarchies and the molding of a society that is, in a certain sense, egalitarian. Yet in the modern world the steady erosion of traditional hierarchies has not produced states that are noticeably freer than those of the past. On the contrary it has produced a "dehumanized mass" subject to manipulation and control by commercial and political interests. This paradox has provoked only a half-realization from liberals themselves. They have evaded it by the use of two propositions. The first is that we live in an era of transition—in other words, we cannot yet judge what are the consequences of the disappearance of feudal and class hierarchies. And the other proposition is that the modern world has opened up a vast potential, whose use depends upon us.

The modern world is not, of course, the product solely of liberal policies and attitudes; the growth of industrial techniques and modern nationalism are both at least as important as liberalism. But liberalism, of all movements, has opened its arms widest and most promiscuously to modern developments, going so far as to regard whatever it dislikes in the modern world as being atavistic or unmodern. It would be a fatal irony if liberals failed to recognize that the domestic dragons have now become almost superannuated; for if we have not yet freed the princess, we are held back by barriers of a different kind—ones that cannot be understood in terms of suffering-situations.

Can One Teach "Political Literacy"?

JUNE 1979

In the burst of conscientious attention to the needs of society that appears to seize academics whenever the supply of students threatens their bread and butter, any discoveries about the usefulness of what they claim to know arouse a special interest. Would it not resolve many of the conflicts of today if the population at large were educated to the point of "political literacy"? A group of people in British public life have thought so and have published a report. Minogue however sets about this report with a profound scepticism and a deft and witty touch; his commentary, in which he predicts that the report will merely make of schools and universities "a breeding ground for quarrelsome bores," is almost unfailingly quotable. He dismantles the doubletalk that endows such terms as "neutrality," "activity," and "deference" with quite arbitrary merits and demerits, and castigates the report for its blindness to what it is feasible to teach and what is not. The context of his remarks is the current political scene in Great Britain; but their applicability to the proper treatment of cant in higher education, like the incidence of that phenomenon itself, is universal.

Kenneth Minogue, "Can One Teach 'Political Literacy'?" This article is reprinted with permission from UNZ.org. Published in *Encounter* 52, no. 6 (June 1979).

The news from the polls is bad. It turns out that people are very misinformed about politics. Some think the Conservatives are the party of nationalisation, others that the IRA is a Protestant organisation. Lots of people never seem to know the name of the prime minister. Some think he was called Harold, but aren't quite sure if his other name was Wilson, or that charming Macmillan they saw on television the other night. The Dorset cottager who thinks we are still ruled by Ethelred the Unready is no doubt an eccentric, but several authenticated cases of confusion between Mrs. Shirley Williams and the Virgin Mary have come to light. Whatever can be done? Fortunately, a Committee has turned up with a timely Report.[1] The teaching profession will once more save the day by developing amongst children the subject of political literacy.

The subject of *what*? Yes, it is an odd expression. A tiny dwarf called "political" is trying to pass itself off as tall by riding around on the shoulders of a giant called "literacy." The inventors of this unlikely circus act are a "Hansard Society Working Party" and what they are working on is called a "Programme for Political Education." The fruits of their labours have just been published by Longman. Within the covers of this Report will be found a discussion of the new concept of "political literacy," guidelines (even better, "general" guidelines) and frameworks (better yet, "overall" frameworks) and (as the pages turn) syllabic dreams of classroom adventures. The main recommendation is an expansion of political education ("a modest requirement of timetable hours," as the Report cautiously words it) and more investment in the training of teachers who can make us all politically literate; and if that doesn't wipe the smile off your face, you're incorrigibly frivolous.

Now the very first element of political literacy—its ABC, so to speak—is to recognize that nothing is quite what it seems. Here in this Report we seem to have a collection of public spirited teachers who have discovered a dangerous void for our society where political involvement ought to be. They present us with a plan for solving the problem. The plan turns out to be a bid for money and time. It has significant costs. Teachers have for many generations encouraged debating societies and given a bit of direction to fledgling political societies after hours. The Report is in tune with the times in seeking money and professional status for a long-standing amateur enthusiasm. It is inevitable that this particular use of public money and curricular time will be disadvantageous to other competing interests. Since the main conception of a political problem found in the Report is in terms of conflict of interests, the reader may appropriately perform the function of reflexivity on behalf of the writers of these recommendations. What seems most appropriate of all is to consider the document as an exercise in persuasion.

The persuader's trump card is to convince his audience that they don't really have any choice at all: *necessity* dictates what the persuader seeks. This old friend of an argument turns up as early as page 5:

"The question is not really whether it is done at all but whether it is done well or done badly . . ."

Another old friend among these rhetorical shifts is to suggest that what is generally regarded as a matter for specialists actually concerns us *all*. And along the lines of "personal freshness matters," we get an insistence that politics is not just something that happens at Westminster, but an activity that affects everyday life. The notion that politics is about conflict, and especially conflict of interests, a notion with great appeal to the pedagogic sense of realism, threatens here to turn every family row into a demand for constitution, negotiated settlements, free collective bargaining, a children's charter, and (to get a bit of practical work done) school assemblies to negotiate with the headmaster or headmistress. The Report is quite explicit that political literacy and autocratic Heads go ill together.

TEACHERS ON POLITICS

There is however, an overwhelming problem about the whole enterprise. Teachers in schools are authorities to whom children go
to learn the dates of battles, the imperfect subjunctive of irregular
verbs, and how to solve quadratic equations. They are not, however, authorities on politics, because no such things exist. There
used to be a vogue for a carefully deodorised version of politics
to be taught in schools under the name of "civics." It was largely
descriptive, and it encouraged liberal and democratic values. Educationally, it was useless, and most children were bored by it; but at
least it was unpretentious, and it did little harm. The authors of this
Report, however, indict it as a timid evasion of the facts of politics,
like sex education limited to a recital of anatomical truths.

To say that such things are inadequate is, however, merely to
recognise one of the most unfashionable and neglected of truths:
that schools are very limited in what they can achieve. In politics,
moreover, most people are devoutly glad of this limitation, since no
one trusts children to distinguish between the kind of reliability
teachers have in genuinely educational matters, and their probable
foolishness in matters political, in which they have nothing that can
be called knowledge, and no experience. And it is a truth on which
all rational men will agree, wherever they are on the political spec-
trum, that there are a lot of screwballs around; and that some of
them are to be found in classrooms. What is to be done when such
people are licensed to guide the political opinions of their tender
charges?

The report is sublimely equable about this problem. Frontal
assaults, they tell us with an odd echo of the language of pornog-
raphy, are not likely to be successful. Deliberate indoctrination
seems more likely to cause apathy and cynicism than enthusiasm.
It would be nice to see a little argument for this belief, which would
undoubtedly come as news to all the Nazi and Communist indoc-
trinators who have not been all that unsuccessful in this century.

It would be nice, I say, to see a little argument on this point; evidence would perhaps be too much to hope for. But all we face is a blank. And this very blankness is another old friend from the repertoire of persuasive devices. If one refuses to take an objection seriously, brushing it aside with impatience as too silly to be considered, one has a good chance of bluffing a critic into thinking that it isn't a very serious objection. In fact, it is very serious indeed, and its avoidance is an object lesson in how the British pedagogue deals with realities.

Even apart from "frontal assaults" of doctrine, the Report does not get the question right. The National Front teacher who spends his time in an exegesis of Gobineau and Rosenberg is one thing; the engineering of attitudes by way of sneering asides about darkies is another thing altogether. If a teacher is adept at this kind of communication he will often carry his pupils with him. And so can any other hot gospeller in the schools—able to convey by sneer and derision what he thinks is a respectable attitude, and what he thinks is too silly for any intelligent person to consider. In this way, whole ranges of possible thoughts have often been made, as it were, "radio-actively" sterile, for many children, for many years. Even the best educators sometimes have this effect. The worst can turn the mind into a devastated area.

In genuinely educational subjects, those in which children learn a discipline of thought having clear criteria of what counts as a good reason, the question of balance or neutrality does not arise. Teachers do not have to guard against "bias" as they teach Latin, physics, or mathematics. Aesthetic judgment in English is not decisive in the same way, but nothing extrinsic to education threatens to swamp an appreciation of the qualities of Hamlet or the "Ode to a Nightingale." And even the dangers of dottiness in modern history are at least limited, however loosely, by considerations of evidence. But the subject of politics combines a maximum of sinister, interested, outside interference with a minimum of agreed criteria of sound judgment.

This does not, indeed, make it unimportant; but it does make it a dubious subject for schools, in which the point of the exercise is training people how to think by immersing them in educationally worthwhile forms of thought. Vast quantities of political discourse consist of worthless and dishonest waffle. Children may have to encounter it at some point, and some may even develop a taste for it, but it is the very last kind of discourse which can stand as an example of clear and critical thinking. And it is necessary to report that these particular teachers of politics, who must be regarded as models of what the subject might be, the *crème de la crème*, as it were, are not always as clear and critical as they might be.

It is obvious that classrooms are as attractive to people with messages as harems might be to Don Juan. How, then, do we formulate the moral responsibilities of a man of strong political opinions who finds himself in charge of a class? The Report formulates the question in terms of the voguish word "neutrality." It does indeed have fears that there may be "gross bias" in the classroom, and thinks that the teacher ought to criticise his own bias and to compensate for it in his teaching. The few words on this theme are a good deal less thunderous than the imposition of a clear duty to avoid bias—a duty such as we might expect to be invoked for a profession, such as teaching, which is not tethered even by such a thing as a Hippocratic oath. A quiet invocation of the idea of professionalism is all we get. These widely acceptable sentiments are undercut, however, by a rather bolder theme:

> Neutrality is not to be encouraged: to be biased is human
> and to try and unbias people is to emasculate them.

There is something "politic" in the bad sense about combining pious advice about the need for fairmindedness with the suggestion that every redblooded he-man will let his biases rip. The latter suggestion will find support (and is indeed supported in the Report) in the currently fashionable pop epistemology which

jumps from the logical characteristics of observation (that it invari-
ably involves selection) to the conclusion that, since "everybody is
biased" or non-neutral, everybody can be as happily partisan as
they like.

The question posed in terms of the misleading idea of neutrality is, of course, one of the central problems of the entire project.
Educational discourse has no problem with neutrality because its
material does not resolve itself into a choice between competing
policies about which one might be either partisan or neutral. But
politics is a maze of *pros* and *contras*, in which every humble little
fact seems to take its place in some scheme of *pro* and *contra*. Hence
the nearest thing a teacher of politics can get to educational remote-
ness is a kind of controlled oscillation between *pro* and *contra*. It
is not merely the only way; it is also required, as a sheer matter of
the practical politics of getting the Report implemented, that all
political groups be offered equal bites at the cherry. The writers
of the Report cannot help but recognise at times that oscillating
between *pro* and *contra* is but a thin caricature of the genuine re-
moteness of educational subjects; but what they do not recognise
is that a teacher in a classroom with a captive audience is exercising a form of pedagogic monopoly which makes genuine freedom
of discussion impossible. For the condition of freedom in politics
is not some set of guidelines about informational neutrality; it is
the competitiveness which makes it easy for people with different
policies to disseminate them. And that competitiveness is precisely
what the classroom prohibits. Neutrality, then, must carry the burden. When it can no longer bear the strain, its employers in this
Report toss it away like a squeezed lemon. Its flavour lingers on,
however, in the meticulous balancing act performed by the Report
in not favouring either of the two *pros* and *contras* it conceives to be
the issues of contemporary politics.

Working-class solidarity, for example, is juxtaposed against

something called "middle-class moderation." When the badness
of an operation called "imposing theory before issues are understood" is illustrated, the three names of theorists used in exemplification are "Burke, Adam Smith or Karl Marx" who, unsuitable
as they may be for the exercise since they are radically different
kinds of theorist, are none the less recognisable standard-bearers
for the three main points of some people's political spectra. "We
would reject the assumptions of those whether of Left or Right"
(the Report fearlessly tells us) "who would have only the correct
attitudes taught." And immediately "socialisation" (presumably
thought to be Left) is juxtaposed against "tradition" (thought to
be Right). This is indeed neutrality of a sort, though a very mechanical sort; and the reader who was enraged by the bold general
remarks about neutrality may find himself soothed in the exemplification. Whether this kind of mechanical seeing "both-sides-of-
the-question" (rather than analysing the very terms in which those
familiar "both" sides are constituted) constitutes a form of education is the point on which attention should focus.

We are, however, far from having exhausted the difficulties
arising from the question of neutrality. For the kind of attitude
here called "neutrality" is, by a common sort of misunderstanding, thought to be essential to the academic validity of politics as
a subject to be taught in schools. And, given such an assumption,
"political literacy" cannot be taught in schools, as civics and religious education have often been taught, as a set of communal beliefs we all share, or which by being taught may reveal to us *our*
way of thinking and acting. Thus, religious education used to be an
induction into Christianity; but exactly the same sort of misguided
attempt to turn it into an academic subject, such as we find in the
present Report, is now turning it into "comparative religion." Similarly, there might be some case for teaching children the way we
engage in the activity of politics. To do this would be to embrace
a belief that it is better, at least for us, to have a free press, regular
elections, an independent judiciary, and all the rest. But this possi-

bility is rejected—and it is worth noting the significantly confused way in which it is rejected.

> It would be wrong, we are told, to define a politically literate person as someone who necessarily shares all values of Western European liberalism. That would be indeed a curious up-dating of the Whig interpretation of history into present-day political education.

We might note, as we pass, the pedagogic display of a bit of flashy and irrelevant erudition. This particular bit of erudition is not only irrelevant but sophistical. What is wrong with the "Whig interpretation of history" is that it is a political position distorting historical understanding; but there is nothing at all wrong with Whig politics, the teaching of which has no necessary connection at all with the Whig interpretation of history. Not all Whigs are bad historians.

The wider issue arising from this remark is, however, the fact that if politics is to be taught at all in schools, there is very little else it can be (apart from ideological indoctrination) except an assertion of what is here called "the values of western European liberalism." Where else can its values come from? The Moguls of India? Confucian China? Genghis Khan? Tribal societies? And in fact the Report does stumble to just this conclusion, except that, having extruded Western European liberalism through the front door, it allows the same thing back through the back window in the form of a tasteless consommé called "procedural values" which it is the business of the teacher to espouse. These values are called Freedom, Toleration, Fairness, Respect for Truth, and Respect for Reasoning. They are in many respects admirable, and in various combinations have no doubt been found in many places at many times. But there is no doubt that this version of them is unmistakably a rather bald summary of what a liberally minded Briton has taken away from his reading of his history.

LIBERALISM WITH ITS HANDS TIED

Training people in political literacy is, then, a training in liberalism which has exchanged its strong patriotic roots for a mess of educational neutrality understood to have resulted from academic hygiene.

But this is liberalism with its hands tied behind its back. It is no doubt an excellent set of values for those engaged in discussion with other liberals; but like the guns of Singapore, it is a defence against attack from the wrong quarter. One important 20th-century problem is that argument between Western politicians has an entirely different character from, for example, argument between Stalin and Trotsky, Hitler and Captain Röhm, or Mr. Teng and Madame Mao. In all the latter cases, the argument is mere froth in a deadly game of power, and the losers usually end up dead. Given that we live in a dangerous world full of power-hungry exponents of ideological truth whose aim it is to do away with degenerate bourgeois shams like parliaments and a free press, the politically literate man begins to reek of Kerensky and the Weimar Republic. It is all like going into a lion's cage to stroke the nice pussy-cat.

But perhaps a bit of danger is just what the Report flavours. It is mortally affeared that people won't take an interest in politics, and hence it seeks to meddle with the character as well as the minds of its pupils.

> The ultimate test of political literacy lies in creating a proclivity to action, not in achieving mere theoretical analysis.

This utterance merely summarises a moral doctrine which underlies the whole Report. At one point, this desirable proclivity to activity is advanced as the Aristotelian mean between passivity on the one band and rebellion on the other. Among the more bizarre recurrences of this general doctrine may be cited the remark:

Socrates was a good man—who broke the law; so did Jesus ...

It is a remark which disposes of Plato and the Gospels in one brisk Liberationist *putsch*; it must constitute a milestone in scholarly revisionism. But perhaps the best clue to the significance of these remarks is a line about "a passive and deferential population, who think of themselves as good subjects and not active citizens." Now the *O.E.D.* takes *"deference"* to be "courteous regard, as one to whom respect is due." How, then, can courtesy get tangled up in this grotesque doctrine about the excellence of activity and the badness of passivity?

DEFERENCE DESPISED

The cause is no doubt to be found in Bagehot's idea of the "deference vote" in British politics, which has haunted the corridors of political science in the form of a caricature of forelock-tugging peasants moronically convinced that only their Eton-educated masters know how to rule. This piece of nonsense has the useful role of explaining away the fact that the lower classes do not always vote for reforming or revolutionary parties. The Tory working-man could be patronised as a "deference voter."

Now the question of why people vote as they do is profoundly mysterious and it is not at all to be confused with the answers people may give to interviewers who ask them for the reasons why they vote one way or another. As with much else in politics, things are not always what they seem, including motives. But on one important such point, most people are more realistic than the authors of this Report. Most people regard politics as a spectator sport, in which the main actors are office-holders or those actively bidding for office. This Report, however, is keen to foster the illusion that politics, like voting and chatting in pubs, is fundamentally participant—cheering and booing are actually taken as politics itself. Now while it is true that no one is necessarily excluded from politics, it is also true that most people will never really take part in politics. It is an activity only for people either with the taste for it, or with very great determination. Any other view is demagogic flattery.

The fundamental presupposition of the Report is, then, a belief in a mode of human conduct called "activity," and it is from this that the muddles about neutrality which I have already discussed take their source. For *neutrality* cannot help appearing, when caught in the upper and nether millstones of the kind of ratiocination displayed here, as a form of the dreaded *passivity*. Hence, too, *deference* as a form of courtesy disappears from sight because it has been identified with *servility*. Now a culture which misappropriates the vocabulary of courtesy in order to express its disapproval of servility (for which there are plenty of available resources) will turn itself into a breeding ground for quarrelsome bores, and it is the latter type of person who seems likely to emerge as the actual prototype of the politically literate man. For if I discuss law with Lord Denning, or astrophysics with Sir Martin Ryle, on the nondeferential assumption that I know just as much about these subjects as they do, then I shall become very tiresome indeed. No classroom, to bring the matter closer to home, could possibly function unless the children in one way or another deferred to the teacher as a teacher. None of this means, of course, that the remarks of the one deferred to are to be taken as necessarily gospel truth; but if some sort of circumstantial pre-eminence were not given to people in conversations, then conversations would never get going in the first place.

The word "deferential" carries a heavy freight of disapproval which, like many corruptions of our language (such as "disinterested," for example), threatens to rob us of one of the essential conceptions of civility. Even more fundamental to the line of argument of this Report is the transformation of the idea of *activity*. Through the slow revolvings of thought, by which sparks of meaning pass from connotation to connotation, a new meaning of the word seems to be slowly evolving. Being active and being passive (or quiet, silent, reflective) used to be two manners of behaviour available to human beings, each valuable in its own way. Now, however, "activity" has come to be identified with essential humanity, while passivity is identified with the character of a thing. (Hence the notion of a "sex object.") To be "fully human" means to strive to get one's way, especially in politics.

BEATING THE APATHY RAP

The change of meaning is a leap from one peripheral meaning to another, and the result is a somersault in which the idea turns into its opposite. A collection of people wanting houses, for example, or more money, think themselves most active when they band together in a demonstration which will induce other people to give it to them. But in fact, of course, such behaviour is peculiarly passive (in the bad sense) because it is dependent. It is a demand for wealth sundered from the creation of wealth. One genuinely active response to such a situation might be to build the houses for themselves, as people have so often done before. By a similar transformation, downing tools in a strike or a go-slow comes to be described as "industrial action." The result is not merely paradoxical, it is surrealistic; and a whole generation of simpleminded people have come to believe that they are being supremely active and courageous in taking part in mass demonstrations, which is precisely where both activity and courage are lacking. Now that all the serious Nazis are dead, for example, some thousands of sheep, who would not have said *boo!* when it mattered to do so, imagine themselves to be lions. It is much harder today to cross a picket line; and correspondingly less common.

There is the occasional disclaimer: though the politically literate are allowed the bracketed alternative of "positive refusal to participate," they would have a hard time beating an apathy rap. But the Report finds a great variety of ways of encouraging exactly the sort of ill-considered reforming activism which has been the curse of Britain over the last quarter-of-a-century. Political literacy ap-

pears as a struggle against strong tendencies towards passive "qui-
etism" in Britain today. The actual situation is that there is hardly
anything in Britain today, from local government to the Health Service, but has been in continuous ferment of hyperactivism. A horde
of reformers has been zealously setting about education at every
level during this period, and has transformed the school system,
not very obviously for the better. There are, it seems, no less than
50 different *A*-level mathematics syllabuses available currently,
with obvious problems for those going into higher education. Far
from passivity being the problem it appears in this report, it is
rather a proneness to activism which keeps the British in a condition of permanent administrative twitching. "Activity," one might
well say, has become the neurotic's protection against activity.

It is thus the final irony arising from the Report's attempt to
teach an academically pure form of politics that it should fail to
comprehend its own most important partiality. For in seeking to
encourage activism, it can raise its eyes innocently to the skies and
point out that it is encouraging "a proclivity to activity," irrespec-
tive of the aims to which that activity should be put. But political
activism is, as we have seen, peculiarly appropriate as an instrument by which a dependent population dramatises a claim on
public resources. We might almost say that the traditional forms
of our political life, revolving round elections and constituencies,
constitute one form of modern politics, while street demonstrations
constitute another. While purporting to be neutral, then, the Report mobilises a set of arguments liable to encourage little but the
production of demonstration fodder.

NOTE

1. *Political Education and Political Literacy*. Edited by Bernard Crick and Alex
Porter. Longman, £3.93. The Report is by a variety of hands, but expresses a single
coherent point of view. Hence there has seemed little point in distinguishing the
contributions of different authors. Nor have I distinguished between the Report
itself, the project papers, and the other material collected in this volume.

Choice, Consciousness and
Ideological Language
1982

Abstract: Because psychotherapists are not moral teachers, they
ought not to advise their clients about evaluative questions.
This means that their advice must be limited to a concern with the
client's view of reality. It happens that in our times, there are prefabricated views of reality on offer from a variety of ideologies—Marxism and feminism being currently the most influential. Ideologists
not only offer prefabricated realities called consciousness—but also
present a set of arguments to show that because choice is unreal,
consciousness is all that matters. Adopting the ideological concept
of consciousness thus becomes a backdoor variant of the ultimate
sin against scientific method: namely smuggling unsubstantiated,
indeed undiscussed, values into therapy.

KEY WORDS: Psychotherapy, Ideology, Consciousness, Morality,
Values, Volition, Choice

It is well known that psychotherapy is in a logically exposed position. It is concerned with how we ought to live, and therefore is part
of a brotherhood which includes Socrates, Luther, the Maharishi

Kenneth Minogue, "Choice, Consciousness and Ideological Language." This article
is reprinted with permission of Springer, publisher of *Metamedicine* 3, no. 3 (October
1982): 351–366. © 1982, Springer, Tiergartenstr. 17, 69121 Heidelberg, Germany.

Mahesh Yoga, the Rev. Jones of Jonestown, and a wide assortment
of priests, ministers, ideologists, gurus and mystics. But while the
rest of the brotherhood has a message to spread, psychotherapists
belong to that part of our intellectual culture whose professional
respectability requires that they should limit themselves to questions of how we pursue whatever we pursue without meddling
with evaluative questions of what is being pursued. The sensitivity of psychotherapists to the criticism that they are really imposing a morality rather than serving the happiness[1] of their clients
arises from the fact that every apprentice intellectual in the twentieth century cuts his teeth on arguments to prove that you cannot
separate the how from the what, facts from values. And it would
be a tricky matter, no doubt, for a psychotherapist to treat, say,
a neurotic cannibal without some suggestion that eating people
is wrong creeping into his professional manner. Psychotherapy
can, at a minimum, hardly help encouraging people to rationalise
the way they think about their conduct. While philosophy, according to Wittgenstein, leaves everything as it is, psychotherapy
must leave at least the goals of the patient intact, and it is in cases
where this condition begins to erode at the edges—in such cases
as homosexuality,[2] adhesion to eccentric religious beliefs, and paedophilia—that ministers to the mind are most likely to find themselves accused of being the undercover agents of some morality
or other.

Psychotherapists are usually well aware that they cannot speak
authoritatively about evaluative questions, but they do feel confident that they can help people to become more conscious of their
situation. The problem, of course, is how consciousness is to be
separated from values, especially within the practice of making
choices which lies at the heart of psychotherapy's concerns. It happens that the related intellectual domain of ideology, by which I
mean here any sophisticated intellectual analysis of society in
terms of some key abstraction like sex, class, race or nation, is also

concerned with the relation of consciousness and choice in a similar manner. It is the parallels between psychotherapy and ideology in this area which I wish to explore.

I

Gouverner, as the French aphorism has it, *c'est choisir*. For our purposes, it can be amended to: *vivre, c'est choisir*. The modern period in European civilization has been one in which more and more people have come to lead a life of choosing. In earlier times, the practice of choice, and hence the exercise of rights, was limited to those in responsible positions, who constituted a small sub-set of the males in the population. In 1531, Thomas Elyot published his *Boke named the Governour*, one of those how-to-do-it manuals which may historically be taken as evidence that a new class of person was arising who had to take decisions but lacked background in the practice. For Elyot, a governor was any kind of boss, and included magistrates, rulers, employers and even schoolmasters. If we move forward a little more than a century, we may see, in John Milton's withering scorn in the *Areopagitica* for anyone so base as to hand over his conscience to some outside "factor," the maturity of this way of life in which a man was expected to make his own decisions, think for himself, and stand on his own feet. Milton, in his simplicity, thought it a religious distinction between Romanists and Protestants: we know better. Before long, men and women would even expect to choose their own husbands and wives.

It may be confidently averred, without too much irony, that this particular historical development was the making of psychiatry, and, in particular, the soft, counselling end of psychiatry, which we may call psychotherapy. For when human beings impose upon themselves the responsibility for leading their own lives, they increase vastly the possibility that they will feel inadequate to the task. Buridan's ass merely starved to death when placed before two equidistant bales of straw. Human beings, admittedly, had an organ called the "will" which was supposed to save them from such an unfortunate fate, but they had to make choices vastly more complicated than which bale of straw to eat. It was therefore hardly surprising that in many people the continuous, almost rhythmic flow of choices which characterise the lives of those who don't end up on the psychotherapeutic couch, should be subject to interruption. Compulsion, obsession, hysteria and many other forms of neurosis are usually understood cognitively as implausible and unlikely thoughts and feelings, but they are no less to be understood as derangements of the machinery of choice. From this point of view, psychotherapists are useful repairmen who work on the volitional machinery and whose success can be measured by whether the flow of choosing is resumed by the repaired patient.

If it is indeed true that volitional disturbance is psychotherapy's *raison d'etre*, then it is unmistakeably ironic that its great period of flowering should have taken place long after the decline of moral individualism had set in. Historians and sociologists generally associate this kind of intense individualism with Protestantism—Max Weber, after all, called it "the Protestant ethic"—and by the end of the eighteenth century, the most pricey and individualist forms of Protestantism were a thing of the past. Philosophically, the high point of an individualist morality has usually been recognised as Kant's concept of the categorical imperative. But from early on in the nineteenth century, individualism came to be seen less as an opportunity for liberation from traditional bonds (which it had been in the early modern period) than as a kind of spiritual fall which had severed the head from the heart, and man from his neighbour. The ideological doctrines whose arguments I propose to examine are, one and all, versions of this rejection of individualism, and the same rejection appears regularly in works of history and philosophy. A sophisticated recent example is *After Virtue: A Study in Moral Theory* by Alastair MacIntyre, who writes: "The surface rhetoric of our culture is apt to speak complacently of moral pluralism in this connection. . . . but the notion of pluralism is imprecise. For it may equally well apply to an ordered dialogue of intersecting viewpoints and to an unharmonious melange of ill-assorted fragments." And the argument he develops reveals the familiar picture of the modern world as a collection of isolated atoms living in a moral no-man's-land.

Let me say at once that this picture of Europeans as isolated and privatized individuals is nonsense from beginning to end. It is true, of course, as Marxists and other ideologists have always argued, that such creatures do not exist; but then, no one ever thought they did exist. Even at the highpoint of individualism, everyone well knew that man was a social animal and could not survive in isolation. The whole idea is nothing more than a logical straw man used to commend an alternative morality of communal integration. Such a morality, like any other, can be commended in a variety of ways, and does not need to engage in historical and sociological distortions. The interesting question is how such a distortion ever became current. The only part of the answer relevant to my present argument is that European casuistry has long emphasised the moral loneliness of man in the face of the ultimate moral questions. The isolation in question, in other words, is a moral abstraction, and the validity of this particular bit of abstraction in no way depends upon the sociological validity of social contract theory. The social contract was an aid in answering a quite different question: namely, whether government was a voluntary construction, made for their own convenience and protection, by men imagined as living in a pre-political state. But these men were always recognised as members of families and clans.[3]

We may thus put to one side the grosser confusions about individualism, and direct our attention to the rise and fall of choosing man. Our question thus becomes: What is the nature of the choosing which in earlier times was thought to be a liberation, and which in later times came by many to be construed as "the burden of freedom"?[4]

Choosing has, as it were, two gears. The top gear is the way in which every act we perform is chosen, because we could at any point have performed a different act, and we could always have performed our actual act in a different manner. Every sentence we utter is a deliberate construction. This is the sense of choosing in which human acts are said to be contingent rather than necessary, because it is logically possible that each of them could have been different; and for this reason persons are essentially different from things. Most people, most of their lives, create a niche of habits and live within that, their choosing being of an undemanding sort which varies the detail without greatly affecting the structure of their lives. Such is the usual condition of families, institutions and indeed whole societies, which can thus be described as having traditions, characters, or ways of life which are tolerably stable in spite of the fact that they are never at rest. This is the kind of choosing which constitutes the virtually irreducible freedom of human beings, and which could never be taken from them short of their being, magically or chemically, reduced to the condition of the zombie.[5]

Choosing's bottom gear is what must be engaged when we suddenly run uphill into what we construe as a deliberative problem. We then assemble all our available machinery for the making of a decision. Puritanism is the whole of life lived in a bottom gear of this kind, in which *everything* becomes, as we say, a matter of *moral* significance.[6] But more commonly, life presents such challenges at intervals, as it did to the unfortunate Hamlet, and we find them difficult to deal with. When we think of a moral problem, we commonly think that it involves a choice between two conflicting moral problems, or two moralities; often, for example, between doing our duty and causing bad consequences, or enjoying benefits as a result of *not* doing our duty. But these perplexities can result from many other kinds of conflict, including judgements of what is likely to happen in the future, and judgements about the condition of our own sentiments. In a real moral perplexity, serious things are at stake, but it is one of the characteristics of the derangements of volition which face psychotherapists that human beings can at times be reduced to the condition of Buridan's ass about things which are entirely trivial.

There are many ways of constructing a taxonomy of choices, but I shall content myself with a simple scheme relevant to my argument: in choosing, we make a judgement upon the *reality* of our situation, the *rules* appropriate to it, and the *future* turn of events. *Futures* we may discard with the observation that many problems only arise from uncertainty about what will happen, and this fact has led men to examine the stars, gaze into crystal balls, cut up fowls so as to examine their entrails, search out pythonesses and gypsies, and employ social scientists.

The more interesting intellectual problems revolve around the rules component of deliberation. This is a component which includes the entire moral and legal side of choosing. The rules issue from an immense variety of sources: from the commands of someone in authority or merely respected, from values held or norms observed, from sentiments of beauty or ugliness, feelings of honour, and much else. What they always issue in, technically, is a duty appropriate to the problem involved: You ought to do *x*. Europeans (including, of course, the European inhabitants of the New World) have throughout modern times exhibited a great thirst to be told what their duties are, because a definitive declaration of duty (unlike a definitive declaration of a right) conclusively solves the moral problem in question. The literature of sermons and the science of casuistry, little cultivated in the twentieth century, were of overriding importance in earlier times because men had an unquenchable thirst for rules that would solve deliberative problems. Throughout European history up till about the end of the nineteenth century, duty was the grand moral concept. It went into battle time and again to control something called desire. Since then, duty has gone rather out of fashion, and shrunk to a somewhat technical status, as in "I will explain to you the duties of your appointment."

Europeans, then, used to have a connoisseur's taste for discov-

ering moral problems in their lives. The novels of Henry James are
a marvellous account of this particular sensibility. Now it will be
clear that the number and the severity of the moral problems which
can be generated depends upon the number of moral rules and dis-
criminations current in any community. The mere liberalizing of
dietary rules for Jews and Roman Catholics has, in recent times,
greatly reduced problems of choice which were increasingly being
found uncongenial. More generally, the more permissive a society
becomes, the fewer will be the moral problems engendered. In
principle, perhaps, one might imagine an almost totally permissive
society in which hardly any rules applied, and this would evidently
be a society in which communal values were very great, and the
individual sense of identity very slight. There would, of course,
still remain choices to be made for so long as individual preferences
remained to be recognised, as when we make a choice from a menu;
and there could be no human society which did not recognise the
economic problem of scarce resources in one form or another, either communal or individual. But these imaginative extrapolations
assume that the will remains unchanged by an erosion of rules in
society. It has been interestingly suggested that what actually happens when humans face a constraint-free environment is that they
merely begin to search for signals from elsewhere—for example,
the preferences of a peer group.[7]

In thus sketching the moral development of the last few centuries, one must be careful to guard against the mistake of thinking that a morality of moral choosing is necessarily identical with a
good life. Much Christian morality, greatly preoccupied with *strug-*
gling against sin, and the melodrama of the romantic movement for
which passion and suffering are the highest value, have tended to
a presumption that the good life is a perpetual deliberative thresh-
ing about. But a good person may well find himself having to make
very few serious decisions, since he might naturally and characteristically tend to the good; and it is also true that many episodes of
great moral turmoil can involve valueless wrestling with phantoms.

Some of the things we do unreflectively are amongst the best, and the worst, deeds of our lives. Modern fiction is largely concerned with moments of this kind.

But in guarding against this misunderstanding, we are not at all diminishing the importance of choice as a feature of the moral life, nor demoting the will as the organ most likely to need psychotherapeutic repair. There are two reasons for its centrality, one intellectual, one practical.

Intellectually speaking, choice lies precisely at a nexus where our criterion for making sense out of the world (determinism, causal explanation) runs headlong into our criterion for making sense of those distinctive bits of universe called persons (freedom, contingency, the fact that a person's acts could have been other than they were). This means that most technologies for the elimination of choice, or the solution of deliberative problems slide down the scale of being and turn human beings into things. The earliest version of this technology appeared early, in the political and forensic rhetoric of the Greeks, and took the form of denying choice by affirming necessity. The defence to a charge of murder is often self-defence, and the elliptical form of the defence is "I had no choice but to kill him." In political life, which is an activity almost entirely conducted in deliberative bottom gear, the temptation to offload many choices onto the broad back of necessity has been so strong as to generate a specific doctrine called reason of state. And necessity appears in the small change of everyday life: One must live, shrugs the prosperous author of best selling trash ingratiatingly, to which the harsh critic replies: I do not see the necessity. In the nineteenth century, the argument from necessity turned scientific. From Marx's capitalists caught up in the toils of a system they could not really understand to Zola's *race, moment et milieu*, there appeared a range of explanations in which human choosing had no part.

Such a drift of the European understanding away from choice towards science and necessity was attractive not only because it seemed to solve the problem of free will and determinism, but also because it promised the removal of pain. For in practical terms, choosing is, as the cliche has it, a painful necessity. Earlier generations may indeed have had a taste for this painful necessity, rather like cold baths and strict diets, but there is no doubt that choices are moments when we are forced to recognise that we cannot have everything. They are moments of self-definition at which the self must, in Hegelian terms, abandon its potential infinitude in order to attain finite actuality, and the price of that is limitation.[8] Or, to put the matter in psychiatric terminology, choices cause stress and sometimes lead people to breakdowns. It has often been noted—most recently in the case of the emergency in Northern Ireland—that a community involved in a really destructive crisis is less subject to neurotic ailments than in normal times. Neurosis is a luxury we commonly indulge when we can. Clearly, there are attractions to choiceless situations, and the interesting thing is that they can appear from two opposite directions: when the stakes are life and death, choice itself becomes a luxury we cannot afford. Alternatively, it might seem, a situation in which all values are equal, and in which all moral rules have gone the way that liberalised dietary rules among Jews and Roman Catholics have gone, would also be a situation in which the pains of choice would be a thing of the past.

II

The ideological argument—and it hardly matters which of the available varieties of ideology available we take—is that choice is unreal. From this is drawn the conclusion that, in practice, deliberation may be analysed in terms of true and false consciousness, I propose to take each of these moves in turn.

The first is a version of a classic argument which is not so much in favour of determinism as against free will. It suggests that the idea of choosing is an illusion we acquire from being so close to that nexus of desires and junction of forces called the mind. Our ignorance of what the outcome of a deliberation will be is illogically converted into a belief in the categorical unpredictability of all deliberation. Seeing it from the perspective of distance, however, we may be led to believe that whatever is chosen is really the outcome of the nature of the person and the forces to which he was subject at the time. The ideological variation on this particular argument is that the forces are all construed sociologically. The human mind is taken to be a field of force which mirrors, or reflects, or represents, the conflicting impulses which jostle for supremacy in society at large.

A decision is thus assimilated to necessity as being the recognition that such and such an impulse is stronger than its rivals. Thus Marx remarks that there are circumstances which determine the actions of private persons which are no less independent of them than the way they breathe,[9] and as his doctrine develops, this general line is used to attack "individualism" in all its forms. Individualism is in one version the doctrine that any society is fundamentally a set of individuals; by contrast, Marx argues that human beings are essentially social, and that in the circumstances of the present, social characteristics are determined by class membership, a picture whose mechanical simplicity is somewhat modified by the recognition of things called "contradictions" which explain the phenomena of conflict. The result of this revision of the traditional account of the moral life is the reduction of moral predicates to sociological ones of a special sort. What we call indecision indicates the presence of a peculiarly intractable contradiction, self-sacrifice means a total alignment to the demands of a movement, deceitfulness means a superficial and unsuccessful attempt to come to terms with contradictions, punctiliousness the unhindered flow of a certain class character into all aspects of a person's life, and so on. Deliberation is a junction of conflict from whose outcome we infer, say, a bourgeois or proletarian character, victimisation by some sort of false consciousness, the beginning of the rejection of ideological illusions, and so on. The point of Marx's emphasis that man is a social being, indeed a species-being, is to diminish to vanishing point any concern with individual character in the generation of an act. Acts "express" and "reflect" social tendencies; hence when Marx comes to describe the acts of individuals in political life, his method consists in translating a chronicle into a puppet show of the abstract categorisations he favours. "Bourgeois society," he tells us as he begins to work on translating Louis Napolean's rise to power into these terms, "had begotten its true interpreters and mouthpieces in the Says, Cousins, Royer Collards, Benjamin Constants and Guizots . . . ,"[10] and here the pluralising of the individual names indicates the beginning of their dissolution into mouthpiece status.

The reason Marx takes this view lies deeply embedded in his conception of the human condition, but the part that concerns my argument is, I think, relatively simple. Marx seeks less to destroy a theory which he thinks is wrong than to discourage a practice which he thinks is deplorable. The practice is that of self-conscious deliberation in terms of individual sentiments and practices. Now in fact it is logically possible for someone to be a convinced determinist in metaphysics and also to insist upon responsibility in ethics. (There are, indeed, some who argue that this is the *only* logically defensible combination.) But Marx seems to have believed that individualism as a social theory (that society consists fundamentally of a collection of individuals) was not only historically but also logically connected with individualism as a moral sentiment. In criticising the former, he seems to have thought that he was removing the foundations of the latter. And the practical point of the endeavour would seem to have been the creation of social conditions in which men need no longer suffer the pains of choosing. Hence Marxism, and in its wake, all other ideologies, have been relentless in their concern to destroy any theory which would seem to attribute to a human individual any independent causal status. Even Hegel's doctrine of world-historical individuals is thus parodied as something called "the great man theory of history," interpreted as if it meant that celebrated historical individuals all alone *caused* the consequences historians attribute to them, and attacked as a failure to recognise that all achievements are in fact essentially collective.

The second argument comes from precisely the opposite direction. Instead of denying the reality of choice, it insists upon taking the conditions of choice with unusual seriousness. The sorts of choice I have described as "living in top gear" may be swept away because they are part of our way of life and are preceded by nothing much in the way of deliberation. Hence they do not count as choices. What then of "bottom-gear choices"? These are seen in terms of a wider perspective. As we look back, we often regret the decisions we have made because one part of our personality or other was uppermost at the time, and hence the choice reflected part of us rather than the whole. Again, when judging indulgently the acts of others, we are inclined to pay attention to mitigating circumstances like poverty, a broken home, alcohol, the stress of the moment, and so on. This type of argument, which begins from the opposite premise from the first argument we considered, nonetheless ends up in the same place, for it can be squeezed so tight as to generate the conclusion that no actual choices made by human beings under real circumstances really count as choices at all. For the only real choice would be one which expresses our full nature, and which is so wholeheartedly taken that no serious questions of doing something different arose in the first place. Even here, however, given that our personalities often have the volatility of quicksilver, the wholehearted choice of today may become the regret of tomorrow, and by this very fact be revealed as subject to invisible constraints which signify that it is not the expression of my real personality.

A third argument arises from developing this same line of thought, and helps to explain the ingrained ideological dislike of any kind of choosing. It depends upon recognising that moral rules of one kind or another are essential ingredients in solving any problem of choice. Now moral rules, indeed any principles of decision, are part of the public world, and are universal and abstract. Their central presupposition, as elucidated by Kant, is that someone in identical circumstances ought to make exactly the decision that I make. But if my decision is determined by a universal of this kind, then it is determined by something outside of me, and hence it cannot be said to be my own choice. Hence every choice, being in some sense determined by an abstract rule, involves us in the paradox that what I chose was actually submission to an external force. But the whole value of choice lies in the fact that it expresses my autonomy, and any heteronomous element must derogate from that. Hence I only express my full nature when I can express myself directly and spontaneously, without the need to deliberate as between choices. In other words, the conditions for saying "I freely chose to do x" have become equivalent to saying "I had no problem of choice at all." Choice has evaporated.[11]

Let us mention one last argument which leads in the same direction. It is again by Marx out of Hegel, and consists of observing that what is really happening at any time is usually different from what anyone thinks is happening. Luther and Calvin imagined that they were destroying luxury and idolatry and bringing Christian worship back to the model intended by the Founder. What they were actually doing, according to Marx, was creating the spiritual preconditions for the emergence of the bourgeois mode of production. Like many of these arguments, this one is, in some degree, a misunderstanding of what philosophers have said. Thus Adam Smith observed in a famous passage that in pursuing their self-interest, supporters of domestic industry were led by an invisible hand to promote the public good.[12] He did not, of course, mean that such promotion was more real in any sense than the pursuit of self-interest; merely, that it happened, and that the pattern of events thus created had the law-like rationality of economic science. But when Hegel[13] talks of men's passions being used by "the cunning of history" to create consequences of which they never dreamed, he is approaching, but certainly not reaching, the doctrine which Marx actually makes explicit. It follows from this doctrine that the actual considerations being entertained in the mind of the deliberator do not represent the reality of the situation as it will be understood by philosophers, historians and economists; and that the understanding of the latter penetrates to the reality of the situation in a way in which the moral considerations actually agitating the mind of the deliberator do not.

And this point brings us back, with the smallest of steps, to that third component of deliberation which we have so far not discussed: namely, the reality of the situation. In our rhetorical vocabulary, "reality" sounds like the bedrock from which we begin our deliberations, but it is in fact the conclusion with which we end. The central question, in deliberation no less than in life generally, is simply: What is happening? What is the situation? This is peculiarly the case in politics, where a trivial fact can turn out to be the sign of momentous consequences, and equally, the most spectacular uproar can mean very little indeed. It very frequently happens that when we replay regretfully some deliberative episode of our life, we find that where we went wrong was in our appreciation of the facts. (And, it should be added, we may still be going wrong even, or perhaps especially, in our new appreciation of the facts.) Now the ideological theory of the facts of deliberation supplies us above all with a *theory* of what is really happening at any time. In Marxism, it is the class struggle, in feminism, the struggle between the sexes, in nationalism a battle for domination, and so on. Ideology is a theory of a fundamental conflict whose reality is obscured by mystifications, deliberate and inevitable, which systematically render our choices nugatory. We often produce consequences we never intended. The road to hell is paved with good intentions. The road to heaven can only be glimpsed by those who can see through the mists which obscure it for us. The technical name, in current ideological language, for the process of beginning to detect this road is "raising consciousness."

A "raised consciousness," i.e., some grasp of the reality of the situation, is undoubtedly necessary for the making of a sound decision; what is relatively new is the belief that there is only one sound opinion on this question and that it comes in the form of a body of ideological knowledge which claims scientific status. Further, such a body of knowledge would not only supply a believer with a solution to any deliberative problems he might have, it would also determine what those problems would be. To put it at its bluntest, the only real moral problems I would have would be those which could be automatically solved in terms of my heightened consciousness. Many of the moral problems which previously agitated my life would be revealed as pseudo-problems, and what I would express as I acted in these new conditions of heightened consciousness would be nothing so insubstantial as merely my own true nature (which, properly understood will come to be recognised as a self-contradictory expression, for how can one person have a real nature all to himself?) but the true nature of humanity itself. And what we arrive at here is again paradoxical: my truest individuality, the occasion when I am most me, is the moment when I am most mankind.

An ideological conclusion thus presents us with an unusual intellectual situation: A philosophical argument which purports to explain the reality of our human condition (by contrast with the fragmentary viewpoints of ordinary experience) also happens to be the practical solution to a set of problems of choice. It is this combination of claims—to philosophical truth *and* practical efficacy simultaneously—which constitutes the distinguishing feature of ideologies. They are all characterised by what is technically known in Marxist thought as the unity of theory and practice.

My concern here, however, is not to analyse the complicated logic of these bodies of thought, but to explore possible analogies between them on the one hand and psychotherapy on the other. And for this purpose, two observations are significant.

The expression "heightened (or raised) consciousness" is

clearly a question begging one. Reality as we experience it is so complicated that there is an infinitude of things, and also of the interconnection of things, we might be conscious of. The claim being made clearly is that in becoming conscious of one set of things pinpointed by a theory—of capitalism, patriarchy or some other oppressive system—one is becoming conscious of something higher and more significant than in becoming conscious of, say, the beauty of the world, man's inhumanity to man or the kinds of inarticulate gropings of consciousness which recently fascinated the practitioners of the *nouveau roman*. To put it bluntly, consciousness is a scarce resource on which there are many claims, and terms like "higher" or "raised" constitute nothing so much as a piece of advertising which declares the superiority of one theory over another. But the question of which theory actually *is* superior is precisely what is at issue here, and this issue is being begged by the terminology which is being used. Nor is it the only issue that is being begged. A more abstract question that arises is whether *any* of the theories which purport to solve both our intellectual and our practical quandaries in one useful economy package is to be taken at its face value.

The second observation is a development of these doubts. I have said that each of these "consciousnesses" is in fact a social theory, and theories, in our civilisation, are abundant and contradictory. We can never be certain of the truth of any of the theories we entertain, even when such theories are couched in such a way that they may be tested. The ideological theories at issue here are certainly not formulated in such a way as to be testable. Such support as they will find is in what Aristotle designated, in the *Rhetoric*,[14] the example. Does the rapist represent the real nature of all men?[15] Bits of literature and random scraps of evidence can be assembled to support this unlikely proposition, but they suffer from all the familiar logical difficulties of any induction, complicated further by the fact that the presupposition itself is less precise than any scientist would be happy to accept. Does capitalism go through crises of successively increasing magnitude until it will be overthrown by the waxing forces of the revolutionary proletariat? Intelligent people can indeed hold this view, and write books supporting it: they are opposed by people no less intelligent. At best, then, the "consciousness" is really a matter of theory, and theory is always contestable—indeed, probably, the more interesting and wide ranging it is, the more contestable it will be.

It is clear then that the most significant feature of ideological rhetoric is the practice of passing off issues of theory as if they were items of perception. If I open my eyes, I can see before me, and thus become conscious of, a stone, a leaf, a door. Others in my situation similarly opening their eyes will see exactly the same things; or at least they certainly would, if these objects were pointed out to them. This is consciousness in the most elementary sense, and is the paradigm to which the ideological uses of the analogy of "consciousness" appeal. To recognise this, then, is to discover that ideological thinking incorporates a doctrine to the effect that there is but one true way of becoming conscious of reality, and only one set of objects (i.e., those designated by the favoured theory) worth attending to. In terms of this perceptual metaphor, ideologies claim to correct the effects of mist, distance, distorting light effects, darkness and any other distortions which prevent us from making out the real nature of some object before us. The instrument of this clarification is the ideological doctrine itself, with its analysis of capitalism, patriarchy, imperialism, or whatever else may be taken to be the source of false perceptions, false consciousness. It is true, of course, that even the simplest perception may be a misconception; true also that all perceptions depend upon some element of theory. But none of this provides the slightest warrant for failing to distinguish between theories and perceptions.

The term "consciousness" in this field thus amounts to a claim to a transparency of understanding which will not withstand criticism. Further, this claim is implicitly made by the entire vocabulary of ideology. The point can best be made by invoking Gilbert

Ryle's[16] concept of "achievement words" whose very use takes for
granted success in the endeavour indicated. If I say that "Smith
refuted Jones" then I am saying not only that Smith tried to show
that Jones was wrong, but also that he succeeded. And when I say
that Smith *realized* that Jones was an exploiter, I am not merely saying that Smith came to entertain a new belief about Jones, but also
that he was right in his new belief. I commend to anyone wishing to
raise his consciousness in this field the game of "hunt the unsubstantiated achievement word" in much of the socio-political prose
he encounters.

It is an ironic implication of this manner of thinking that ideologists thus "reify" people. Ironic, because "reification" is a technical
expression describing precisely that depersonalisation which ideologists believe results from false consciousness and victimisation
by a system of oppression. Ideologists are concerned to reveal to us
static blocks of understanding described in such terms as "workers' perceptions of the state" or "womens' [*sic*] perceptions of marriage." But these are evidently objects which cannot in any sensible
way be "perceived" at all. They are composite abstractions about
which we entertain beliefs, and these beliefs are in a constant state
of change. They are not static pictures by which we are victimised.
To employ a perceptual vocabulary where issues of theory arise is
to present the world as infinitely more static, and even more irrational than it actually is.

III

There are many possible developments of the set of distinctions
I have so briefly sketched, but the one that seems most to require
emphasis is the danger that psychotherapists, in distancing themselves from the purveyors of moralities may find themselves indistinguishable from the purveyors of consciousness. For it is clear
that the end of the road marked "higher consciousness" is a mi-
rage where all the pains of choice will have been eliminated and
human nature will flow directly into spontaneous self-expression,

thus healing the split between the head and the heart. And it is also clear that were that destination even to be reached, human beings would have ceased to be creatures who hold values at all. To "hold" a value is to recognise it, to be capable of examining it, and possibly to reject it in favour of some competing value. So long as human beings have this capability, then they are likely to come into conflict with each other; conversely, the only fundamental solution to social conflict is the entire removal of the very capacity to abstract oneself from an impulse and to examine it as a value which we may either support or reject. The regulative ideal of psychotherapy is the mind that functions perfectly and can bring peace to itself. The corresponding regulative ideal of the ideologist is a society of which the same can be said. From some points of view, they may be confused as the same thing. But this is a serious mistake, which depends upon thinking choice unreal and a higher consciousness a matter of true perception.

This particular danger, however, is remote. However much the individualist morality of past centuries may have gone into a decline, contemporary societies clearly buzz with a plurality of opinions and impulses. Society is many "consciousnesses" and none of these different consciousnesses can be regarded as problems to be solved in terms of the highest consciousness; they must be seen rather as the solution which each of us has temporarily arrived at in our encounter with the world. It is up to a point possible to take a connoisseur's pleasure in the sheer variety of these consciousnesses, an attitude reinforced by the recognition that, however well argued they may be, their view of the world can never, in the nature of things, be demonstrated. Hence while there are certainly better and worse understandings or "consciousnesses" of the world, there are none which can be equated with perception, none, that is, which provide us with a god-like access to things in themselves. For the rest, it is the business not of psychotherapy, but of politics to hammer out sufficient accommodation between these "consciousnesses" to allow us to get on with the business of life. The most to which psychotherapy can aspire is to prepare a conscious-ness agenda paper for the committee meeting of deliberation, in which the moral component makes the final decision on what the action will be. It is better to be conscious than unconscious, but consciousness is not omnipotent, and psychotherapy can only lose both its character and its usefulness if it succumbs to the assump-tions of ideological thinking.

NOTES

1. Aristotle instructs us that all advice is concerned with happiness, and goes on to define happiness as "prosperity combined with virtue" (*Aristotle*, Book I, Chapter 5, 1360b). The point is that the happiness of the advised is ultimately pre-supposed by the concept of advice, by contrast, for example, with the concept of command. Aristotle is here thinking, for rhetorical purposes, of what most people will recognise as the causes of happiness, and he lists such things as good birth, plenty of friends, health, large stature, etc. He is not here concerned with what are arguably the true sources of happiness.

2. On homosexuality, see Bayer. There is, of course, a vast literature on cults. On the general issues involved, the most extensive discussion is, of course, by Thomas Szasz.

3. Quite how this idea became current is, I think, one of the more interesting questions in the history of European morality. The real answer, I think, lies much less in the myth of the social contract (which was always known to be a myth) than in a growing awareness that what at first looked like a religious heresy (the emer-gence of conscience as an overriding guide to life) was actually a new manner of life. It looked at first like nothing so much as a form of moral decadence, but came in time to be discussed in the form of characterisations of human nature as domi-nated by egocentricity and self-interest. The analysis of egoism might appear either in moral discussion or in what we should now call economic thinking, and it might mean either the implausible philosophical doctrine that every action, even the most saintly, is at bottom the pursuit of a selfish interest; or, quite differently, it might merely refer to selfish behaviour. Only a whiff of cynicism is needed to compound this brew into the fiction known as "economic man" which stalks grimly through the pages of such writers as the early Marx, rather like Frankenstein's monster. On different aspects of this development, see, for example, Keohane, and Hirschman.

4. Thus the title of Erich Fromm's famous book *Escape to Freedom*, which was published in Britain as *The Fear of Freedom*.

5. Here we approach a specific frontier of the person/thing and the man/animal distinction. In our century, we have become aware of the possibility of reduc-ing human beings to something like a mindless condition through drugs, or the deprivation of food, sleep, light and sensory stimuli. This is, however, an extreme situation, whose consequences, while no doubt horrible, would not be entirely

predictable once the conditioning controls were removed. Hardly had the technology of chaining the most elementary physiological mechanisms of men and animals been invented before it became metaphorically used to describe much less dire and dreadful social influences, such as advertising and family life. I have discussed this theme in "The myth of social conditioning" in *Policy Review* 18, Fall 1981; reprinted in Arnold Beichman, Antonio Martino, Kenneth Minogue, *Three Myths*, The Heritage Lectures, 7.

6. As MacIntyre (1981) remarks: "We are so accustomed to classifying judgements, arguments and deeds in terms of morality that we forget how relatively new the notion was in the culture of the Enlightenment. . . . In Latin, as in ancient Greek, there is *no* word correctly translated by our word 'moral.'" And he goes on to describe the narrowing of the word from its earlier width as meaning "practical."

7. See, for example, David Riesman et al.

8. Hegel (1952), paragraphs 6 and 7. " . . . the ego is also the transition from undifferentiated indeterminacy to the differentiation, determination, and positing of a determinacy as a content and object," etc.

9. Marx, Vol. I, p. 356.

10. Marx, Vol. II, p. 104. The Eighteenth Brumaire of Louis Bonaparte.

11. But not, it should perhaps be emphasised, the possibility of regret. The pains of choosing are obviously not the only pains of the human condition.

12. Smith, Book IV, Chapter 2, p. 421.

13. Hegel (1975), p. 89.

14. Aristotle, 1356b.

15. See, for example, Brownmiller and Millett.

16. Ryle, p. 143.

The Roots of Modern Dogmatism

JUNE 1983

Abstract: This is the text of the Latham Memorial Lecture 1983 delivered on May 10, 1983, at Sydney University. To quote Kenneth Minogue it is a lecture "which takes off from Hegel and Marx and which explains the way in which a certain kind of philosophy has become in modern societies a loyalty that competes with patriotism and everything traditional. I wanted to call it, parodying a lecture of Hayek's, "Universals: True and False."

I have spent the last few years thinking about ideology, and I crave your pity for it. Ideological thinking is narrow, repetitive, limited in range and saturated in rancor, and, I tell you frankly, I shall be glad to see the back of it. But I have now almost finished assembling my thoughts, and my theme of Universals, true and false, is obliquely related to them. I must begin by trying to indicate the kind of argument I wish to present.

It is a species of philosophical analysis, stiffened by intellectual history. And it may help if I explain what I am trying to do by way of an image. It is taken from the puzzles which used to feature in the

Kenneth Minogue, "The Roots of Modern Dogmatism." This article is reprinted with permission from the publisher of *Quadrant* 27, no. 6 (June 1983): 38–46. © 1983, *Quadrant*.

children's corner of newspapers. The joining together with a pencil
of a series of numbered dots eventually produced some whimsical
animal such as a rabbit. Philosophers discover less commonplace
beasts, whose shape cannot be so easily discerned by moving from
one already numbered dot to the next. For example, Jean Jacques
Rousseau in the 18th century lived among many people who hated
the *ancien regime* and yearned for a true community. Some were
clear about one feature of this community, some about another, but
it took Jean Jacques to delineate the whole thing, in the *Contrat
Social*, right down to some nasty hidden claws it contained in the
concept of freedom associated with it. Rousseau was a relatively local hero of this type of philosophical practice, but there have been
some, like Plato and Aristotle, who have delineated animals of such
ubiquity that we may still read their works and experience revela-
tions about how we think.

    That the philosopher reveals things which people had not seen
before—not at least in all its wholeness—might seem to align him
with the psycho-analyst, who purports to reveal hidden determinants of thought and feeling locked away in the subconscious. Such
a comparison needs to be treated with caution. The things a philosopher may discover are not hidden. They are all there on the
surface, like the aesthetic properties explored by the critic. They
merely need to be pointed to by an acute and experienced observer.
And this means that once the job has been done, those who follow
can perhaps build upon it, or recapture what has been forgotten.
This is why the history of philosophy is part of philosophy itself
in a way in which the history of science is not itself science. Now
the animal that concerns me (if I may be permitted to continue the
image) is called ideology, and the work of delineating its character
was done by Germans early in the nineteenth century. It consists in
what Marx made of certain doctrines of Hegel. Hence the first part
of my talk will describe this particular intellectual adventure, and
also attempt to clarify what I take to be its true character, for it was
soon overlaid with other preoccupations. I shall then draw some

implications from my argument which will, I hope, illuminate the character of modern intellectual and political controversy and exhibit what I believe to be a problem that lies at the heart of modern Western civilization.

I

I must begin by stipulating with brutal simplicity what I mean by ideology. It is a doctrine to the effect that the world we live in is characterised by a variety of subtle forms of oppression or domination, and that life inevitably consists in either submitting to domination or struggling for liberation. This simple formula, of course, describes no actual belief held by any actual person. It is, rather, a kind of cocktail gin or mixer, always found in combination with moral and political beliefs specifying the oppressed, the particular modes of oppression and much else. But I believe that it is the element which allows these actual beliefs to flow—like the gold which symbolized understanding for the alchemists of old—with a marvelous light. For our beginnings, we must turn to Hegel.

II

Hegel turned world history into a story of the progress of mankind. The theme was the growth of freedom and self-consciousness. The central character of the story was, for technical reasons, not mankind itself, but something called *Geist*, or Spirit. From a temporal point of view, *Geist* is a process of development, an unfolding of potentialities. As a striving to develop, *Geist* is free and creative, and this constitutes what Hegel called its "universality." On the other hand, to actualise itself, *Geist* must incorporate itself in material things, especially individuals, with particular interests and passions. In terms of this machinery—whose development constitutes Hegel's dialectical logic—the career of such a figure as Alexander the Great can be understood at two levels. At the level of the particular, Alexander may be understood historically, through the culture to which he belonged and the ideas and aspirations which explain what he did. At the universal level, Alexander is a world-historical personality whose "task" or "mission" it was to destroy the oriental despotisms to the East and to diffuse the more advanced conceptions of freedom and objectivity which had been created by the Greeks.

This machinery sounds somewhat cumbersome to us now, and as Charles Taylor has recently been arguing, as a synthesis, it has now quite dissolved.[1] Nonetheless, Hegel was using this machinery to throw light on a problem which is by no means superannuated. I refer to the ever-fascinating question of the character of the sort of modern society in which we live. It is evidently very different from any society before it, but how? Hegel answered this question by way of a theory of the development of the whole human race. Again, let us sketch it out.

Imagine a primitive tribesman of long ago, living, as we tend to think of him, essentially as a member of his tribe. The tribe itself is constituted by custom, the tribesman unable to conceive of himself apart from it. Indeed, he probably imagines that there is little else in the entire world, rather like Papageno when he meets Tamino in *The Magic Flute*. Tamino explains that his father rules over many peoples, and therefore he, Tamino, is a Prince.

"Regions?" exclaims Papageno, "People? Prince? Tell me, do you mean to say that outside this place there are more regions and people?"

Tamino: "Thousands."

Such a tribesman has, like Papageno, little that we should recognise as an inner life, no subjective individuality. Nor, on the other hand, has the tribe developed anything in the way of political institutions, which would be abstract and involve a historical sense of the tribe's past. Man and nature are here imagined to be so similar as barely to be distinguishable.

Now in elaborating his account of human development, Hegel appropriated from epistemology the long-established distinction between universal and particular. In any process of understanding, the identification of an actual thing is impossible unless we can characterise it in some general way, as tree, or spade, or at worst blob or blur, while to specify it, on the other hand, we must recognise its particularity as this or that tree or spade, blob or blur. Hegel used this apparatus in its Aristotelian form, in which universals can never be encountered except as embodied in some actual thing. Thus we may find scattered through Hegel's writing such remarks as:

> If anyone wishes to marry or to build a house, etc. the result is important to the individual only. The truly divine and universal is the institution of agriculture, the state, marriage, etc. . . .[2]

The development of mankind, as Hegel argues it can be gleaned from history, is thus in part the growth of the complexity of the institutions of human life (the state, marriage and the like) and, relatedly, the growth of its activities, such as technology, art and philosophy. And this process, like the philosophy of Hegel itself, gains its strength from the fact that it is an endless scuttling back and forth between the universal and the particular, between the objective and the subjective, so that the complementary conditions of human life are spun out of the warp and weft of human life, through a steady process of abstraction and objectification on the one hand, and the development of subjectivity on the other. Even the very expression "tribesman" with which we began is anachronistic in its suggestion of a possibility of the separation of the tribesman from the tribe which, *ex hypothesi*, would not have been possible at this early stage.

Nearly everything that Hegel wrote is a reflection upon the basic theme. It is the subject matter of the philosophy of history, in which freedom emerges first as a glimmer of possibility in the oriental despotism and is then brilliantly explored and developed in its objective form by the Greeks. But precisely because of this gift for objectivity, the Greeks were deficient in their capacity for exploring subjective individuality. In the *History of Philosophy* Hegel treats the fate of Socrates as a tragedy in which subjective individuality comes into conflict with the abstract objectivity of the Athenian state and Greek culture. With the fall of Rome, *Geist* retreats into its own subjectivity, only to emerge with the beginnings of the modern world. The history of the modern world, Hegel believes, is like the coming of "a bright and glorious day. This day" (he goes on)

> is the day of Universality, which breaks upon the world after the long, eventful, and terrible night of the Middle Ages; a day which is distinguished by science, art and inventive impulse; that is, by the noblest and highest, and which Humanity, rendered free by Christianity and emancipated through the instrumentality of the Church, exhibits as the eternal and veritable substance of its being.[3]

This passage is one that ends the Philosophy of History, and you will see that, among his many talents, Hegel was a good man to orchestrate a climax. Perhaps we might elaborate the idea a little further by switching to another area: namely, Hegel's logic. You might suspect this to be an unpromising and sterile area, but you would be wrong. For, as Hegel remarks,

> It may be well at the commencement of logic to examine the story which treats of the origin and the bearings of the very knowledge logic has to discuss. For, though philosophy must not allow herself to be overawed by religion, or accept the position of existence on sufferance, she cannot afford to neglect these popular conceptions. The tales and allegories of religion, which have enjoyed for thousands of years the veneration of nations, are not to be set aside as antiquated even now.[4]

And then he proceeds to discuss the story of Adam and Eve in the Garden of Eden. Our first ancestors are to be found at the beginning in perfect and unreflecting harmony with nature, until Eve eats of the apple at the serpent's prompting. Hegel takes the view that the story has misleadingly externalized the temptation:

> . . . the truth is [he tells us] that the step into opposition, the awakening of consciousness, follows from the very nature of man: and the same history repeats itself in every son of Adam.

For the original harmony with nature and innocence of our first parents belongs to nature, and cannot survive the emergency of spirit, of self-consciousness, of the human capacity to separate itself out and consider things in abstraction. And then

> The first reflection of awakened consciousness in men told them that they were naked. This is a naïve and profound trait. For the sense of shame bears evidence to the separation of man from his natural and sensuous life. The beasts never get so far as this separation, and they feel no shame. And it is in the human feeling of shame that we are to seek the spiritual and moral origin of dress, compared with which the merely physical need is a secondary matter.[5]

Hegel thus takes the story of Adam and Eve as a parable, and in the twist he gave to it, it happens to constitute one of the basic formal patterns of ideological thinking. In the beginning is a primal innocence, a harmony which must be shattered. Man falls into separation and self-consciousness, into the possibility of pursuing his own narrow and particular ends, and when he seeks these "apart from the universal, he is evil; and his evil is to be subjective."[6] But it is the task of Spirit, which has shattered this primal harmony, also to restore it at a higher level, for what Hegel calls "the second harmony" must spring from the labour and the culture of the spirit. "Except ye become as little children," he quotes from the gospel, but adds that we must not *remain* children. The way down is thus the way up, the path to the heights. Or, to put it in Hegel's own technical language, the descending into the particular. And it is in this way that Hegel deals with the suggestion that it is philosophy itself, the pride "which leads man to trust to his own powers for a knowledge of the truth"[7] which constitutes the original sin. What thought has disrupted can only by thought be put together again.

Now I remarked earlier that Hegel's central preoccupation is very close to our own. Let me explain what I mean. Original sin is notoriously disruptive of social and familial harmonies. Each of us is not only conscious of our separation from each other, but also equipped with powerful desires likely to bring us into conflict with our fellows. Such desires are characterised as vices: greed, pride, ambition, sloth and the like. Even brothers fall out. If Cain does not always actually kill Abel, he spends a lot of time engaged in fisticuffs, or walking off in a huff. It thus seems that the condition for human harmony is, if you will forgive me continuing to use this suggestive terminology, the submission of the particular individual to some universal scheme.

The history of social and political thought is a history of a concern with order and justice, often understood as some sort of functional harmony. Or, in a more modern idiom, we all have roles to play, and it is best if we identify our lives with them—men as providers, women as wives and mothers etc. And this instinct for order which runs very deep can appear in many forms. One of the most abstract and exiguous of these, I remember, was what Professor John Anderson used to excoriate as the "ideology of service: in which young people were simply told that virtue was the subordination of one's own inclinations to *any* larger cause. Such simple views respond to a modern world composed of self-willed people equipped with distinctively modern moral organs such as will, conscience and personal opinion. Such people seek to live their lives in terms of rights. If one believes in the importance of order, this feature of the modern world must induce, and often has induced, a profound sense of anxiety which leads to a strong conviction, seldom entirely absent from anyone of the age of about forty, that everything's going to the dogs.

And yet, the dogs are still waiting. They may not, in the end, wait in vain, of course. We just don't know. All we do know is that the history of modern societies has from about the sixteenth century onwards been one of steady dissolution of traditional roles and accepted conventions of subordination. Generations well before our own have believed that the process has gone as far as it possibly could, only to discover, usually horror-stricken, that it can indeed go further. Consider the knocks taken by such disparate figures as the husband and the professor in our own days. Yet the consequence has not quite been the feared disorder. It is now clear—it has, in some respects of course, been clear for centuries—that we Europeans have evolved a quite new form of human association. It has been less clear, but it is certainly true, that much of the vocabulary and many of the locutions we use simply serve to conceal from us its essential character. This particular problem is tangential to my present business, but let me at least say that while the traditional image of order resembled a pyramid, or perhaps the model of classification known as the tree of Porphyry, the modern reality of order more closely resembles those fantastic shapes of recombinant molecules often used to popularize the hypotheses of chemistry. The philosophical lineage of this newer mode of self understanding includes Montaigne's *Essays*, Hobbes's account of the contractual and rule-governed character of human virtue, Montesquieu's account of *monarchie*, Hume's view of the passions, and we might perhaps add in some respects John Anderson's article "Mind as Feeling."

Hegel's philosophy is thus an attempt to understand modernity in all its aspects, and part of the way in which he approached this task was to give an account of human progress in terms of the emergence of the universal or rational side of the human spirit and its contrast with the particular and subjective side. His insistence upon the dialectical relationship of these ideas is a way of blocking off the rationalism which merely *subordinates* the personal and particular to some abstract universal, the sort of rationalism in which the passions must accommodate themselves to a grand plan. It is the universal element in human life which allows us to be self-conscious, to construe ourselves as part of a wider scheme both of concepts and institutions. But it has also been Hegel's achievement—often thought to be a notorious achievement, in the bad sense—to make universality a character incapable of standing on its own, necessarily yoked to the world of passions and particularities without embodiment in which it could have no reality. Any attempt to interpret the world must necessarily take account of these features of human experience, whatever terminology it may use.

III

Among Hegel's Universals was the State. It was the highest realisation of the human community on earth.[8] There were, indeed, higher realisations of *Geist*—art, religion and philosophy itself. But as a life-form, the State transcended all the political forms that had gone before it.

Hegel died in 1831, and in the 1840s the young Marx, who had never been taught by Hegel but was greatly influenced by disciples, wrestled with the Hegelian philosophy and came to a famous conclusion:

> The executive of the Modern State is but a committee for managing the common affairs of the whole bourgeoisie.[9]

Law, morality and religion were all consigned to the class of false and mystificatory beliefs. What, we must ask, had become of Hegel's universals?

In the autumn of 1843, Marx wrote an essay "On the Jewish Question" which was published the following year. In the course of castigating his erstwhile associate Bruno Bauer, who had taken a liberal position about the civil rights of Jews, Marx attacked the idea that the equal relations of citizens in any way transcends or cancels out social and economic inequalities. In civil society, wrote Marx, man

> acts as a *private individual*, regards other men as a means, degrades himself into a means, and becomes the plaything of alien powers.[10]

Man is discovered to be living in two quite separate spheres, which Marx ironically calls, in these early writings, an earthly and a heavenly world. The earthly world consists in the unequal and alienated life of society, while the heavenly life consists not merely in the fantasies of religion, but in the abstract promise of civil life. Like religion, the state must be seen through: revealed as a shadow masquerading as a substance. It is another of those dream compensations of men who have become instruments of a process they do not understand. The perfect political state, Marx tells us, is "but its nature, man's *species-life*, as *opposed* to his material life." And Marx italicizes the idea of opposition here because the process of criticism, as he understands it, consists in separating out the reality from the promise. Underlying Marx's critique of the state, as David McLellan has recently written

> lay the possibility of forming a truly free association of citizens in a state conceived, on the Hegelian model, as the incarnation of reason.[11]

But in this particular essay, Marx had not yet thought through his position. The *idea* of the state might actually represent man's species-life, even though the states that actually existed in Europe contradicted the real interests of their members. But as with everything else Marx was to analyse in the modern world, the state turned out to be a false universal, an illusion masquerading as a philosophical concept. Just such a pattern of criticism continued to be a staple of Marx's thought for the rest of his life. It was as if he imagined that such a universal had actually been born, but actually, this blessed event had happened nowhere else than in their imaginations. Hegel had, for example, imagined that the Prussian bureaucracy was a "universal class" but this too was an illusion. Marx believed, of course, that a true universal class was actually in the process of being born. It was not, however, a bureaucracy falsely supposed capable of harmonising the interests of all classes in society, but (I quote McClellan again)

> the proletariat whose needs and aspirations coincided in the long run with those of humanity as a whole.[12]

These disagreements between Hegel and Marx are explicitly concerned with religion and the state, but the real issue lies in the role of philosophy. That issue may become clear if we employ a metaphor. On Hegel's view, the philosopher is someone who has managed to reach a mountain top from which he may survey the pattern of human endeavour as a whole. His trips to the mountain-top, however, must be brief and limited, for the atmosphere is so thin that life cannot be lived at that level. Hence, even the philosopher must return from these intellectual adventures and live his own life the way others lead theirs. The actual lives of individuals can never be anything but fragmentary—abstract, in Hegel's special use of the word—and wholeness, concreteness can be found nowhere but in the understanding of the philosopher who can put it all together. Marx, by contrast, starts with a vision of actual human suffering. Such suffering came to be most dramatically symbolised for Marx in the condition of the working class in mid-nineteenth-century Europe, but in fact Marx believed that everyone suffered, everyone was subject to the degradation of domination by outside things, everyone was alienated. To put the matter vulgarly, Marx believed that it wasn't good enough that philosophers might enjoy a vision of coherence while the rest of the human race soldiered on in the dismal valleys of abstraction. It was necessary that the whole human race should not merely share but actually *live* this vision. It thus came to seem plausible to Marx that philosophers were wrong in thinking their visits to the mountain top to be merely a temporary release for the happy few from the burdens of abstraction. What they had actually done was, unwittingly, to lead the human race through the Sinai of history to the very edge of the promised land. Behind them, the toiling masses of humanity laboured on in a wilderness rendered increasingly inhospitable by the passage of time and hardship. But now Marx and his contemporaries too had reached the mountain top and could see over to the land of Canaan. And what Marx was proposing was to lead the masses down into that promised land.[13] Such was the drama Marx had in mind as he scribbled down that famous thesis on Feuerbach: "The Philosophers have only interpreted the world. The point is to change it." Here is a remark to stiffen the sinews and summon up the blood, and it is certainly true that many a follower of this doctrine has gone on to disguise fair nature with hard-favour'd rage. Here, then, is a philosophical resolution of a problem which calls for commitment rather than demands to understanding.

The first stage in the attempt to change the world, and one highly congenial to Marx and all the intellectuals who, then and now, shared his commitment, was an intellectual operation which Marx called "criticism." This particular term has a long and fascinating history going back to the rational investigation of the Bible in the seventeenth century, but in Marx's usage it is a process of exposing error whose final outcome is to produce in society a special condition called a "crisis." The two words are etymologically related, which is convenient, because on Marx's view the point of the one is to induce the other. The first stage of this operation was an attack upon Christianity, which Marx usually generalised as "religion." What he said about religion had paralleled what he said about the state. Religion was another of those abstract and impractical visions of the Promised Land whose function was to enervate men and discourage them from taking their destiny into their own hands. Everywhere Marx looked, in fact, he saw a special kind of debilitating unreality in which the possession of the shadow in thought inhibited men from seeking the substance in life. Nothing is more ferocious in the early Marx than his detestation of what he called "the *Hegelian* miracle apparatus"[14] by which metaphysics produces merely intellectual solutions to real problems.

The critical practice of the Young Hegelians consisted in discovering that the ideals and aspirations, indeed the very *meanings*, of human thought and practice were actually the secret of human evolution. It rejected the kind of realism which consists of reducing dreams and aspirations to mere illusion which evaded the grosser realities of the human condition. It was not in the least cynical. On the contrary, it was a kind of supercharged idealism which identified reality with the actualisation of the idea itself. The religious conception of love and forgiveness, for example, was by no means taken to be merely a sentimental illusion cherished by alienated man. It was, rather, an insight into the character of a true society. Thus we find Marx elaborating Hegel's view of punishment as the doctrine that the criminal in his punishment passes sentence upon himself. Marx comments that this is merely the *ius talionis* in speculative disguise, and goes on:

> Plato long ago realised that the *law* must be *one-sided* and take no account of the individual. On the other hand, under *human* conditions punishment will *really* be nothing but the sentence passed by the culprit upon himself. No one will want to convince him that *violence* from *without*, done to him by others, is violence which he has done to himself. On the contrary, he will see in *other* men his natural saviours from the punishments which he has imposed on himself, in other words, the relation will be reversed.[15]

It is well known that Feuerbach, who powerfully influenced Marx's view of religion, invented a transformational method of interpreting Hegel, in which subject and predicate were reversed. Marx's ingenious use of this method of reversal here shows what transformations it can accomplish. It also helps us to see the extent to which, in Marx's thought, human beings *belong* to the community even more closely knit than a family. He is thinking, in other words, of what in traditional political philosophy is called a "despotism." Crime is *anything* that separates us from the community, and must be followed by reintegration.

Punishment is, by its very nature and circumstances, the human institution most easily susceptible to being criticised as a False Universal.[16] In respect of the state itself, Marx soon came to the belief that a false universal was masquerading in place of the true, but it took him some time to clarify just what he was going to posit as the true universal in this area. Sometimes he described it as "democracy," sometimes as "emancipation" and sometimes as "communism," but since the true universal is humanity itself, these ideas, adopted for polemical purposes, may be discarded. The real universal is species-man. For Marx, universality begins in the fact that human beings, by contrast with other earthly creatures, are conscious of themselves as members of the same species; they belong to their own human world, and it is this self-consciousness which cannot but guide them in their actions. Marx tells us that man duplicates himself in consciousness, intellectually, and in a parallel way, he "duplicates himself" in reality by his productive activity. Hence the object of labour is "the *objectification of man's species-life*," but the objects are in effect "stolen" from him by the fact that he must use these objects to live, work in competition with his fellows, and distinguish his time into a free activity called leisure and a period of enslavement called work.[17]

Perhaps the best way of saying what Marx was getting at is to suggest that mankind is, under capitalism, robbed by abstraction, because this formula captures the way in which Marx seeks to unite philosophy and the world. Hegel, of course, knew perfectly well that humans, as self-conscious creatures, act in awareness of a universal element of which they are a part: the family, the state, perhaps even humanity itself. What they are aware of, however, is merely an abstract universal at best, one that has been conjured out of practice. They may, for example, see the state merely in terms of its external character as restricting, by its laws and demands, their freedom. Only the philosopher, released briefly from practice, can arrive at an understanding of the true or concrete universal, such as Hegel believed himself to have expounded in the *Philosophy of Right*. Now Marx saw the intellectual inadequacy of ordinary people in terms of a division of labour imposed upon men by the structure of society, rather than an intractable consequence of the difference between action and speculation. It was thus necessary, and it was possible to convert the abstract universals of our modern world into the concrete universals of philosophy. Such conversion could not possibly leave philosophy unchanged; philosophy could no longer remain the academic, indeed esoteric, practice of an iso- lated few cut off from the workaday world. The problem lay thus in the division of labour, especially that between mental and mate- rial labour. We may thus say that those who in communist regimes have sent university professors out to toil in the rice paddies and restricted places at universities to the children of manual workers may have a pretty crude idea of the solution, but they have certainly grasped what Marx believed to have been the problem.

It is in these terms, with one qualification to be mentioned, that we may interpret the central theme of this portentous philosophi- cal adventure in reasoning which has proved so dazzling to mil- lions of bookish men. What, Marx demands in the *Contribution to the Critique of Hegel's Philosophy of Law*, is the positive possibility of a German emancipation? And he answers as follows:

> In the formation of a class with *radical chains*, a class of
> civil society which is not a class of civil society, an estate

which is the dissolution of all estates, a sphere which has a universal character by its universal suffering and claims no particular right because no particular wrong but *wrong generally* is perpetrated against it; which can no longer invoke a historical but only a *human* title; which does not stand in any one-sided antithesis to the premises of the German state; a sphere, finally, which cannot emancipate itself without emancipating itself from all other spheres of society and thereby emancipating all other spheres of society, in a word, is the *complete loss* of man and hence can win itself only through the *complete rewinning* of man. This dissolution of society as a particular estate is the *proletariat*.[18]

Now the rhetorical brilliance of this passage is such that it may well confuse us as to its import. Those first few sentences are like the riddles which heroes must answer in order to pursue the grail or get the girl. What is a class that is not a class? What is an estate that is the dissolution of all estates? There is a smell of magic in the air, and an even stronger smell of religion, for the doctrine advanced here asserts, or perhaps parodies, the view that the meek shall inherit the earth. Further, since we read this passage through the spectacles of hindsight, we know that this doctrine was to project into modern life a whole new political party and a new style of politics. We think that we understand the terms "bourgeois" and "proletarian" because we know how they came to be defined and how the idea was developed. They are, in fact, interestingly technical terms. "Proletariat" is, philosophically speaking, a blank which can stand for any set of people believed to be oppressed. It is a word taken from the politics of early Rome, where it signified the lowest of the classes called out for military purposes, the group which had nothing to contribute to the defense of Rome but their offspring (*proles*). "Bourgeois" had signified anything from city-dweller to (in some towns such as Geneva) a particular legal class of person having specific rights and duties. But what "bourgeois" signifies, in terms of this philosophical argument, is everyone in respect of being conscious of himself or herself as an individual, conscious, to put it in the favoured language of those days, of the separation of man from man. This is why generations after a proletarian revolution, rulers can still discover a phenomenon which the Soviet authorities have called "bourgeois remnants in the consciousness of the people." What thus emerges from Marx's thought is a purely abstract set of meanings waiting to be filled by local circumstance. Ideology, in other words, is here a pure theory awaiting some circumstantial content. An evil society is diagnosed, a theory propounded, a revolution envisaged, a better society adumbrated, and a world will emerge in which—well, in which what?

It isn't clear, and Marx, of course, did little to help. He thought that communism was inevitable, and desirable, but felt the need to say little about it. It was already a foetus in the womb of history, and undoubtedly, as it emerged, would produce also the tastes needed to sustain it. To describe it in 1848, even had that been logically possible, would have been merely to produce one more utopia for a public which would treat it like an item on the menu of the future, and Marx would have no truck with such bourgeois frivolity. To put before people such a picture of the future would be to invoke the voluntarist apparatus of choice, the determination of life by (necessarily individual) preferences, and that (Marx believed) was precisely the feature of modern life from which all other evils flowed. For preferences are inevitably particular, and the true community will, of course, be a universal, something necessary rather than contingent. This, presumably, is why Marx says virtually nothing about the type of society around which his remark notionally revolves, except for the odd frivolous remark about hunting, fishing and literary criticism. But for us, who know of the effects upon the world of generations of believers, the question of the character of this future world has more than a passing significance.

The best account of it I can give is to say that it seems to mean that everyone will, as it were, "live philosophy." For philosophy will, by its critical activity, be instrumental in bringing this new society to birth, and it will then dissolve into the very interstices of the emerging communion of mankind. No longer an isolated specialism of the universities, philosophy will become the very texture of our life and work. To translate this back into the Hegelian language whence it came, it amounts to saying that we shall all live at the level of the universal. What, then, will become of particularity? I'm not quite sure of the answer to this question, but I think it runs as follows: what Hegel had called "particularity" consisted, in this area, of the private transactions and domestic passions of individual men and women living in states, and all such things, in their separation of man from man, are what Marx took to be expressions of the structural domination of bourgeois society. Reflection had, as it were, been hijacked by the dominant class who had reduced the oppressed to a mechanical condition of abstract subservience. The oppressors had succeeded in acquiring power, but oppressors and oppressed alike had, in the process, lost their humanity. To realise the full potential of humanity thus requires the abolition of particularity understood in this sense. Once again, *The Magic Flute* in its account of the esoteric progressivism of Viennese freemasonry states the issue in its most transparent form. You may remember where the Third Priest has doubts about whether Tamino can stand the trials ahead, and ends by remarking: "He is a Prince!" To which Sarastro replies:

"Much more, he is a Man!"

All particularities, then, such as husband and wife, prince and subject, debtor and creditor, even the particularities of lovers who raise each other irrationally above the universal of humanity, will therefore dissolve into the rationality of man to man, constitutive of the species life of humanity.

We know from Marx and Engels that this condition will be the end of politics. It will also be the reason why the state will wither

away. It will also be the end of tragedy, for this new universal subject Man (no longer *Geist*) will take into its own hands the conscious direction of its own destiny. It is an important part of Hegel's
doctrine that historical actors cannot understand the significance
of what they are doing because they are absorbed in the parochial
ties or particularities of their passions and purposes. The cunning
of Reason, it will be remembered, sends men and passions into battle for it, leaving these particularities to suffer the pains and losses,
while Reason itself remains unscathed. But with the coming of the
new society, all battles are won, and these usurping particularities
will dissolve into that of which they are fundamentally composed—
universality, on the one hand, and matter on the other. Hegel had
thought that the universal can actualise itself directly in material-
ity, in the productive process which purely expresses the species
life of mankind, with man and product as two inseparable sides of
the same concrete reality, leaving *nothing* outside it—not God, not
individual passion, not philosophy or reflection itself.

IV

In this literature of the 1840s, then, is to be found delineated a pure
theory of ideology, a suitable peg on which one might hang almost
any set of grievances, almost any proposal for radical change. It
happened that Marx and Engels spent the rest of their lives elaborating this idea in terms of the circumstances of workers in the fac-
tories of nineteenth-century Europe, and that the arena into which
this theorising came to be channeled was that of the politics of
competing parties. We therefore regard communism, anarchism,
nazism, etc. as political doctrines, and working backwards from
this judgement, we think of all political doctrines such as liberalism
and social democracy as being ideologies. But it has also struck the
imaginations of many people that ideological doctrines can generate a fanatical kind of loyalty and are therefore distinguishable from
the ordinary elements of political competition with which we are
familiar.

When we observe the strong elements of ritual (in communism, for example, Lenin's tomb, the liturgical expressions, the passion for doctrinal purity) which are found in all ideologies, we are often tempted to consider them forms of surrogate religion. Such a view would help to explain the evident futility of discussion across ideological lines. For what is there to discover if one possesses the truth already? It would perhaps even help to explain the curious duplicity of ideologists, who demand in liberal democracies civil rights which they propose to subvert the moment they have the power to do so. Such a view would in addition cast light on many of the phenomena of ideological conversion, and disenchantment, leading to the exposure of (as the title of a famous book had it) "the god who failed." Ideologies have therefore been discovered to be not politics, but religion.

This type of conclusion might well cause a certain impatience. Is it not, at best, essentialism, at worst a piece of trivial semantic demarcating? Since this particular conclusion happens largely to be one I don't wish to support, I have no wish to defend it in substance, but I do think that it responds to a legitimate and interesting question. Things are not always what they seem, and to call ideologies religions does help us recognise certain features of their strangeness, of what distinguishes them from genuinely political allegiances. My argument, however, is that the view that ideologies are religions does not really capture what is at stake. Our civilisation is hospitable to religions. We keep inventing them all the time. They fit easily into our political and social life, asking for nothing more than the right to practise and to evangelise. Quakers may be reluctant to fight in wars, but they are perfectly happy to serve their country in some other way.

The significant thing about ideologies is that they are hostile not merely to religion but also to patriotism. They constitute not merely a separate loyalty, but a separate kind of loyalty. We sometimes think, for example, that a member of the Irish Republican Army is just a kind of supercharged patriot. But this is a serious mistake. Like many nationalists, such people often detest the actual religion, character and beliefs of the people on whose behalf they purport to be fighting. Their real allegiance is to a country laid up in the heavens, and they are prepared to kill and maim lots of actual Irishmen in serving it. Australian nationalists may be found, of an ideological kind, who regard your actual Ocker as a deplorable betrayal of the early promise of Australian history. Wherever nationalism may be found in ideological forms, it includes a strong component of detestation of the actual *patria*. And what this fact suggests is that an ideology is a special *kind* of philosophical loyalty. It regards patriotism as merely one of those false universals against which it must struggle. Its own loyalty lies elsewhere. The same is true of feminists, who often dislike the actual women of today, or those communists who presume to correct the consciousness of actual workers.

I take the view, then, that many of the puzzling features of ideology can be explained by recognising it as a kind of philosophy. And in calling ideology a kind of philosophy, I must take the opportunity of apologising to professional philosophers who, inclined in any case these days to blackball Hegel, may well find themselves squirming at the thought that they are being identified with a set of vulgar political activists. Hegel himself, incidentally, notes that the word "philosophy" can cover some strange things, and in the *Logic* has a passage on "what the English call philosophy," wherein he includes a footnote observing:

> Among the advertisements of books just published, I lately found the following notice in an English newspaper. The Art of Preserving the Hair, on Philosophical Principles, neatly printed in post8vo, price seven shillings.

Any reader of Shakespeare will remember that the word "philosopher" commonly signified to the Elizabethans a practical Stoic, one who would repress his groans at the dentist. Philosophy is one of those upmarket expressions to which mountebanks and publicists may, and do, lay claim.

Ideology is philosophical in that it is a doctrine which purports to explain the character of reality (and therefore cannot be identified with any *particular* science) and because it rests upon no other foundation than its own evident rationality. It is therefore not a religion. Whether it satisfactorily explains reality, and whether its standards of evident rationality are cogent are, of course, quite separate questions, and ones which have produced little in the way of a literature that professional philosophers would take very seriously. The implicit claim is, however, that an ideological doctrine possesses a universal perspective of such scope and magnitude that even professional philosophers themselves feature within it as little more than myopic pedants unwittingly serving the interests of domination. Claims of this kind and scope are by no means unprecedented. In another part of the intellectual forest, for example, may be found all manner of doctrines (usually forms of mysticism, packaged in the modern world as techniques of the will) which claim to be the source and foundation of everything in our culture. Some versions of sufism exemplify this claim, and so does theosophy. In some respects, these doctrines may be recognised as forms of gnostic religion. But for my purposes on this occasion, all that matters is that whoever is drawn towards some version of an ideological doctrine, however superficially, begins to take upon himself or herself some of the rhetorical apparatus and mythology of philosophy.

By "rhetorical apparatus" I refer to the fact that the posture of the philosopher is that of a rational man awakening from the deep sleep of practical involvement. The exemplary legend of his process is the life of Socrates, who spent a lifetime obeying his *daimon* and attempting to rouse his fellow Athenians from the sleep of everyday life. They were so grateful to him that they gave him a cup of poison to drink. Hegel, as we have seen, was greatly interested in the career of Socrates, to which he interpreted as a tragedy in the

Greek sense: a clash between the abstract universality of the Greek *polis* and a subjectivity which had developed too far for its culture to be able to tolerate. Like the ideologists who have remotely taken off from his thought, Hegel was an optimist, and thought that the resolution of the famous case of the People v. Socrates was ultimately to be found in the further development of *Geist*. Similarly, the ideologist believes himself to be, like the Hegelian Socrates, on the side of the future. His superiority lies in his sense of having grasped the universal in a world composed of people still blundering around amid particularities, some of which are masquerading as universals. And in some degree, great or small, the ideologist may be recognised as an exponent of the practice of criticism directed at the delusive universals—the idols, as he might see them—of the society in which he lives.

We have seen that Marx rejected the modern European state as a false universal disguising bourgeois domination. Hegel had seen the state, in his complex philosophical vision, as an entity necessarily wider than the political thoughts that might be generated within it; and in practice statesmen make demands upon their subjects by claiming that they have a more rational and informed understanding of what the community needs than the population at large. Marxism, like other ideologies, "unmasks" this claim, and thus makes its own bid for universal status.

The objectivity of markets is, in a similar way, exposed as a mechanism which, for all the purported equality of the exchange relation, allows the rich to exert the power of wealth. Feminists discover in the family a disguised form of patriarchal domination. It might be thought that academic activities, as the disinterested pursuit of truth, might escape this form of criticism. Not so. In ideological terms, everything that happens "in society" is part of a struggle, partly overt but mostly disguised, between the oppressors and the oppressed, and the very worst form of mystification is the illusion that anything is outside this struggle. Hence the ideological view of academics resembles what the famous Punch cartoon said about the role of the cavalry in battle: they are there to give a touch of class to what would otherwise be nothing more than a vulgar brawl. No universal is in principle beyond the possibility of destructive reduction to base particulars. Sanity has, by psychiatrists calling themselves critical, been unmasked as a form of domination by the capitalist way of life; so too has Reason, particularly by the Frankfurt School; many apparently peripheral things have been subject to the same kind of criticism: the idea of an educated accent, for example, has been taken as a device by which the elite bends the mass to its will.

It is a further implication of the ideological hijack of the idea of philosophy that political controversy takes place between, on the one hand, a set of possessors of the truth whose sole ground of action is the very rationality of the *praxis* in which they are engaged, and on the other, a collection of particular interests. Since they argue at the level of the universal, they have left behind, indeed transcended, all particularity; while those who disagree must be explained in terms of their failure to have achieved this sort of transcendence. There are many consequences of this conviction, and they may help to explain the often baffling failure of minds to meet whenever any discussion takes place between ideology and its critics. One of them is that ideological criticism in politics need sometimes consist in nothing more than listing positions and associations (party membership, company directorships, etc.) which are taken as *ipso facto* proofs of vested interest, and hence unsound argument. By contrast, any attempt to do the same thing in reverse leads to indignant complaint that an ethical commitment is being smeared, sullied, bashed or witch-hunted. Another consequence is the tenuous evidential connection between an ideological commitment and any corresponding regime based upon that commitment. There is, of course, a long history of the adulation of ideological regimes at times when it is fashionable to believe that they incarcerated or embodied the universal,[19] but many believers have retreated in good intellectual order from the discovery that the regimes were in fact monstrous. However bad they may be, they have begun to ask the right question, and as we all know, philosophers take questions more seriously than answers. Our own society, by contrast, is a swarm of particulars distracting us from the quest for the true universal.

My argument is, then, that the true contours and the inspirational dynamic of ideology are to be discovered not in religion, nor in the politics which usually provides its substance, but in a special sort of philosophical doctrine. Most intellectuals, and some philosophers, cannot reject the call of ideology without an inexplicable sense that they are rejecting something which has a legitimate claim on their loyalty. This inspirational core of much modern discussion is certainly not hidden, or esoteric, but it is usually in the background because the foreground is dominated by political polemic.

But it is polemic irradiated by a strange enthusiasm, whose cause cannot properly be brought out into the light and examined, because it is essentially incoherent. Universal and particular are (as Hegel had insisted) inseparable aspects of the real world, and the idea of living at the level of the universal, or abolishing, especially, that sense of our own individual particularity from which come conflict and frustration, is at best a dream. But the lure of this dream has entrenched at the heart of the modern world a doctrine whose critical import is systematically destructive of any universals, ideals or standards which we may generate, and whose only positive implications are in the strictest sense impossible. They compose a vision already current in the eighteenth century, and which appears in *The Magic Flute* as follows:

(The Three Boys) Soon to announce morning, the sun will arise on her golden path, soon shall superstition disappear, soon the wise men will conquer. Ah, gracious peace, descend, return again to the hearts of man; then the earth will be a heavenly kingdom, and mortals like the gods.

The problem is, we can't play the part of gods. Even that of angels is beyond our reach. Our situation would be less unfortunate if this vision of a true and heavenly harmony were out in the open, where its feasibility could become an explicit subject of discussion. But the very doctrine itself decrees its own discretion, and leaves humanity on a logical treadmill dreaming of universals which can never be.

NOTES

1. Charles Taylor, *Hegel*, Cambridge University Press, 1975, p. 538: " . . . by his actual synthesis is quite dead. That is, no one actually believes his central ontological thesis, that the universe is poised by a Spirit whose essence is rational necessity."

2. *Hegel's Lectures on the History of Philosophy*, trans. E.S. Haldane, London: Routledge and Kegan Paul, 1963, Vol. 1, p. 424.

3. Hegel, *The Philosophy of History*, trans. J. Sibree, New York: Dover Publications Inc., 1956, p. 220.

4. *The Logic of Hegel*, trans. William Wallace, Oxford University Press, 1904, p. 54.

5. *Ibid.*, p. 55–56.

6. *Ibid.*, p. 57.

7. *Ibid.*, p. 54.

8. Taylor, p. 465.

9. Karl Marx and Frederick Engels, *Collected Works* (henceforth cited as MECW), London: Lawrence and Wishart, 1975, Vol. VI, p. 486 (*The Communist Manifesto*).

10. MECW III, p. 154.

11. *Marx: The First Hundred Years*, Ed. David McLellan, London: Fontana, 1983, p. 143.

12. *Ibid.*, p. 150.

13. My use of this image is a tribute to Lewis Feuer's discussion of the whole subject in *Ideology and the Ideologists*.

14. MECW IV, p. 137.

15. MECW IV, p. 179 (*Economic and Philosophical Manuscripts*).

16. As when, for example, an execution of a criminal whose justice is contested

is called a "judicial murder." As I was writing this, I came across an example of this way of thinking when the defence counsel for a murderer electrocuted in Alabama in April 1983 was quoted as saying: "John Evans was burnt alive tonight (in) the State of Alabama . . . tortured tonight in the name of vengeance and in the disguise of justice." (*Times*, April 25, 1983).

17. MECW III, p. 277.

18. MECW III, p. 186.

19. See, for example, George Hollander, *Political Pilgrims*.

The Conditions of Freedom and
the Condition of Freedom

1984

I

The Liberal tradition is often traced back to John Locke. This is entirely appropriate. Locke was a very tricky customer, and so is liberalism. First you think you understand it, and then you realize that it has slipped through your fingers. The study of Locke can yield the same sensation. It is possible, for example, that we now celebrate the tercentenary of the writing of the *Two Treatises of Government*, but it is also possible that that particular anniversary has already happened: or, indeed, that it will only come in 1989, which is certainly the anniversary of the document's publication.[1] John Locke's general evasiveness—including his consistent refusal even to admit himself the author of his most famous political work—is well known. An interestingly similar evasiveness is characteristic of much of contemporary writing on liberalism.

Liberals descend from the Whigs of the late seventeenth century, but in the 1830's they began calling themselves "liberals," presumably because they thought it appropriate to run the flag of

---

Kenneth Minogue, "The Conditions of Freedom and the Condition of Freedom." From *The Prospects of Liberalism*, edited by Timothy Fuller, Colorado College Studies no. 20 (Colorado Springs: Colorado College, 1984).

liberty up their masthead, rather than other possible flags such as reform, progress or democracy. Yet in the twentieth century, and particularly now, i.e., one hundred and fifty years after that interesting change of name, it is still necessary to ask: Are liberals in favour of liberty? The question is necessary because, particularly in the United States, many who call themselves "liberals" are in favour of more and more central regulation, while others who call themselves "conservatives" are in favour of less regulation. On the face of things, at least, the more regulation seems to take us some distance beyond the point at which political names are usually very bad political descriptions. It takes us, rather, straight into paradox.

There is one easy way of dissolving the paradox. It consists in recognizing that from about 1880 onwards, a certain influential collection of liberals was influenced by socialist arguments in favour of greater state regulation. Instead of actually becoming socialist, however, these liberals assimilated this new alien element to liberalism by the simple device of contending that only the state could provide the *conditions* of liberty for all members of the community. Thus it was said that no individual could properly be free unless he had been somewhat educated and had a full stomach. Thus was derived the liberal allegiance to *compulsory* education and (in time) the welfare state. The sophisticated arguments tending in this direction were presented, in Great Britain, by writers such as T.H. Green, Bernard Bosanquet and L.T. Hobhouse. A historic realignment of liberalism had taken place. Up to this point, Whiggism and liberalism as political traditions had been at the forefront of the rationalizing passion to liquidate whatever was merely traditional or inherited in European societies and thus to break the bonds of government and community. From this point onward, liberalism seemed to go into reverse. Liberals became the party of a centrally fostered community, and much of the inheritance of John Locke and Adam Smith passed over to those who called themselves "conservatives." The curse of Babel had struck again!

In this context of confused aims and purposes, the issue of

liberty as a central criterion of European political life has become obscured, and what I propose to do in this paper is to sketch out, in something like historical terms, what I think liberty means in the European political tradition. My task will be facilitated if I refer initially to a notable analysis of liberty given by Isaiah Berlin in his *Four Essays on Liberty*.[2] Berlin popularized a distinction between negative and positive liberty, and did so with all the more urgency because it seemed at the time he was writing[3] that one of these two kinds of liberty was a dangerous and disruptive imposter. Berlin's fundamental concern was that some totalitarian regimes of the twentieth century had oppressed their subjects while simultaneously claiming that this very oppression constituted a kind of higher liberty. It was plausible to see this kind of practical political claim as being a muddled, or possibly unscrupulous, misuse of Rousseau's famous argument in the *Social Contract* that sometimes the punishment of malefactors amounts to "forcing them to be free." Similar arguments are deployed in the *Philosophy of Right*, in which the supposed opposition between the state and the individual is dissolved as a misleading abstraction. Hegel reveals that there is an important sense in which the individual may be said to will the community and its laws, a sense which is not even contradicted when a particular individual is being punished in terms of those very laws.

It was these arguments which were transformed into a philosophy of self-realization by the English Idealists (notably T.H. Green). Berlin criticizes this tradition root and branch. He tells us: "Once I take this view, I am in a position to ignore the actual wishes of men or societies, to bully, oppress, torture them in the name, and on behalf, of their 'real' selves, in the secure knowledge that whatever is the true goal of man (happiness, performance of duty, wisdom, a just society, self-fulfillment) must be identical with his freedom—the free choice of his 'true', albeit often submerged and inarticulate, self."[4]

Positive freedom thus stands revealed as a kind of confidence

trick familiar to the demagogic politics of our century, and indeed
as an exemplification of that particularly gross corruption of our
political language satirized by George Orwell in the conception
of Newspeak in which things turn into their opposites—peace is
war, freedom is slavery, and so on.[5] Professor Berlin recognizes, of
course, that Rousseau and Hegel were not a pair of cheap crooks,
but he does seem to treat them rather as sorcerers' apprentices
who dallied dangerously long with paradoxes affrontive to common sense. The safer path is evidently to hold firmly to the
common sense notion that freedom means not being hindered.
With such an intellectual ballast, we shall not lose our balance and
succumb to philosophical paradox and totalitarian practice.

Berlin's treatment of liberty is a work of intellectual hygiene,
distinguishing the noxious from the clean. It is possible, however,
to argue that he has, to develop the metaphor of hygiene further,
thrown out the baby along with the bathwater. Such, in fact, is what
I propose to argue, though the reasons will take some time emerging. The clue to what has been left out can be found in the way
that publicists often link liberty with courage. It is very curious
that the idea of "fighting for freedom" is a cliché among publicists
and politicians, yet barely considered by philosophers, who are too
busy with the microscopic work of mapping our usages of the word
"free." Let us, instead, replace the Berlinian distinction with a different division of the subject consisting of three elements, one of
which I shall largely dismiss from consideration.

Firstly, freedom has sometimes been taken to involve a kind of
spiritual mastery of our emotions and responses, an idea most familiar to our civilization in its Stoic versions. It can, of course, be
found in many civilizations other than our own. In discussing this
notion of freedom, Berlin suggests that it is very likely a response
to despotic government in which the individual feels helpless to influence the outside world and responds by turning inward. I think
he is probably right about this. Perhaps the growing popularity

of occult versions of this idea in contemporary society might be taken as evidence for the view that freedom as spiritual mastery is a response to a sense of helplessness. Modern industrial societies, whether or not they are actually developing despotic characteristics, do seem to give many of their inhabitants a strong sense of helplessness. Whatever the force of this suggestion, it is clear that the idea of spiritual mastery is concerned not with freedom, but with power, with which freedom is often confused. It is certainly not a political idea.

Secondly, there is situational freedom which is, I suppose merely another name for Berlin's negative liberty, and which corresponds to what Thomas Hobbes called "the silence of the law." Here, the concept of freedom is a way of stating a relation between a will and its environment. Alone, this doesn't tell us very much, but what it does tell us is often relevant to political freedom. We shall briefly consider it again later.

Thirdly, there is what I shall call "the condition of freedom," which is how people live in what we in the West would recognize as a free society. It is this third kind of freedom which seems to me to be central to the entire subject of freedom.

II

Modern man has gut-level response in favour of freedom. He becomes sentimental about the suffering of caged birds, and yet all the great achievements of animate nature—from swearing parrots to adult human beings—are the direct result of training and education, which take away freedom in the most obvious sense possible. Hence the fundamental contrast at the heart of our subject must be that of civilization *versus* freedom. A Chinese Mandarin observing the comings and goings of the nomadic tribe beyond the Great Wall thought (in one sense, quite wrongly) that they were marvelously free, but he was not tempted to admire them. He much preferred civilization. Aristotle had a similar view of the Scythian tribes to the north of the Hellenic world. He thought them undisciplined. It was the proud boast of those who served the Great Turk that they were slaves—slaves of the supreme power.

Indeed, we may extend this point beyond the conceptual contrast between freedom and civilization to observe that it has always been both the desire and the satisfaction of most people most of the time to serve—to serve other human beings, to serve institutions, or perhaps to serve ideas. With respect to what is relevant to the service, service is the deliberate abandonment of freedom. We do not begin to understand the problem of freedom, then, until we realize that it initially stands in direct contrast with the idea of civilization and all that that involves: the spread of culture and courtesy in relations between human beings.

It was the ancient Greeks who first practiced a manner of living which combined civilization with freedom. They are thus recognized as the creators of what I call the condition of freedom: a subject so large I can but point to its salient characteristics. The condition of freedom grew out of the political structures of ancient Greece. It arose essentially because Greek cities were governed by a negotiating group, none of whose members was strong enough to subdue the others. All civilizations begin in violence, and usually in conquest, which is the easiest way to generate government. Legitimacy begins as naked power and softens into convictions about the natural order of things. The most common of the progressions from conquest to legitimacy seems to be despotism. Among the Greeks, however, political life developed out of the cooperation among equals, and everybody was perfectly clear that this fundamental postulate of equality was an artificial one. Indeed, some of the institutions of Greek political life—such as the lot, and the use of the *klepsidra*—testify to the deliberate contrivance of this equality.

Because superiority is such a tempting, natural way of associating with others, we can hardly resist the hypothesis that, in the beginning, it was sheer inability to achieve the desired superiority

which led to the development of a form of government generated by
equals out of deliberation. No doubt many features of thought and
belief among the Greeks combined to produce this outcome. We
do know that by the end of the classical period, the Greek view, as
expressed by Aristotle, was that government by public discussion
among equals had come to seem the best of all manners of governing, and much preferable to the civilized despotisms of the east.

It is clear that to achieve citizenship, a Greek had to succeed
in avoiding submission to a natural superior. His freedom was the
legacy of his courage. Freedom appears first and pre-eminently as
the condition enjoyed by warriors who had succeeded in not being
subdued. But in the riper stages of the condition, it is also clear
that, as a matter of pride, one citizen would not *wish* to subdue
another. Such a domination would be about as satisfactory as being condemned forever to play a game against someone tediously
inferior in skill. The condition of freedom is thus the discovery of
the pleasures of public association between those who are, in the
relevant respects, equal and independent.

Paradoxically, there is a sense in which this achievement involved a loss of freedom: The Greek citizen took to heart the principles of government. He was self-moving, but moved within the
limitations of those internalized principles. He had thus abandoned the particular freedom, common in the cat-and-mouse
relations of servility, of following his own inclinations once the external hand of government had been removed. Freedom, to put it in
familiar modern terms, involves a kind of internalization, and it is
to this point that most theories of positive freedom refer, however
obliquely. This element of self-government implicit in the condition of freedom explains the Western abomination of corruption,
which is determination by external inducements. The spread of
corruption is the death of freedom. The great example in Western
civilization of the morality I am sketching is, of course, the Socratic
refusal to skip town in order to avoid the death penalty of the Athenian court. On this point, as on many others, Socrates was clear:

mere survival is the value of slaves, while the value of the freeman is integrity. Thus, a free man is a great deal more rigid and inflexible than a slave.

From this last observation, it is clear that those who sustain the condition of freedom are a good deal less rational, in a certain sense of rationality, than those who do not. This also is paradoxical—indeed, part of the same paradox. The free do not always have the freedom to treat everything according to its merit, or to find means, suitable to whatever ends they may *happen* to pursue. To say this is perhaps to equivocate excessively on the meaning of rationality. It is clear that Socrates did everything he did in the name of Reason. But his reason was, to use once again the modern idiom, value-saturated, and very different indeed from the instrumental rationality with which we are familiar in policy studies. Still, the kind of Reason which Socrates took as his guide to the examined life was bound to bring many practical disadvantages in its wake. In many ways, it limits rather than enables. Socrates and Plato were well aware of this. Speaking amongst his fellow citizens, Plato could contrast the unworldliness of the philosopher on the one side with the slavish shrewdness and involvement in practical affairs of the orator on the other. What was categorically true of the distinction between the philosopher and the Greek man of affairs was also in a more general sense true of the contrast between the Greek citizen and the slave, or the slavish inhabitant of one of the neighbouring despotisms.

It would seem, then, that the condition of freedom is, in practice, disadvantageous, and that its emergence was merely an accident of the history and geography of Greece and Rome. How are we to explain, then, that the emergence of the condition of freedom, instead of being merely a parochial episode in the rise and fall of civilization, turned out to be (as Hegel, who was fascinated by the subject, called it) "World-historical"? The answer is to be found in the enormous and dazzling military successes of free communities.

From Marathon onwards, relations between Europeans and

those ruled despotically have been preponderantly a succession of episodes in which small, well-organized armies defeated large, unmanageable ones. Once again, freedom is linked with courage, but it cannot be linked exclusively with courage. We may assume that the distribution of courage among human beings is not dramatically different from one culture to another. For example, we would be foolish to assume that the Greeks were more courageous or virtuous than the Persian hordes whom they so frequently defeated in battle. It is clear that in order to understand why such communities as Greek cities survived and prospered as they did, we must focus our attention on courage *in combination with* elements of self-discipline. Without this combination, a certain communal spirit could be lost. When citizens of such communities began to lose these vital qualities, as the Romans rightly felt they were losing them when the Republic became the Empire, they begin to project them in imagination upon barbarians, as Tacitus did in the *Germania.*

Aristotle is unambiguous about the connection between courage and freedom. In defining a slave, for example, he links intellectual with moral features. In Ernest Barker's fussily elaborate translation, Aristotle says: "A man is thus by nature a slave if he is capable of becoming (and this is the reason why he also actually becomes) the property of another, and if he participates in reason to the extent of apprehending it in another, though destitute of it himself." The passage in brackets which Barker has added suggests, no doubt rightly, that some men have been reduced to slavery through difficult circumstances. This addition is unnecessary in the context since Aristotle is talking of natural, not legal, slaves. The two classes are quite distinct. Still, there is a hint that anyone who *can* be enslaved has preferred slavery to death, and thus the initial and fundamental characteristic of slavery.

To value freedom highly would be absurd if it were freely available to anyone. In fact, an admiration for the condition of freedom involves an admiration for the qualities that make that condition possible. Among these qualities, courage has always been pre-

eminent. The presupposition of this assessment is that human beings live in a world where freedom may sometimes be threatened
because some men try to dominate others. Even within a free *polis*,
or a free state in the modern world, the conservation of freedom is a
difficult business, requiring both constitutional safeguards and an
intelligent and vigilant political class. The dangers of this conservation are much greater in relations between states. Hence freedom
has always been thought to depend upon a resilient patriotism.
"Our Trimmer is far from idolatry in other things" as Halifax put
it. "In one thing only he cometh near it: his country is in some degree his idol . . . and he would rather die than see a spire of English
grass trampled down by a foreign trespasser."[6]

This element of patriotism was pre-eminent in the Roman Republic, but it has played a relatively small role in the development
of modern European states. As far as Europe is concerned, only
city-states offered a suitable environment for the continuation of
freedom in the classical mould. As Europe emerged from the ruins
of Rome, freedom reappeared with a variety of new features. As in
ancient Rome, successful warriors and members of the feudal nobility, in cooperation with the independent powers of church and
town, created freedom. The whole idea of representation, which
later developed into government by consent, was an early product of this new condition. In this short treatment, the point to be
emphasized is that the early usages of freedom were elaborated in
terms of the idea of Christian individuality: the belief that each person is spiritually of equal value.

This new belief was an advance on classical ideas in a number
of important respects. In the first place, it made freedom universally available, whereas in the ancient world, it had been merely
the condition of those privileged few who were located at the apex
of the hierarchy of rationality. The slave who did not participate
in reason was, as we have seen in Aristotle, a natural slave. This is
the point made with such force by Hegel in one of the great books
on freedom—*Lectures on the Philosophy of History*. Hegel says that

in the ancient world some were free, whereas in the modern world, all are free. In the ancient world, fully human action was restricted to the free citizen. The lives of most human beings were burned up in the cyclical repetitions of necessity. In Christian thought, by contrast, each person's life on earth was taken to be an unrepeatable spiritual adventure full of spiritual significances likely to be at variance with the world's judgment of importance.

This notion of spiritual adventure not only extended the condition of freedom to all but also neatly solved what had been a difficult problem in classical thought—the recognition of *what* it was that was enjoying the condition of freedom.[7] The Christian notion of the individual person as an independent substance not assimilable to a universal principle of reason pervading the universe itself, allows of a different conception of a situation in which men are free. However much the Greeks must have recognized (as we all do) the more evident marks of human individuality, their rationalism continually led them back to the ideal, the universal. It led them to construing human acts as *expressions* of something deeper, rather than as *performances* of individuals. In modern Europe, freedom took on a new meaning: it was to permit the playing out of a game, a test, a trial, of vast significance to each of the players.

What emerged was what we may call an opportunity theory of freedom, in which (if we may parody the old mafia joke) life offered everyone an opportunity that couldn't be refused. Freedom was exercised not merely in the *agora* but in all stations of life, and by all sorts and conditions of men and women. It did not matter whether these men and women made recognizable changes in the texture of inherited life, any more than whether they needed to participate in politics directly in order to be counted as having consented to the laws as was Locke's view. In the latter case, mere residence was enough, while in the former, merely being human and alive was enough.

The act of choosing and the organ of choosing, namely the will, came to be at the centre of the European view of what distinguished the human from the non-human world. One expression of this fundamental sentiment was a continuing drift of opinion away from serfdom, slavery and other forms of life which were not, even in principle, chosen. In this sense, all Europeans were "individualists." However they lived, it could be presumed that they had chosen to live that way, even if their manner of life seemed to replicate that of their parents and grandparents. There are, by contrast, many civilizations in which this presumption would make no sense at all. The word "individualist" tended, of course, to be applied more commonly to the colourful cases in which an individual broke with his background. The meaning of the word thus began to shift towards "eccentricity," or "egotism," senses of the word which distort our understanding of the real situation.

Europeans became self-consciously choosing creatures, while the range of things they were aware of choosing continually expanded. Equipped with only the most basic elements of life, the European individual came to regard religion, and ultimately morality, as optional extras available with a wide range of possibilities. One may well ask just how far this process might go before reaching total self-destruction. This is a question I do not wish to confront directly in this paper. My central concern is merely to elucidate what Europeans mean by freedom.

This task compels us to keep a steady eye on common sense realities. One of these common sense realities is that most men, in most places at most times, are in the same general situation: they are members of a community in which they perform daily duties necessary to their individual livelihoods. This was as true of the early modern Indians and Chinese, who were presumed not to be free, as it was of Europeans. Given this anthropological similarity of the myriad ways of life, what distinguishes the supposed freedom of Europeans? The answer to this query lies in the paradox that Freedom is only Freedom when it is given up. Life for a free individual is a sequence not of duties or customs but of commitments: to work, marriage, social arrangements, and so on. We are continually giving up our freedom, spending it as a currency with the full understanding that it is subject to the considerations of opportunity cost. Hence a free life, superficially considered, is no different from an unfree life. More deeply considered, though, the difference is categorical.

European thought has concentrated primarily on differences in political institutions. Europeans are ruled not by a despot, but through a constitution, administered by chosen representatives whose business it is to make the laws under which they live. Hence part of the European idea of freedom has always been that it is a condition in which we live under laws which, in some sense, we have made ourselves. Beyond these familiar considerations, it seems most important to stress that Europeans mean by freedom a condition in which they live "under" law, rather than under the domination of custom, which is much more concrete. Custom is, metaphorically, a sponge that mops up large numbers of small decisions about the manner and the details of what we do. It is usually beyond the range of discussion and challenge. Law, by contrast, is abstract and disputable, leaving more opportunity for self-expression and imagination in our response to it.

It is thus a consequence of the condition of freedom that we have come to understand human life as the continuous response of a will confronting other wills, subject to abstract rules which allow us a variety of modes of response. The rationalism so prevalent in Western civilization can thus be seen as something greatly facilitated by the condition of freedom. The free man has more problems, and problems of a greater variety, than the man who lives in a traditional society, even though in any human community there will always be traditional pockets and a strong tendency to establish restful regularities.

In spite of what has changed since the time of the Greeks, we still encounter the paradox we noted in the classical condition of freedom. The free European is less free in a situational sense than the flexibly pragmatic subject of a despot to the extent that the commitments he undertakes and inherits become binding duties even when external determinants are removed. This point is difficult to bring into focus, but it is of central importance. All human beings have loyalties which can keep them steadfast even in the face of death. Hence it would be absurd to argue (though it has often been argued in the rhetoric of free peoples at war) that either heroism or initiative are created by freedom. What may perhaps be true is that a heroic steadfastness, in terms of an abstract commitment which must be continually reinterpreted according to changing circumstances, is the characteristic freedom provides that is so important in practical affairs because of its enormous military value.

Thus the condition of freedom depends upon a morality of integrity rather than a morality of survival. This may be a contrast of characters, or, more plausibly, of the different moods experienced by the same people. It tends to connect freedom once more with the morality of warriors, and freedom becomes an element of aristocratic behaviour. Just as aristocratic rights have spread through a community, so too has the chivalric or aristocratic ethic: one of the many clusters of values found in modern European society. From the point of view of freedom, then, Europe has always contained people characterized by the courage to sustain it. It has also contained an underworld of professional survivors—the equivalents of Falstaff and Good Soldier Schweick—who have taken the argument of rationalism to its logical conclusion and asked: "What is honour?"

My argument thus far is, then, that the condition of freedom emerged with the ancient Greeks, continued with the Romans, and re-emerged in medieval Europe, to be developed further in a variety of interesting ways in our modern world. I have said little about the Romans because they were less rationalistic than either the Greeks or the moderns. There remains one question of great importance with which I will conclude this section. It consists in asking: Is the condition of freedom identical as it passes through history, or ought we to make a sharp distinction between the freedom achieved by the classical world and that which we have achieved in the modern world?

As European thought has evolved through the continual revival of classical ideas, many have been revived in opposition to recurrent threats of servitude or despotism. By suggesting not only that the moderns ought to recover the ancient notion of freedom, but also that Europe's monarchical institutions were a barrier to that recovery, Machiavelli, and his school of classical republicanism, caused constant irritation to the practice of politics in Europe. European thought on freedom has been expressed most clearly as the hatred of despotism as opposed to the love of liberty. Hence monarchies have often been mistaken for despotisms. There is another view, to which Hobbes subscribes, which suggests that what distinguishes the modern notion of freedom from the ancient is more significant than what unites them. As we shall see, this issue is the nexus of myriad problems.

III

Amongst Europeans, things are never still. Dynamic Europe is the world's first civilization dedicated to Heraclitus: fashion, including moral fashion, is a river into which one never steps twice. From about the end of the seventeenth century, a new feature of European moral life emerged which I shall call oppositionality. Its components are entirely familiar to intellectual historians, and the only interest of what I have to suggest in the next few paragraphs lies in the connections made.

One of the new developments in European moral life was born out of the classical republican tradition pioneered by Machiavelli. It consisted of the emergence of opposition parties as regular participants in the politics of Great Britain. The division between Whigs and Tortes dates from the Exclusion Crisis of 1679. Soon after the Revolution of 1688, loose groupings of politicians representing different policies vied for dominance in the King's government. The *Oxford English Dictionary* tells us that the term "opposition" was first used in politics in 1704. It was at about the same time that dismissal from office became an ordinary incident of political life rather than a perilous storm in which the dismissed minister was likely to lose his head, rather than merely his post. The nervousness attending the accession of George I, which led to over forty years of Whig ascendancy, interrupted this process without in any way blocking it. Early in the reign of George III, we find Edmund Burke presenting his celebrated definition of a party as "a body of men united, for promoting by their joint endeavours the national interest, upon some particular principle in which they are all agreed."[8]

Yet the development took a long time, and it was still possible for a politician called Dunning in 1828 to be thought to have produced a delicious paradox in referring to "His Majesty's Loyal Opposition." Even today, nothing short of a national crisis incites people to consider a coalition, a government of many talents, to provide what is needed to unite their nation.

In France, by contrast, nothing of the same sort happened. What did develop, though, was no less portentous than the British development of a political opposition. Pierre Bayle moved to Holland and, in publishing his celebrated *Dictionary*, gave a profound impulse to the tendency to stand outside one's own culture and criticize it from what appeared to be the standpoint of reason. Early in the eighteenth century, the French went on to develop a literature of criticism purporting to be the response to France and to Europe of a visitor from another civilization. Montesquieu's *Persian Letters* were a famous case of the device, which seems, in its experimenting with alien perspectives, to be a unique feature of European civilization. Voltaire's *Lettres Philosophiques*, in which the glories of England are used to criticize what Voltaire thinks is bad in France, is a brilliant extension of the method from civilizations to nations. Thus, throughout the eighteenth century, the French *philosophes* developed an intellectual form of oppositionality which is interestingly parallel to the English case. Within the very bosom of a country which ideally—at least according to the official ideal—was united in loyalty to a monarch, fidelity to the Roman Church and patriotic attachment to the old French ways, there had developed a highly articulate and influential set of people who dallied with republican ideas derived from the classical world, with deism, skepticism and materialism in religion, and with rational, rather than French, criteria of action. They admired English liberties and Newtonian physics.

The condition of freedom had thus given birth to oppositionality: a new ideal of a rational man as one who exercised an independent judgement on matters which membership of his community would previously have foreclosed. Merely to be a Frenchman was not necessarily to admire the Bourbon monarchy, to adhere to the Catholic Church or even to support the King in his foreign adventures. Indeed, the finest flower of oppositionality, the ultimate proof of one's independence of spirit, might well be found in systematically rejecting all of the positions which one's social and notional position might seem to entail.

Still, subject to a crucial qualification we shall consider in a moment, oppositionality came to be a stable element of the modern world. In other words, we are here dealing with a permanent change of mentality rather than a fully evolved alternative seeking to take over the government. For example, oppositionality became a typical adventure of young people, but the young grow old in the end, come to adopt the ways of the establishment, and discover that oppositionality sometimes goes with irresponsibility. For another thing, the dogmas of oppositionality are constantly being stolen by flexible and ingenious defenders of the current order. Hence the constant changes in moral fashion in modern societies combined with a steady, if irregular, drift in a permissive direction. Further, the distinction between the establishment and the opposition (or, in one of its limited manifestations, the counter-culture) is a purely formal one whose content changes according to circumstances.[9] This is how oppositionality emerged in the West. It became an interesting and permanent resource of the condition of freedom, bringing a further disruptive, and also dynamic element into modernity.

Oppositionality was, in important ways, fundamentally parasitic upon the establishment within which it thrived. In times of war or any other threat to the European way of life, establishment values and resources became necessary to keep society going. Oppositional modes, like permissiveness, which were fundamentally the popularization of aristocratic discretion, required in-built moral restraints and sensibilities if they were not to become brutish. What we find here, then, is another version of the paradox familiar to libertarian supporters of the free market. This very desirable thing can only flourish if it works within a framework supplied by non-market values and rules, ranging from regulations about contract, and about weights and measures, to such matters as loyalty, integrity, a sense of craft and a love of beauty. Otherwise, we are doomed to live in a madhouse of rational optimizers struggling to satisfy their own desires. Similarly, oppositionality may also tend to destroy patriotism, authority, self-restraint and other modes of behaviour whose value may not be realized until some major crisis arises.

What makes this problem more serious is a further very important fact about oppositionality. It could be developed at many levels and in many moods. Its typical exponent was the village schoolmaster who, in the name of "thinking for himself," espoused republicanism under a monarchy, or pronounced himself an atheist by establishing himself as an *esprit fort* in the midst of a pious or even merely observing community. Bohemians and avant-gardes are other common oppositional phenomena, which sometimes generalize themselves into a rejection of everything "bourgeois." Marxism is a movement which rides the waves of this rhetoric of self-presentation. But beyond such rhetorics, there is the possibility of pushing oppositionality to a point where it ceases to be a cultural development and turns into an account of the entire human predicament. Consider as a typical example some remarks of Alexander Hertzen:

> Education snares us before we are able to understand things; it makes children believe in the impossible and cuts them off from a free and direct relation to the world. As we grow up we realize that everything is awry: both ideas and life; that what we were taught to look to for support is rotten and flimsy: while what we were warned to avoid like poison, is wholesome. Intimidated and mystified, trained to obedience and rules, we finally find ourselves at large, each groping for the truth as best he knows how . . .[10]

This is oppositionality approaching the point of saying: "Evil be thou my good." That so sensible a man as Hertzen should understand and express such a viewpoint makes all the more evident the spread of such a point of view in the Europe of the last century. The conviction that one is a spark of goodness adrift in an evil world has a long history in Western civilization, and seems to have drifted in from the East. An early Christian sect called the Ophites saw the serpent in the Garden of Eden as a liberator warning Eve against the evil Demiurge who had created the world. It is plausible to suggest, therefore, that there is one level at which oppositionality could become entangled, for historical or temperamental reasons, with suppressed currents of thought having an unmistakably religious character. Various forms of the human condition—femininity, homosexuality, work, or race—could become the vehicle of such all-embracing oppositionality as to persuade sectarian believers that modern Western civilization, which represents man's triumph after a long contest under difficult circumstances, had actually produced the most dire and dreadful human condition imaginable. What has been most astonishing about oppositionality at this level is the way in which it seems to have grown more persuasive in direct proportion to the improvement (in common sense terms) of living conditions.

I introduce this idea of oppositionality for two reasons. Firstly, because it constitutes a new development in the condition of freedom. As I have already mentioned, medieval men were often free in a sense which may be contrasted with the experience of those who had been despotically ruled. Oppositionality supplied, at the very least, a completely new context for the uses of freedom. Freedom now became the completion of practices and theories which in an earlier time would have been regarded as entirely disruptive to the very fabric of a community. Freedom could be spelled out as a list of civil rights, and the larger issue of freedom turned into an agenda of liberations from a variety of restrictions. Thus, many things which not so long ago would have carried the death penalty—drugs, homosexuality, the right to plot revolution and subvert the loyalty of the state's civil or military servants—became rights associated with freedom and the object of impassioned campaigning. So far, paedophilia has not managed to pick up much support, while nearly everything else has. What follows from this is that the condition of freedom, as it has emerged in modern times, while recognizably akin to that of the ancient world so long as we retain oriental despotism as our point of reference, is nonetheless strikingly different, and ought to be recognized as, in important respects, an entirely different kind of thing: The Condition of Freedom: Mark II.

The second reason it is necessary to introduce the idea of oppositionality into a discussion of liberty is because of the need for a rectification of names. Semantically, there are too many wolves getting about in sheep's clothing. Isaiah Berlin's "positive" liberty (which, in his view, is commonly used to subvert liberty) is only the half of it. The general point can best be made by distinguishing between piecemeal oppositionality, which has become an integral part of the modern Western world, and total oppositionality, which construes the modern world as an evil system that must be destroyed.

Somewhere towards the end of the nineteenth century, liberalism was infiltrated by oppositional arguments to the effect that the provision of the conditions of liberty for all must become the central priority of politics. According to these arguments, the purpose of liberty was to achieve something called "self-realization." In England in this respect, the succession of thinkers runs: Locke, Adam Smith, Bentham, John Stuart Mill, Green, Bosanquet and Hobhouse. Early in the twentieth century, this succession of names often looked like an ordering in terms of the profundity of their doctrines. The English idealists could be presented as a considerable advance upon the crude simplicities of Bentham and James Mill. Green's criticism came out of the same stable as that of Marx: Hegelian idealism. Like Marx's criticism of the liberals, Green's criticism of his predecessors looked both deep and uplifting. In fact, both men were trading on a philosophical vocabulary to command a message no less practical than that of their predecessors, though very different in effect. They all believed that the complexity of modern social conditions, combined with the abrasive self-seeking of modern industrial conditions, required considerable growth in the power of the state such as to bring about a great advance in social welfare, or social rights.

Whether all of this was desirable or not is no doubt arguable, and possibly beside the point altogether since it has all come about. It has often been rightly pointed out that, desirable or not, welfare is not the same thing as liberty. Indeed, the growth of the new, centralized bureaucracies, which were required to bring these desirabilities into the world, has led us to a world of planners, experts and regulation. These new developments have diminished our sense of liberty, and perhaps even our appetite for it. Further, such is the Wonderland World of confusion into which we have moved that with every increase in apparently desirable social rights, liber-

als have come to feel more and more unhappy and discontented
with the world in which they live. How can we explain a situation
in which the more successful people are in achieving their policies,
the unhappier they become?

The answer, I suggest, lies in the fact that total oppositionality
is an interestingly subversive and somewhat metaphysical doctrine
which converts features of temperament into characterizations of
the world. It is adept at generating conclusions which run directly
counter to the evidence before one's eyes. Hence one cannot but
suspect its dread hand working away beneath the trend by which
each new improvement of the conditions of life of modern Westerners seems merely to intensify the liberal conviction of the hollow-
ness, indeed the horror, of the current world. The shibboleth of
criticism has been appropriated by gloom, pessimism and despair.
As welfare state budgets increase, we constantly learn not merely
that the poor are still miserable (which might easily have been pre-
dicted) but that increasing expenditures are needed to prevent the
situation from getting worse. I cite these familiar features of the
contemporary world merely to provide context for the present confusions about liberty and liberalism. What more directly concerns
me is the way in which the idea of individuality, which is central
to our modern condition of freedom, is being semantically eroded
from within.

The attempt to destroy modern individualism comes in two
forms which are no less effective for being directly contradictory.
One line of attack is that individualism is part of bourgeois egoism
and ought to be replaced by a sense of community and love for our
fellow men. The other is that individualism is an excellent thing,
but that the conditions of repressive modern societies entirely block
its achievement. Evidence on the first line of attack can be found in
such disparate fields as the early writings of Marx[11] in which individualism and rights are asserted to be forces of egoism, and in
the current tendency for the word "individualism" to be used to
mean aggressive and selfish behaviour. The identification of indi-

vidualism with egoism is sometimes supported by an assemblage of remarks made by European, and especially British, moralists from the seventeenth to the nineteenth centuries, which occasionally add up to a fully-fledged theory of psychological egoism. Thus the *Maximes* of La Rochefoucauld and sundry remarks of Bentham and Hames Mill are marshalled to prove that the capitalist man is essentially selfish, and hostile to his community. There appear to be intelligent people who take this line of argument seriously,[12] but it is evident that they have little understanding of either liberty or individualism. It is indeed true that the communities of Europe are different, more flexible and deliberate than the communities of other lands. But the most astonishing fact about Europe is not its selfish individualism, but its dazzling skill in creating ever new, cooperative arrangements to reflect its developing interests.

The United States is, from one point of view, nothing but an heroic stage of community construction. As for selfishness, this charge would seem to confuse two senses of egoism. The doctrine of psychological egoism is not one that denies the existence of agreeable and benevolent behaviour as a transformation of egoism rather than as a series of basically non-selfish impulses. Few people are convinced by it, but even if they were, it would not show that modern Europeans were more selfish than the peoples of other cultures. In terms of consideration for the less fortunate, Europeans, in their individualism, have been no less considerate and creative (probably more so) than other peoples.

The direct attack on individualism, therefore, is both feeble and misconceived. But the belief in a higher and better form of individualism is more destructive to the understanding of liberty. The central concept is repression, which can be identified with any experience of frustration. Since all human life involves frustration, the idea that modern society is "repressive" finds frequent verification. Individualism, we have argued, necessarily involves self-limitation, in the simple sense that whoever concentrates his energies on reading philosophy or training to be an Olympic runner cannot simultaneously be a professional violinist. Such limitations also, of course, constitute an exploration of an individual's own desires, but few individuals are so coherent and sure of their character as not to have moods of frustration, regret and even desolation at the road not taken. We may thus see how plausible it is to suggest that real individuality consists in the full development of all possible experiences: vocational, sexual, cultural, sensational and so on. Who would not wish to be a hunter in the morning, fisherman after lunch and literary critic in the evening? In Marx's version of this thesis, it is the division of labour which destroys freedom. The idea is that man is a creature of needs, varying with his historical situation. Individuality consists not in the chosen exploration of the strongest legitimate possibilities (with the consequences that some will not be explored at all) but in the *achievement* of the satisfaction of needs. Species-man is promised a release from the frustrations of the world, and the kind of oppositionality we have called total finds a theory by which it can identify itself with the tradition of liberalism.

The contemporary world has, to a large extent, been constructed along these lines. For example, everyone can travel, but only at the cost of turning travel into a different thing called tourism. Cooks Tours take over from Sir Richard Burton and Mr. Stanley. A few strong and highly articulated desires as the basis for life as a moral adventure have given way to a bundle of diffuse impulses which can *all* be satisfied because they are vague and will accept a range of substitute objects. By general consent, a new kind of human being has tended to emerge.[13] How far we have gone along this path, and how we should judge it, are large questions. We may, in time, come to recognize that the new liberalism has absorbed elements of total oppositionality, and come to espouse the organic conception of the individual as a bundle of impulses which must all find some kind of satisfaction.[14] The development of true community and an egalitarian, non-repressive society means that we must give up *desires* and settle for a bundle of *needs*, as judged by our peers. The freedom to participate in the decisions that affect our own lives adumbrates a future in which *all* decisions will be taken communally. In principle, this means that the community becomes a despot which owns all of its members and which can dispose of them as resources in pursuing its projects. In practice, it almost certainly means that much more specific despots will emerge to tell people what to do.[15] Perhaps this is the way many people would in fact like to live. It is certainly a long way from the condition of freedom, and it is the very opposite of what liberalism has traditionally demanded.

IV

This very brief sketch of the history of our civilization in terms of the idea of freedom will perhaps make clear why I conclude that Isaiah Berlin's argument in "Two Concepts of Liberty" should be regarded as a healthy refutation of totalitarian dangers rather than as the last word on the subject. Some features of the view of liberty as self-realization can, as Berlin argues, be incorporated in totalitarian rhetoric. It is also true, however, that, properly considered, some features of what preoccupied Spinoza, Hegel, and even Rousseau, belong to the sphere of those "unthinkabilities" which I have argued to be the necessary support of the condition of freedom. The condition of freedom is to espouse one version of the positive view of freedom.

But just as the positive view is not entirely the bad thing Berlin thinks it is, so also the negative view is not as beneficent. This is a point which events have reinforced since Berlin wrote—most notably in the appeal to negative freedom by the student militants of the sixties, which aimed at bringing about the total dissolution of all authority and order in the universities. These events must lead us, if other things have not, to think anew about Berlin's judgement that "Pluralism, with the measure of 'negative' liberty that it entails, seems to me a truer and more humane ideal than . . . the ideal of 'positive' self-mastery by classes, peoples, or the whole of mankind."[16] Attractive, and indeed, in many circumstances, sensible as this judgement is, it does not recognize the way in which some of the tenets of modern liberalism can be reformulated as attacks upon repression. Such attacks may erode the condition of liberty.

Liberty as an idea begins in political practice, and to political practice it must be returned. If there were no danger of being dominated and subdued, then liberty would never have been worth valuing in the first place. Hence an idea of liberty, which has narrowed its focus to a point where it is purely concerned with the abstract question of removing more and more restraints from human actions, will move towards absurdity because it forgets that men live in societies in which the question of domination periodically arises. To say this is not to commit oneself to the absurd view that all life is struggle or that the striving to dominate is the central feature of human existence. The whole point of a free society is to release us from such tendencies and to allow us to associate freely as equals. But in the end, liberty is not merely a situation to be enjoyed, but a capacity to be exercised. Those who lose this capacity will soon have no freedom left to them.

Perhaps the best way to sum up this argument is to say that we must not put all our evaluative eggs in one basket. There may come a point with liberty—as there certainly has come a point with democracy—at which it is really better to abandon the grandiose and to explore what we value in less pretentious terms. This is what Hobbes did, and he remains our best guide to the project. So far as self-realization is concerned, his argument that we may discover a *summum malum* in human affairs, but not a *summum bonum*, remains the most economical way of invalidating the errors in the positive conception of liberty. Hobbes grasped one of the important points in the positive conception of liberty by saying that laws are like hedges which help us on our way. This is why the laws we have adapted to are usually less onerous (because our imaginations have adapted to them) than new laws, or the laws of other communities. Hobbes dealt with liberty in the context of his whole civil philosophy. There is no other way of dealing with it adequately.[17]

NOTES

1. For a typical view see G.A. Sabine, *A History of Political Theory* (London: Harrap, 1938), p. 442. For Peter Laslett's review of the argument and contention that the Two Treatises were originally designed in the context of the Exclusion Crisis of 1679, see the introduction to *Locke's Two Treatises of Government: A Critical Edition with Introduction and Notes* by Peter Laslett, Cambridge: Cambridge University Press, 1980. For the more recent argument that Locke was writing in support of the Rye House Plot of 1683, see Richard Ashcraft.

2. Oxford: Oxford University Press, 1969.

3. The third essay, "Two Concepts of Liberty," had been Professor Berlin's Inaugural Lecture at Oxford in 1958.

4. *Four Essays*, p. 133.

5. The idea is explained and theorized, of course, in an appendix to Orwell's famous Novel *Nineteen Eighty Four*. See Plato's *Crito*.

6. *Halifax: Complete Works*, Ed. J.P. Kenyon (Harmondsworth: Penguin Books, 1969), p. 96.

7. An excellent discussion of this and related issues may be found in Charles Norris Cochrane, *Christianity and Classical Culture* (Oxford: Oxford University Press, 1939).

8. Thoughts on the Cause of the Present Discontents, in *Burke: Select Work*, Ed. E.J. Payne (Oxford: Clarendon Press, 1878), p. 86.

9. For example, the conversation of the environment used to be part of the establishment and has recently become an important part of contemporary oppositionality.

10. "From the Other Shore" in Alexander Hertzen, *Selected Philosophical Works* (Moscow: Foreign Languages Publishing House, n.d.).

11. E.g. "The *droits de l'homme* appears as *droits naturels*, because *conscious activity* is concentrated on the *political act*. *Egoistic* man is the passive result of the dissolved society, a result that is simply *found in existence*, an object of *immediate certainty*, therefore a *natural* object. The real man is recognized only in the shape of the *abstract citoyen*." Etc., as Marx so often says, "On the Jewish Question," Marx & Engels, *Collected Works*, Vol. 3 (London: Lawrence & Wishart, 1975), p. 167.

12. I have commented on this tendency in the case of both C.B. Macpherson and John Dunn. See "Humanist Democracy: The Political Thought of C.B. Macpherson," *Canadian Journal of Political Science* 4, no. 3 (Sept. 1976), and "The Prison Cell of Political Theory," *Encounter*, Sept. 1979.

13. See, for example, David Riesman et al., *The Lonely Crowd* (New Haven: Yale University Press, 1950).

14. I have discussed some of these issues in *The Liberal Mind*, New York: Random House, 1963.

15. The London *Times* of 27 October, 1980, contains a report on the Chinese control of Tibet. When, says the reporter, Alan Hamilton, "I asked a senior he laughed uproariously and said: 'It takes many soldiers to teach the people socialism.'"

16. Berlin, op. cit., p. 171.

17. Hobbes deals with liberty in Ch. 21 of *Leviathan*: and it is in Ch. 30 that he writes: "For the use of laws, which are but rules authorized, is not to bind the people from all voluntary actions: but to direct and keep them in such motion, as not to hurt themselves by their own impetuous desires, rashness, or indiscretion: as hedges are set, not to stop travelers but to keep them on their way."

The Goddess that Failed

NOVEMBER 1991

Radical feminism comes from the same stable as Marxism: it is an ideology revealing the secret of the world. That secret is that our apparent freedom masks the fact that we are dominated by an oppressive system which invades every corner of our lives. The famous doctrine that the personal is the political is one formula expressing this secret. Once it has been revealed, there's only one thing to do: struggle against the evil system and liberate mankind.

Feminism tends to accept from Marxism an overarching understanding of capitalism as the basic form of oppression, but it has its own names for the evil system: "patriarchy" or "phallocentrism." Like Marxism, feminism is prone to fragmenting into different understandings of the strategy by which the system is to be understood and destroyed. Feminists face, however, a serious problem from which Marxists are free. They are uncomfortably torn between the thesis that women are indistinguishable from men, and the very different thesis that women represent a sane and healthy value system, quite different from the brutalities of masculinity.

Kenneth Minogue, "The Goddess that Failed." This article is reprinted with permission from the publisher of *National Review* (November 18, 1991).

The spiritual dimension of feminism is something called "raising consciousness." This is the activity of learning the doctrine,
meditating upon its implications, and applying it to every aspect
of life. It also involves accumulating the materials of indignation,
so that a constant and ruthless hatred may be directed against the
system that feminists now realize is bent on seducing everybody
into compliance. The fully raised consciousness discovers confir-
mations of the truth of the doctrine everywhere: such, of course,
are the fruits of any spiritual enthusiasm. It also appeals to the
vanity of believers, because the feminist finds herself living among
sleepwalkers who do not realize what their real situation is. The
distinction between elite and mass—so foreign to the realities of
Anglo-Saxon life—is thus central to the ideological belief.

All feminists (like all Marxists) are intellectuals in the sense
that they understand the world in terms of theory, but many of
them are inevitably, as the old joke goes, intellectuals without an
intellect. The basic materials of the theory were put together by
Marx, whose work is essentially a collection of devices for mobiliz-
ing proletariats and turning any set of circumstances into a theorized project. Ideologies basically mimic philosophy, and a few
theorists are good enough to rise beyond the Salvationist practical-
ity of ideology and achieve the academic level from which the materials of belief had previously derived. It is thus not quite a solecism
to talk of "Marxist philosophy," and perhaps the same is true of
some feminist thought.

Not of much, however, because ideologies are essentially practical. Even the most arcane realms of logic and metaphysics are
judged in terms of what the believer imagines to be their bearing
on the political struggle in the here and now. Nothing is more familiar in these circles than the pseudo-philosophical cry that there
is no neutrality anywhere. As the old American trade-union song
had it, "You can either be a union man or a thug for J. H. Blair."
Feminists have had no difficulty in consigning the whole history of

science and philosophy to the exile of oppressive patriarchal doctrine whose point is to exclude women.

What became unmistakable in the 1960s, however, was that ideologies are remarkable sets of abstract propositions lacking both the competence of practice and the reflectiveness of theory. An ideological movement is a collection of people many of whom could hardly bake a cake, fix a car, sustain a friendship or a marriage, or even do a quadratic equation, yet they believe they know how to rule the world. The university, in which it is possible to combine theoretical pretension with comprehensive ineptitude, has become the natural habitat of the ideological enthusiast. A kind of adventure playground, carefully insulated from reality in order to prevent absent-minded professors from bumping into things as they explore transcendental realms, has become the institutional base for civilization self-hatred.

Feminists have, however, been so far protected from one major disaster which bids fair to destroy the plausibility of Marxists: they have never attained the total revolutionary power they seek in order to engineer society closer to their ideas. Just such power was acquired by Marxists in many of the less sophisticated parts of the world, and their governmental bungling has left whole populations impoverished, demoralized, slaughtered, and genuinely oppressed. This tragic tale is fitting commentary on the arrogance of ideologists, and in fact, the best commentary on it is in Marx himself: the remark in the *Theses on Feuerbach* that all theoretical mysteries find their solution in practice. The solution here is one of the few certainties in social science: If your rulers start taking Marx seriously, run for your lives. Millions have done so, but survival is only to the swift.

PARASITES OF THE MODERNITY

The comparison with Marxism reveals the essence of the feminist movement. For like Marxism, feminism is parasitic on the development of modernity. By the end of the eighteenth century, modern European society was sketching out the possibilities for all of a kind of freedom and abundance not previously enjoyed even by kings. Marxism orchestrated a hopeful enthusiasm among those who had so far seen few of the promised benefits. On this ground, it could claim to be progressive, though it encouraged the kind of snatching at benefits which destroyed those very benefits. But Marxism had another side: it appealed also to the many who were demoralized rather than challenged by the opportunities opened up by the modern world. It promised these people a secure and changeless place in a future world, a world without risk or failure. In this sense, it was an attempt to put the clock back. The result was that societies, like the Russian, which fell for the Marxist sales talk and tried the revolutionary shortcut to the future ended up in desperate straits pleading for help from the liberal democracies of the West.

Feminism is a similar exploitation of the impatience of less able women who want to make a fast leap into a future of free and easy equality. How else might one explain the astonishing indifference among feminists to the skill, ability, and resourcefulness on which the success of the Western mainstream has been based? How else to explain the lunatic demand that an amendment to the Constitution should immediately give women 50 per cent of all elective offices? All that matters to these simple people is that they want it, *now*, and all problems are theorized away as prejudice, stereotyping, and the resistance of the "malestream."

Yet, as with Marxism, there is a curious backward-looking element in feminism which bids fair to be as destructive of the opportunities of Western women as Marxism has been of the countries it dominated. A good example of this tendency is the campaign to turn women against men on the grounds that they are all rapists. No one doubts that some men are rapists, but this in no way establishes that all men are. A dim sense of unease with this logical point is part of the reason why the concepts of rape and of sexual harassment are constantly being stretched by feminists, so that it now appears possible for a woman to have been raped without even realizing that it has happened.

A raised consciousness in this area plays with propositions of the form "X per cent of women have experienced sexual interference before the age of Y," where X is a very large number and Y as low as you care to make it, and "sexual interference" defined so broadly that it can include hearing an older sibling discuss his/ her adolescent sexual experimentation. Statistics of this kind are known in the trade as "advocacy numbers." The point is that the feminist, who in her hatred of patriarchy *starts* from this basic proposition, feels justified in choosing to entertain any fiction at all which will dramatize true consciousness.

It is along these lines that we discover an important but little-noticed convergence between radical feminism and Islamic fundamentalism. By campaigning against the thing called "date rape," the feminist creates immense hatred and suspicion between men and women, so that the feminist advice to any woman going out on a date is to establish a virtual contract governing what will happen in the course of an evening. This is to destroy the free and easy relations between men and women which have long characterized the Western world—and only the Western world. It parallels the fundamentalist campaign to restore the old ways in the Islamic world. "It is a well known fact," as a Jordanian member of parliament recently remarked, "that putting men and women in the same room is like mixing benzene and fire."

BACK TO THE HAREM

Feminists, in other words, are well on the way to reinventing the harem—special quarters in which women traditionally lived entirely separate lives untainted by the lusts of men. As with Marxism, the way forward turns out to be the way back. But anyone contemplating this remarkable situation is likely to have a further thought. Political doctrines always invite the question: *Cui bono?* Who is it, one might ask, that would benefit from dormitories filled with attractive young women who have been worked up into a state of hysterical mistrust of men? One of the most influential fragments of feminism has been its lesbian wing.

There are good reasons for thinking that late-twentieth-century feminism, now a generation old, has reached something like its apogee. One reason is that it has been able to ally itself with all the other ideological "minorities" which have succeeded in playing upon the guilts of the American mainstream and extracting a variety of collective privileges. American males of this generation seem to be polarized between a Rambo-like fantasy life and a remarkable wimpishness when charged with the supposed crimes of their ancestors or even themselves. Like everything else in American life, this disposition is unlikely to last. The minorities will themselves fall into conflict over scarce goods, and collectivist privilege (which clashes in any case with the basic individualism of American life) will begin to dissolve.

An even more important vulnerability of radical feminism is the fact that it is based upon an illusion. It imagines that everything it demands corresponds to the establishment of justice. But in a modern society, justice is simply the gloss that special interests paint over their demands. Justice, in this wildly extended sense, is a matter of fashion and taste. It is within living memory that many people (including women) waxed indignant over giving equal pay to spinster schoolteachers on the ground that they would spend it on cosmetics and foreign travel, while men were supporting a family. Such judgments change all the time. Many simple people, after all, used to believe devoutly that socialism was the unchallengeable wave of the future. Lost in a dream of absoluteness, feminists are ill equipped to face the inevitable somersaults of modern moral pluralism.

The most important vulnerability of the feminist project, however, lies in its evident bad faith in relation to its environment. Whatever complaints women may have in modern societies, they are as dust beneath the feet of women in all other societies. Yet every feminist success is greeted with a redoubling of complaint-mongering and tooth-gnashing at the horrors of patriarchy. This is a tiresome form of behavior which will in time wear out its welcome. Camille Paglia's charge that feminism is an "adolescent whine" is a salutary recalling to evident reality of believers lost to all sense of outside opinion.

REWRITING THE RULES

Not so lost, however, as to have rejected the benefits of what they most violently attack. The basic fact about feminism is that it is financed by the "malestream" and that its respectability results from exploiting the ranks and respectabilities of supposedly male-oriented universities. Feminists have got to be professors on the ground that they can do academic work just as well as men. But having been admitted to the game of academic life, many feminists have decided that it is "masculinist" and patriarchal, and that there is a superior feminist understanding of the world which ought to replace masculinist science and philosophy. They thus resemble those tiresome children who demand to play adult games but, on being admitted, find that they can't play, or won't play, and demand that everybody else accept a new set of rules more congenial to them.

False consciousness generates contradictions. Living amid fantasies, feminists on the one hand demand that female Marines should be given a combat role just like the men, and on the other hand thrill to the alleged sufferings of Anita Hill distressed over some pornographic remarks. What do they want? To be clinging to vines, or out there in the desert beside Rambo zapping America's foes? The men were understandably muttering: "If you can't take the heat, get back to the kitchen." Logically, American feminism is a mess—but who cares?—as long as the men knuckle under and the benefits keep rolling in.

The future of radical feminism in America is tied to the fate of all the soft, non-revolutionary ideological enthusiasms which are currently trying to march through the institutions. It seems likely that Americans will soon tire of the grievance-mongering which plays upon their guilts. It is difficult to think that a movement which replaces the fun and poetry of life with mediocre theorizing—which turns *Romeo and Juliet* into a disquisition on the oppressive character of heterosexism—will long dominate even the academic world on which it has so successfully battened in recent times.

Can Scholarship Survive the Scholars?

FALL 1991

I

What is education for? Even to ask the question is to set out on the wrong foot. We may certainly ask, What is a training in singing or strategy or business management *for*? and we shall get an appropriate answer. Education, however, is logically on a different level, and to ask, What is an educated person good for? leads us into the same error, and for the same reasons, as the question, What is a just man for? in Book 1 of the *Republic*. Education, like virtue, relates not to specific areas of life, but to life as a whole.

But practical men are great functionalists. What often interests them is the point, the nitty gritty, the bottom line, what bang for the buck, and similar descriptions which constantly emerge from this practical payoff. They are well aware that at both schools and universities, pupils do learn skills—literacy, maths, languages, and so on—and that these skills are very useful in businesses and bu-

Kenneth Minogue, "Can Scholarship Survive the Scholars?" This article is reprinted with permission from the publisher of *Heritage Foundation* 4, no. 4 (Fall 1991). © 2015, Springer, link.springer.com. This essay is adapted from the keynote address Mr. Minogue presented at the Heritage Foundation's First Annual Leadership Conference for Academic Excellence, sponsored by the Salvatori Center for Academic Leadership, held on March 25 and 26, 1991, in Washington, D.C.

reaucracies. This makes it plausible constantly to be adjusting educational practices in such a way as to produce the skills which from time to time are thought necessary. That this kind of rationalism is often self-defeating is my central theme, but for the moment I want to press on with the question of education itself. Recently, the American philosopher John Searle sketched out what he thought constituted an appropriate liberal education for our times. It included a lot of things worth knowing—cultural traditions, some science, a foreign language, political economy, and communications skills, etc.—and the hope was expressed that this knowledge could be acquired in a way that "combines intellectual openness, critical scrutiny, and logical clarity."[1] These are the words by which Searle would want to characterize the academic tradition.

There are other ways of approaching this difficult question. One of them is by linking education to a conception of the human condition, as Michael Oakeshott does, who construes human life in terms of a conversation of mankind. Education thus becomes learning how to participate in this conversation. I think this is an important addition to, or modification of, our received ideas, partly because it rescues our understanding of education from severe intellectuality. It helps us recognize the importance of manners and dispositions in characterizing education, and it is hard to imagine this better done than in some words Oakeshott quotes from an Eton schoolmaster of a past generation:

> At school "you are not engaged so much in acquiring knowledge as in making mental efforts under criticism. . . . A certain amount of knowledge you can indeed with average faculties acquire so as to retain; nor need you regret the hours you spend on much that is forgotten, for the shadow of lost knowledge at least protects you from many illusions. But you go to a great school not so much for knowledge as for arts and habits; for the habit of attention, for the art of expression, for the art of assuming at a moment's notice,

a new intellectual position, for the art of entering quickly into another person's thoughts, for the habit of submitting to censure and refutation, for the art of working out what is possible in a given time, for taste, discrimination, for mental courage and mental soberness. And above all you go to a great school for self-knowledge."[2]

Voices from the past like this one are valuable in releasing us from the worst of all parochialities: that of our own time. But I find this passage especially valuable because it focuses our understanding of education on dispositions—those elements of our personality which, among other things, make our virtues real and settled. An educated person must be understood not merely as a collection of skills, but also as a bundle of dispositions.

II

I put it this way for personal reasons. I went up to the university (in Australia, quite some time ago) with great excitement, and I must have found what I was looking for because no one has been able to prise me away from universities ever since. I love places of learning, and I love the philosophical self-consciousness that goes with them. I can identify with Oakeshott's account of his own school-days:

And when with inky fingers a schoolboy unpacked his satchel to do his homework he unpacked three thousand years of the fortunes and misfortunes of human intellectual adventure. Nor would it easily have occurred to him to ask what the sufferings of Job, the silent ships moving out of Tenedos in the moonlight, the terror, the complication and the pity of the human condition revealed in a drama of Shakespeare or Racine, or even the chemical composition of water, had to do with *him*, born upon the banks of the Wabash, in the hills of Cumberland, in a Dresden suburb or a Neapolitan slum. Either he never considered the question at all, or he dimly recognized them as images of a human self-understanding which was to be his for the learning.³

But to be self-conscious is to wonder about the tradition one is entering. I certainly had a vibrant sense of that tradition. I found it easy to understand myself as a link in a chain. I was inheriting marvelous things from the past—so much that no lifetime suffices for their enjoyment—and my duty was clearly to transmit them to the young: not merely, indeed, to transmit but also to spark enthusiasm, to shape their tastes so that they might share my pleasure in an elegant sentence, a profound thought, a beautiful image, or a passage of events from the past. All this I absorbed easily enough, but in our century a tradition must not only be absorbed, but grasped.

We come to grips with a tradition by way of stories, formulae, concepts, and symbols. In my generation, the stories were about cultural heros like Socrates, who died for challenging (as it seemed) the popular beliefs of his time, or Galileo, who had been forced by an obscurantist Inquisition to recant beliefs we now all know to be true. The basic formula I learned was that the academic tradition was a disinterested pursuit of truth. Liberty and democracy were of course also involved, and I found the whole package deeply satisfying. It was satisfying because it gave me a conviction that *in* believing in these things, I was on the side of the angels—as no doubt I was, and still am. But you will already have observed that my understanding of the Western intellectual heritage was already tinged with the most dangerous of literary genres—melodrama. I was abridging my understanding of the past by taking sides in long-gone quarrels.

Further, this understanding of the academic gave me something else that I soon came to distrust in myself. At first I thought it arose from the Australian background where, European social complexity being largely absent, society dissolved all too easily into a critical elite and an unreflective mass. In the case of many of my teachers—and one very influential one in particular, the philosopher John Anderson—the key concept was criticism. Criticism —from a Greek root meaning "judgment"—had, of course, been popularized by the skeptical Pierre Bayle (his dictionary of 1699 was "critical") and passed into the vocabulary of the philosophers of the Enlightenment. Kant's great critiques made the term philosophically respectable, and it had then been absorbed into the language of Marxism, where "critical" referred to a standpoint-transcending reflexivity that allowed its practitioners to rise beyond the illusions of conventional people. Criticism was an adventure of the spirit and it had for us bookish scholars the color of heroism. Like St. George, we prodded a few dragons, such as censorship, and were not consumed by fire. In our gentle Anglo-Saxon world, the dragons were pretty tame. A taste for melodrama thus came to be combined with self-satisfaction.

It was all perhaps magnificent, but it certainly wasn't scholarship, or even properly academic. That it wasn't became abundantly clear in the 1960s, when an exhilarating version of this formula swept the world. One of the difficulties is that criticism combines a reference to feeling as well as to thought. The expression "Ugh!" is thus the lowest level of the critical attitude, and it didn't require much in the way of intellectual patter for many conspicuously unreflective people to congratulate themselves that in rejecting the world in which they found themselves, they were being models of academic vitality.

Such simple vanity would not be worth our attention if it had not had the effect of ravaging the universities. And before moving to my central argument, I cannot resist making a comment on this popular doctrine which identifies the academic tradition with criticism. That tradition is, according to some widely acclaimed contemporary thinkers (such as Jurgen Habermas), "emancipatory," and emancipation intellectually involves the criticism of that from which one must be emancipated. To criticize (in this context) is to find defective, and there is nothing whatever that is not defective from many points of view. What is the use of a camel if one is looking for a horse? The academic tradition, however, is concerned not with the discovery of defects, but with understanding and explanation.

Let me add just one further example of a process I propose to specify in general terms. I also picked up in those halcyon days long ago another simple truth which was destined for a prominent career in the educational world. It began as the simple piece of practical advice that, since it was impossible to know everything, the vital skill to get from one's education was that of knowing where to find whatever one needed to know. To be educated was thus knowing how to find one's way around dictionaries, manuals, encyclopedias, and the theorists away from their scholarly concern with learning toward a ferocious concentration on skill; it is an idea closely linked to the attempt to encapsulate the academic tradition as essentially critical. The professor of history, for example, no doubt knows a great deal about the past, but what is really educated in him is the critical sophistication he brings to thinking about historical narratives. The task of education, it was concluded, is to distill this sophistication and teach it to graduates, to undergraduates, indeed as the mania took hold, to schoolchildren—to whom it was soon being solemnly explained that there were different versions of historical events, and that past versions were not to be taken "uncritically."

III

I have indulged myself in this autobiographical syllabus of errors because I want to draw a conclusion, and it seems to me that confession is not only good for the soul but also the quickest way to explain an illumination. And my illumination is this: that no tradition can ever be satisfactorily caught in a concept or a formula. The way we usually communicate traditions is by way of story and anecdote—in a word, legend. The point about stories is that, being collocations of contingencies, they can be theorized in many ways: consider what theologians have done with a page or two at the beginning of the Book of Genesis. The way to kill a tradition is to believe that any particular theory of what the story means is true. If we really believed this, then we would toss the story away as no more than a frivolous bit of icing on our intellectual cake. And this is the reason why, I think, literature and history have always been at the center of education, however indispensable philosophy and science have also been. To be educated meant to have learned and reflected upon Homer, Herodotus, Virgil, and Horace, and of course the Bible.

A mind educated in this way, along with its modern variants, is likely to be an interesting junction between contemporary understandings and an imaginative sympathy with the deeds and customs of times past, and the interaction between these elements provides the materials for a lifetime's reflection. It provides, indeed, the capacity to lead a reflective life, which is, I think, something rather wider than the examined life which Socrates took to be indispensable to a fully human condition. I think it is necessary today to emphasize this character of reflectiveness, partly because the term is well-equipped to defeat vulgar attempts to give it a specific content, and partly because it saves what is valuable in the current identification of education with criticism.[4]

No abstract formula that explicates a tradition can be better than a partial truth, and criticism (like its political analogue freedom) has a tendency to destroy what it feeds upon. Just as there must be a given subject which is free, so there must be an accepted material on which criticism does its work. Criticism might perhaps be compared to the process of fermentation. Criticism apotheosized, if I may be allowed to be a little fanciful, is like bubbles without a liquid to be bubbles in.

The definition of a tradition is not that tradition itself, any more than a description of an effervescent liquid is the champagne itself. But those who put criticism at the center of education have embarked upon the project it is—of composing an abstract characterization of the dynamic thing that is a tradition of education. And if one takes one's bearings from the partial truth of criticism, one must immediately advance to recognize—and here I use words which would once have made me wince to utter—that education also requires reverence for authority, a piety toward what we have inherited. Yet in all the stories I had learned, authority was the enemy. Authority was the *demos* of Athens, the Inquisition, the Churches rejecting Darwinism, and the censoring prudes who attacked Freud. The Middle Ages were virtually characterized in the Renaissance manner as a period lost to human creativity by an absurd reverence for authority. The Scholastic philosophers, it was well known, had revered Aristotle so much that they could not even see what was before their very eyes. My philosophical education reflected this judgment. Philosophy died with Aristotle, and was only reborn in the century of Bacon and Descartes.

It is only recently and then curiously in the philosophy of science, that the point has been emphasized that almost all of our knowledge comes by way of the authority of books, dictionaries, encyclopedias, newspapers, etc., and that while thinking for oneself and adopting a critical attitude is indispensable, only madness can come from trying to think everything out for oneself.[5] No one, of course, seriously tries to do this, but the contemporary form of our civilization may be recognized as one in which a kind of bumptious ignorance is free and generous in uttering worthless judgments. There was a time when simple people did not know how to frame a general opinion; we have succeeded in abolishing simple people.

IV

This, I suggest, is the intellectual matrix from which our well-recognized troubles have come. And there is no doubt of the pattern of reasoning that has generated these troubles. It is a pattern of reasoning that most of us find hard to resist, and what is most terrible about it is that it emerges from the rubble of each disaster, untouched and eager to sell us another bright idea about what went wrong and how to improve matters. The critical spirit construes the human condition in terms of the solving of problems, defines a defect and proceeds to specify the ways in which it can be remedied. It is happening even as I write. "We're developing ideas for a strategy about how to meet the goals" the new secretary of education has just remarked, referring to sex education goals for the year 2000 agreed on by President Bush and state governors.[6] This is instrumental rationality, or rationalism, or assimilating education to the ambitions of social engineering, and it is a game any number can play, from one to 250 million or so.

The rationalist has no difficulty at all with our original question: What is education *for*? Education having made him critical, he knows that its business is to emancipate people, it is to disseminate skills and teach individuals to lead critical, rational lives. This intellectualism is so modish a doctrine that a whole tribe of philosophers is currently engaged in trying to extract from the concept of rationality the correct ideas that will allow us to construct a properly just society. Like Plato, but without his judgment, they believe that improvement is all a matter of getting the ideas right. But a program whose basic premise is the achievement of infallibility is an absurdity for human beings. Worse, it destroys virtue. Universities, like all human institutions, depend upon certain virtuous dispositions—civility, good manners, tolerance, and the like—and no one is more deficient in these virtues than someone who imagines he has hit upon the right idea. Such a belief, you might say, would be a form of megalomania, and you would be right; but there is a lot of it about.

Education has thus become a province of human life dominated by rationalism. Battered by numerous instrumental criteria of relevance, it has lost its autonomy and succumbed to the ambitions of outside interests. It has become the victim of its own success in accumulating, over the centuries, a great wealth of prestige, buildings, ornaments, access to commerce and government, and so on. It was thus ripe for plunder, and its own custodians have proved so easy to seduce by appeals to their self-importance that it has

found itself defenseless. Businessmen have sought to turn education into an instrument for disseminating the skills that from time
to time they imagine necessary for prosperity—though in the spirit
of the eighteenth-century maxim that men are never more harm-
lessly employed than when making money, it should be added that
businessmen have also known how to be disinterestedly generous
in their dealings with universities. This caveat is less true of governments that have followed the Enlightenment path of attempting
to solve problems of social disharmony through education. But the
freelance idealists undoubtedly are the most dangerous, those who
want to use the university to build a better society. They are most
dangerous because, in their total ignorance of what education is
about, they cannot distinguish it from their own blind enthusiasms.

V

We must thus return to our basic question about the real character of education. Let me make a negative and a positive point. The
negative point is that education cannot be taken to be a productive
process that turns out a standard product. In making this point,
we should perhaps distinguish education from training. Whoever
successfully studies mathematics will be able to solve a range of
mathematical problems, just as the student of a foreign language
will only graduate if he can read and speak that language. But an
educated person is something other than simply the location of
skills, and I have suggested reflectiveness as a possible characterization of that additional feature. It is a characterization entirely
compatible with the fact that many young people can successfully
graduate from universities, acquire skills, and make smart remarks
at cocktail parties without being educated.

The positive point is that education is a procedure which brings
into contact with our cultural inheritance that part of the young
who show signs of responding to it. Not everyone has the capacity
to respond, any more than everybody has either the desire or the
capacity to become an athlete; and if we forget this, and cram the

university full of people eager merely to exploit its resources and its prestige, we shall simply admit barbarians into the city.

If education is the cultivation of an inheritance, then the essence of an educator is that he is a custodian, and in fact this role is etymologically entrenched in the history of educators. The first virtue of custodians is to love and care for the thing entrusted to them. Just such a virtue is exhibited in the Socratic saying that wisdom consists in knowing what one does not know. This profound saying—it would take a whole philosophy course to unpackage it— is a salutary specific, uttered near the beginning of the academic tradition against the characteristic academic vice of dogmatism. The case of the actual founders of universities in the twelfth-century Renaissance is rather different. They were entirely immersed in a civilization that juxtaposed the virtue of humility against the endemic human tendency to pride and self-admiration. Their explicit business was to resurrect from fragments an intellectual tradition of which they knew little more than that it was a supreme achievement. "We are dwarfs," wrote William of Conches, who so infuriated Abelard, "but we stand on the shoulders of giants." Their successors struck out in many bold directions, but never forgot that the cultivation of their inheritance was the only thing that could protect them against the light-headedness of a generation that imagined it had arrived at a final truth. Against this kind of shallow folly, we must remember the words of an unmistakably educated man, the poet T.S. Eliot:

> And what there is to conquer
> By strength and submission, has already been discovered
> Once or twice, or several times, by men whom one cannot hope
> To emulate—but there is no competition—
> There is only the fight to recover what has been lost
> And found and lost again and again: and now, under conditions
> That seem unpropitious.
>
> (*East Coker*, V)

There is no doubt that Eliot would have recognized and approved the image of human life as a conversation, and education
as teaching the young how to take part in this conversation. A conversation is something that flows, and in the course of its rhythms,
we play different roles, talking and listening above all. There is a
rhythm too in the alternations of activity and passivity, and also
of criticizing and being criticized. There is also, however, a meta-
phorical analogue of criticism which identifies it with "putting
down." It is thus very easy for the critic, particularly in his inter-
course with the dead, to stand triumphantly above them and in the
vanity of his ignorance, to specify their deficiencies. Hobbes once
observed that men often praise the dead in order to diminish their
competitors among the living, but the tactic can work both ways.
The professor who denigrates the dead puffs himself up among his
students. The vulnerability of the dead is the Achilles heel of the
educational tradition.

With the arrival of self-conscious expressions of this spirit, such
as modern ideologies, the whole of our civilization goes under the
hammer of criticism, and the ideologist stands above everything,
in his self-ascribed intellectual eminence, proclaiming the final
achievement of truth. These pseudo-philosophies—Marxism and
feminism and their many derivatives in particular—have no place
in universities because they reject all that we have inherited from
the past as being mere error—the debris of an at last revealed oppression. No doubt scholarship can get to work on them and make
of even them theories bearing some relation to reality. Theory can
turn anything into anything—it is an alchemy of the imagination—
but it is a futile exercise, because the attitudes entrenched in this
kind of practical enthusiasm are incompatible with the specific element of humility that is essential to education.

VI

We thus find ourselves, I believe, in a very complex situation, and
the real problem is getting it right. What my reading of the situa-

tion suggests, at its broadest, is that when truth goes, what is left is power. Currently we blunder around in a fog when this basic truth has not, and perhaps cannot, be fully realized. When the celebrated Stanley Fish remarks: "All education decisions are political by their very nature," he is drawing a conclusion that inexorably followed from the basic project of identifying education with criticism. But it is a curious utterance, because it only has force if construed as: "It is true that all education decisions are political by their very nature." What is somebody who does not believe in truth doing uttering a remark of this kind? He is both speaking and not speaking at the same time. All such remarks implicitly refute themselves. Similarly, those who denigrate our cultural inheritance as emerging from the "dead white male point of view" are committing the *ad hominem* fallacy. From a logical point of view, much of the challenge to education survives only by such an insistent and relentless defiance of elementary canons of logic and clarity that our will weakens, and we capitulate in favor of the terms of those who shout longest. It is a replay of Socrates against the Sophists, and what the Sophists knew is that winning an argument is partly a triumph of the will.

These logical considerations are so elementary that it is almost embarrassing to advert to them. But they point to something significant in the real world. Another way of describing Fish's utterance is to say that it is *parasitic* on taking for granted conversational practices (i.e., a recognition of truth) which it challenges when used by others. And no one can survey this scene without becoming aware that the barbarians who are challenging culture have nothing positive of their own. Ideologies like Marxism were parasites on the Western philosophical tradition; these successors are parasites in that way, on parasites. They not only exhibit a conspicuous intellectual sterility, but are institutionally uncreative as well. Creating nothing of their own, they nonetheless want to take over institutions created and defended, often with some degree of heroism, by people whom they abuse and denigrate—doing so quite safely now, because the victims are dead. What appears here in the realm of logic as fallacy is bad faith in human conduct.

It is clear that these are people without the courage or creativity to strike out on their own. Now the very fact that this pretty dim crew have been able to get as far as they have must impel us to consider the elements of rottenness in universities on which they have battened. The cartelization of academic oligarchies, the proliferation of vacuous pedantries in journals which no one wants to read, the collusion with profitable nonsense in the field of social and political engineering, the promiscuous acceptance as academic of whatever was handed over on a golden plate—these are the signs of a tradition gone fat and flabby, and there are moods in which it is hard not to feel that these parasites are the scourge we have deserved. After such fleshpots, what better for us than a spell recovering our spirits in the desert?

My feeling is that the academic world has expanded too far, and that it must retreat back to the scholarship where it belongs. I do not doubt that the positive resources necessary for renewing our spirits are there. What that requires is a clarification of just what the university is, even though no such clarification can be final. Myself, I rather like the image of the ivory tower, because it meets head on all the nonsense about our inescapable involvement with society, but it is not to everybody's taste. But there is no doubt that a professor must again become recognizable as something different from the worldly opportunist so many have become today. I am well aware of the many inevitable involvements we all have in practical affairs, but I believe that (rather like priests on a job) we must always have a high awareness of when our academic vocation operates.

If we don't, we may be tempted to slug it out with the vulgarians who talk about such things as "academic superstars" and whose only criterion of whether a department is admirable is whether the media hangs around. The only real leadership in the academic world must come from those who can strike a true academic note. Only by striking such a note can we serve the many people in universities who have been confused by the patter about justice used by the barbarians; only then will they learn not only what harmony to sing, but also that they are not singing alone.

NOTES

1. John Searle, "The Storm over the University," *New York Review of Books*, 6 December 1990, 42.

2. Michael Oakeshott, *Rationalism in Politics*, expanded ed. (Indianapolis, Ind.: Liberty Fund, 1991), 490.

3. Ibid.

4. For a recent example of that identification, see Ronald Barnett, *The Idea of Higher Education* (Bristol, Pa.: Open University Press, 1990).

5. The story is told of a friend writing to Mary Shelley (the daughter of William Godwin and Mary Wollstonecraft) about the education of her son. "No doubt," said the well-wisher, "you will want him taught to think for himself." "Not at all," replied Mary Shelley. "Let him be taught to think like other people. That will be quite sufficient."

6. "New Education Chief Stresses Commitment," *New York Times*, 19 March 1991.

Totalitarianism
Have We Seen the Last of It?

FALL 1999

... totalitarianism has shaped, or, if one prefers it, distorted
the political and governmental scene of the twentieth century.
It promises to continue to do so to the end of the century.
—*Carl Friedrich and Zbigniew Brzezinski, 1965*

There is no perfect way to put the question, but it has to be asked:
Was totalitarianism a twentieth-century aberration, or did it reveal
something profound in the modern West, something we still must
reckon with? One difficulty in posing the question is that since
the fall of communism, the very idea of totalitarianism has largely
evaporated. It is a rather crude idea, yet it has been central to the
way freedom has been construed in our time.

It is the idea of totalitarianism itself that makes the question
difficult to pose. That idea began its life describing something
imagined to be admirable—Mussolini's *stato totalitario* as a heroic
national enterprise. In the second half of the century, however,
the term became an uneasy addition to the lexicon of political science, uneasy because it combined under a single rubric the rather
different experiences of Nazism, Communism and Fascism. Carl
Friedrich and Zbigniew Brzezinski, in their influential book *Totalitarian Dictatorship and Autocracy* (1965), thought totalitarianism could be boiled down to six basic characteristics: an ideology, a
single party typically led by one man, a terroristic police, a commu-

Kenneth Minogue, "Totalitarianism: Have We Seen the Last of It?"
National Interest 57 (Fall 1999).

nications monopoly, a weapons monopoly and a centrally directed economy. Marxists were always unhappy with the idea, both because it put them in the same box as the Nazis, and because their undeniably totalist conception of communism, by contrast with actually existing communist states, claimed to generate freedom rather than servitude. On the other hand, radical philosophers such as Foucault interpreted Western civilization itself as a kind of concealed totalitarianism—a form of oppression without an oppressor. The idea thus lacked focus.

The first thing to clarify in asking our question, then, is the meaning of totalitarianism itself. In this task, we must be cautious of entanglement with the melodramas of twentieth-century politics. If in the twenty-first century we should be threatened by freedom-destroying ventures seeking to create an ant heap society, the one thing we can be reasonably confident of is that they will not feature men in jackboots. Far from being announced by the drumbeats of revolution, they are likely to be stealthy and insidious. For what one must never forget about all totalitarian experiences is that they are created (though not necessarily sustained) by idealists thirsting for virtue.

To expound an idea is to plunge into abstraction, which is why, from the beginning of Western thought, the idea of a perfect society has taken a philosophical form. The traditional civilizations with which the classical Greeks were familiar all imposed some overarching scheme on human life, and virtue consisted in fitting into one's place. The imaginary societies of the Utopian tradition merely rationalized this type of arrangement. Karl Popper, in *The Open Society and its Enemies* (1945), fingered Plato as the great exponent of what Popper called "the closed society," and in *Laws*, Book V, we find as perfect an account of such a society as one could wish for. The first best society involved community in womenfolk, children and all possessions. Ownership would have been banished from life, and

all possible means have been taken to make even what nature has made our *own* in some sense common property,
I mean, if our eyes, ears, and hands seem to see, hear, act,
in the common service; if, moreover, we all approve and
condemn in perfect unison and derive pleasure and pain
from the same sources—in a word, when the institutions of
a society make it most utterly one, that is a criterion of their
excellence than which no truer or better will ever be found.

Plato, then, could conceive of the complete extinction of individuality long before individualism became central to Western society. The essence of totalitarianism is the project of transforming
human life by making people, conceived of as the *matter* of perfection, conform to some single overriding *idea*. All of these idealisms
turn nasty when it is discovered that human beings are unsuitable
material for crafting social perfection. And since human beings are,
in totalitarian terms, merely social creatures, to be valued only for
their potential in creating perfection, those found lacking may be,
and of course have been, dispensed with fairly ruthlessly. Marx, in
his much later version of the idea contained in the *Economic and
Philosophic Manuscripts of 1844*, deplored distinguishing between
the individual and society because the individual, in his view, was
inconceivable except as part of society.

What makes Marx central to the totalitarian project is his clear
recognition that it was incompatible with the modern Western idea
of the individual as a unique soul or self capable of bearing rights.
To be made suitable *matter* for a perfect society, individuals had
to be reduced to a form of generalized social substance. This is
why Marx construes consciousness as merely a mirror, generally
distorted, of reality, and an individual as nothing else but a particular instance of social being. Death, Marx concedes, "seems to be a
harsh victory of the species over the *particular* individual and to
contradict their unity. But the particular individual is only a *particular species-being*, and as such mortal." This, also from the 1844

Manuscripts, is so far as I know Marx's only reference to death. This line of thought makes the disposal of quite large numbers of people as surplus to the requirements of social transformation entirely a technical matter. Death is merely a biological event, and the communist practice of referring to the people as the "masses" takes on an exact significance.

Society, then, cannot be reconfigured in terms of an idea if it consists of individuals each pursuing his or her own projects. A perfect society must consist of a population exclusively devoted to some shared enterprise. People have no value except as they contribute to the success of that enterprise. This, of course, means that totalitarianism directly contradicts what we understand by a "civil society," described by Michael Oakeshott as one in which individuals freely associate together in self-chosen projects. The idea of "inalienable rights"—indeed, any idea of individual rights—is, properly, incompatible with social perfection. The idea of rights has, however, become so elastic that it can now be used to cover any kind of imagined perfection.

MANAGEMENT AND SPONTANEITY

Totalitarianism is the imposition of some idea of a collective enterprise on a society conceived of as plastic. As Maxim Gorky said of Lenin: "the working classes are to Lenin what minerals are to the metallurgist." We may add one further characteristic to this analysis: the enterprise will generally be *productive*. "Communism," Lenin declared in 1919, "is the higher productivity of labor—compared with that existing under Capitalism." Indeed, production to satisfy human needs has been at the heart of virtually all the popular utopias of modern Europe, and in these terms the military project of the Nazis may be counted, if not eccentric, at least as unusual. A world that had abolished slavery, and was technologically inventive, hardly needed to bother with imagining slave labor, and even in the case of the Nazis a central part of their appeal was the promise of *Autobahnen* and Volkswagens.

It is an important implication of this idea that the productive enterprise must be one in which all share equitably, indeed usually equally. Unequal distribution has always been recognized as the ultimate cause of political conflict, and conflict is what the perfect society will have transcended. A totalitarian state would thus be a state in which everyone lived the same kind of life: as contributory to, and benefiting from, the productive enterprise. Hence Lenin in the period of War Communism sought to replace the vagaries of the market by rationing, which, of course, had the added attraction that it gave him vastly more control over his followers.

Totalitarian projects come in various shapes and sizes, but they all have in common the idea that each version is what real human nature demands, being the most natural way for human beings to live, superior above all to the coercions and makeshifts of the way we live now. This means that, in some sense, the project of perfection should emerge from people themselves. It must not seem to be imposed. A good society is one in which spontaneous goodness replaces civil coercion. Soviet man was envisaged as a dedicated producer, and Lenin was keen about *subbotniks* (volunteers who worked without pay on Saturdays) because they served to confirm that there was an element of popular enthusiasm for labor discipline. The trick is to derive the right policy from the masses themselves. When, for example, the Chinese revolution came to the village described in William Hinton's documentary *Fanshen*, the cadres did not teach a doctrine. Instead, they asked the Leninist question: Who depends on whom? It took the peasants some time to cotton on to what this signified. At first they thought, in the falseness of their consciousness, that they depended on the landlord, who provided the land and the seeds. Slowly they came to understand that actually it was the landlord who depended entirely on their energy and labor. The peasants were oppressed and exploited, but they had to be taught to "speak bitterness." The later campaign to "let a hundred flowers bloom" was designed to produce useful criticism of local cadres, though when the Great Helmsman discovered that the Party itself had become the object of criticism he moved to an "antirightist" campaign that soon chopped down these blooms. A lot of management has to go into the spontaneity.

While the unity of totalitarian projects is to be found in the implementation of a single idea, policy requires complex judgements on a variety of more mundane issues that that idea does not determine. Thus, success in producing the goods depends on getting the technology right, and in 1959 Mao took the whole of China on an adventure called the Great Leap Forward. Absurd targets were wrung from the leaders of the communes right down to the peasantry. These targets were based on socialist theory created by Stalin's favorite geneticist, Lysenko, who had caused a sensation (and much Western incredulity) by claiming that environmentally acquired characteristics would be inherited by the next generation. Sowing seed deep in the ground no doubt startled bemused peasants, and led directly to a catastrophic crop failure. This failure was further compounded by the fact that the peasants were often not in the fields to harvest such corn as did manage to come up because they were too busy in backyard furnaces making steel out of old woks, iron fences and any other suitable materials to hand. The Chinese leadership, in classic despotic style, could not understand why the promised grain production had not eventuated, and blamed the peasants for concealing corn. The fatal famine that resulted replicated in many respects the Stalinist disaster of the early Thirties in the Soviet Union, and even more people—an estimated thirty million—died.[1]

These were, of course, spectacular results of revolutionary failure in unusual circumstances, but the basic components of the disaster are by no means uncommon. All you need is managed popular enthusiasm and a set of rulers in the grip of some grand moral or technological idea. And here we come to the crucial point as far as our opening question is concerned: *Contemporary conditions are friendly to both the enthusiasm and the grand technology that are the preconditions of totalitarianism.* Education, for example, has been the plaything of social engineers throughout the century. No utopia is complete without incorporating the idea that children are the plastic materials of social perfection, and it has been a notable achievement of many teachers in the twentieth century to stultify education without producing the promised generation of peaceful communitarians. Meanwhile, the rising power of genetics promises possibilities of human perfection such as the eugenicists of a century ago (who merely achieved racism) could only dream of.

Modern democracies do indeed lack the coercive apparatus of the old totalitarian states, but they have acquired remarkable talents in imposing orthodoxies upon their subjects. The respectability that once haunted the lives of conformists has now been replaced, in such institutions as universities, by a schedule of prohibited beliefs and required sensibilities enforced by professional discipline, compulsory indoctrination and in some cases criminal prosecution. (For a specific example of the management of popular attitudes, consider the attack on smoking.) There can be no doubt that the West exhibits in abundance the conditions in which we might all be subject to an imposed social unity implementing some scientific fancy.

THE EROSION OF CIVIL SOCIETY

Totalitarianism is essentially a crafting of society in terms of an idea, and the problem it faces is the problem recognized by Plato in *Laws*, namely, that individual human beings think individually rather than socially. From this point of view, Christianity and totalitarian projects are initially faced with the same problem: the fact that each individual is his or her own world. What Christians call pride, the placing of oneself rather than God at the center of the universe, becomes in totalitarian terms a form of alienation induced by a divided society that is to be transcended.

This is one sense in which critics have often taken totalitarian projects to be essentially religious. Ordinary projects are to be judged in terms of desirability, while religious projects are matters of identity. They are not normally to be disputed about. But there is one vital difference between these two doctrines in religious terms: Christianity posits a world after death in which the defects of the here and now can be remedied. Totalitarian theories raise the stakes by insisting that perfection must be achieved on earth. If all we have is this mortal life, it follows that activism is likely to become more frenzied. And the minds of the people can only be focused on politics if Christianity—or any religion that posits an afterlife—can be demoted to the status of an illusion.

What directly blocks totalitarianism is individuality, which must be replaced by social consciousness. Now all totalitarian theorists have recognized that what sustains individuality in the modern world is the family; indeed, since Plato these theorists have identified it as the source of social imperfection in any society. This is why in all communist revolutions, the family has been a direct object of attack. The Chinese tried to replace domestic life with canteens, and in many communes men and women were required to sleep separately in dormitories.

Religion and the family have thus been notable barriers to the success of the totalitarian enterprise. Both are institutions of civil society that impede the totalitarian project of first atomizing society into pseudo-individuals, and then totalizing these fragments by submerging them in the solidarity of a productive enterprise.

What is the strength of these barriers now? In the United States, Christianity remains strong, though it cannot (for constitutional and other reasons) be dominant. But churches throughout Europe are in steady decline, less it would seem as a result of deep thought about the rationality of Christian practice than from nothing more profound than dislike of the inconvenience of meeting the demands of what is derided as "institutional religion." Families are breaking up in record numbers, leading to a steady increase in single-member households. Totalitarian rulers devoted immense energy to combatting religious belief, and to getting women out of the household and into the labor force where, treated as equal with men, they could be assimilated to the grand productive project. What Stalin and Mao worked for in vain has today fallen effortlessly into place with the triumph of the religion of convenience and the spread of modern feminism.

It is almost as if totalitarian ideas were less projects than prophesies. A variety of liberations seeping through Western societies has made unnecessary the melodramatics of earlier totalitarian repression. Individuals have learned to follow their impulses, with less concern than before for constancy and coherence. One casualty has been the family as a lifelong commitment. Again, many women have been persuaded that unless they join men in the workforce, they lack freedom and dignity. Hence, the individual and the family, those gritty units on which so many revolutionary projects were shipwrecked, have in large measure dissolved.

And what has emerged resembles the classical idea of a vast household, which is how the Greeks conceived of despotism. In a despotism, all initiative had to flow from the despot himself, and everything both public and private belonged to him. In earlier modern times, European rulers sought to determine the religious beliefs of their subjects, but such repression generally faced active subjects—nobles and bourgeois—impatient of any control beyond what was needed for keeping the peace. Besides, the fact that kings were "above" peoples, and therefore in some degree alien to them, limited their power, in contrast to democratic governments that could claim actually to speak for those who elected them. The so-called "enlightened despots" of the eighteenth century sought to impose uniformity on their realms, often by the use of the teacher and the torturer. Revolutionary and totalitarian rulers were their successors and used the same techniques.

The paradox of twentieth-century government, however, is that it is often the apparent virtues of governments that are most damaging to freedom. Easier divorce and the provision of welfare have removed the material necessities on which families were sustained. And just as these pleasing liberations have jeopardized social institutions, so it is also the agreeably facilitative activities of government—the subsidies and provision of education, health, medical advice and more—that have turned the state into a gigantic household. As has long been recognized, therapy replaces political repression, and it is generally more effective.

In other words, our situation is a confusing one. If we look to the substance of what most of us want to do, we are remarkably free, and it would be absurd to smell repression. If, however, we look at the formal features of how we are ordered, at the processes by which governments increasingly intrude into our lives, we find ourselves threatened with a kind of enslavement. The progress of what we might call "soft" totalitarianism thus depends on the way in which our character changes as our attention is fixed upon the substance of our lives rather than its form.

THE PARADOX OF DEMOCRACY

The broad answer to the question I have posed in the title of this essay is that totalitarianism, properly understood as both an impossible and an irresistible political and social vision, is one of the profound drives of our civilization. The signs of its vitality seem to me to be abundant, and I have been suggesting that certain vital barriers to totalitarianism in the past no longer stand in its way. I shall content myself now with sketching out several features of the modern world that would facilitate the emergence of a "soft" (which is to say, relatively bloodless) totalitarianism.

The first of these is the evolution of government from a limited role as guardian of civil peace to its current dominance as an all-purpose provider of services ranging from pensions and medical care to equalization and whatever gets construed as "social justice." It is as part of this drive to improve the lives of its subjects that governments have taken ever greater regulatory and discretionary powers, which must be financed by rising taxation.

Charity has been nationalized, and its range has enormously expanded under its new name of "welfare." In each Western nation, the story has been somewhat different, but none has been unaffected.

Charity used to be the province of the church, and governmental expansion into the welfare industry is merely the continuation of the compulsion Western states have to appropriate the responsibilities that used to be performed in civil society by churches, universities, cultural organizations, professional associations and the rest. Such an aggrandizement of state power has been accruing since late medieval times, though there have also been periods of retreat. As the state moved into the sphere of education, it became difficult to resist the temptation to mix education with public instruction. Indeed, the move into education is in part the consequence of the nationalization of charity. When, for example, governments start supplying medical services to the poor, they cannot help soon involving themselves in determining how people live their lives, with the result that most countries now have such a figure as a Surgeon General dispensing good advice about some "national strategy" to determine optimal levels of obesity, suicide, deaths from heart disease or lung cancer, and much else. The rising level of illegitimacy and the dangers of AIDS have led governments to the tricky art of telling people how to manage their sex lives. And as governments have taken over ever more responsibility for the financing of education, they have become insistent that currently favored doctrines and conditions (for example, about access to education) be implemented by schools and universities.

Some of these developments go back to Bismarck's Germany in the late nineteenth century, but most have emerged in this century, often quite recently. All such policies responded to the specific problems, real or imagined, that an agitated journalism and a responsive democracy could conceive. What is seldom understood is that these policies amount to a profound transformation in the respective moral weight of governments and citizens. For is it not obvious that in the contemporary world it is governments that increasingly spend on moral imperatives such as justice, welfare and public education, while individuals, able to enjoy national provision of these necessities, are left free of any obligation to do other than indulge themselves? The very term "individualism," signifying a principle that governs the choices people make, has become synonymous with selfishness and indulgence.

Similarly, governments benefit from expert advice and are thus sources of wisdom and solutions, whereas their subjects constantly cause problems by folly, addiction, lack of self-control and other vices. It is little wonder that high-minded bishops and journalistic pundits are capable of taking the view that the higher the taxation the more civilized the society.

All this has been done in the name of democracy, even though some measures (for instance, those imposing toleration upon populations given to racism, sexism and the like) may very well lack popular support. But the outcome of these separate developments has been to highlight what might well be called a paradox of democracy. As things currently stand, populations that are evidently both selfish and foolish enjoy the right to elect governments that are both morally and intellectually superior to them.

One can only wonder how long this can be allowed to continue. Indeed, the spread of proportional representation in European countries—a system that muffles the decisiveness of the popular voice—suggests that politicians are already beginning to take the problem in hand. And we may be sure that the removal of the benefits of democracy as we currently enjoy it will be done in the name of democracy itself. As a direct consequence of the state's accretion of both morality and wisdom, the private realm has steadily been absorbed into the regulated society. Put politics in command, advised Mao, echoing the totalitarian tradition; an army of academics took that advice and promptly set out to demonstrate that everything is about politics. Similarly, the feminist slogan about the personal being the political supplies a license for governments to invade both the kitchen and the bedroom. The confusion has become such that political issues come to be described as "ethical," and vice versa.

AGENTS OF HOMOGENIZATION

The ultimate question in considering the advance of totalitarian tendencies must be: who is promoting them? The answer might seem to be that nobody is pushing them at all. And it may well be true that the present totalizing drift of Western civilization is largely the unplanned outcome of a host of responses to specific conditions. In other words, totalitarianism must ultimately be attributable to our basic problem-solution logic. It may just be that we cannot leave well enough alone.

But I do not think that this is the full story, for in some ways it is precisely the invisibility of agency in this drift that is most striking. Consider on this point the fact that our inherited morality of right and wrong is currently being replaced by a form of manners and morals called "political correctness." This is a codification of a collective sensitivity that stereotypes the supposed responses of women, Hispanics and other people classified as "minorities." It is a very odd form of morality indeed, and not the least of its oddities is that many of its human vehicles spent much of their lives denying that there was a single right way of judging moral and political issues. Such a denial seemed to them so evidently sensible that they did not recognize it as a doctrine at all, and they dismissed its critics as "right-wing reactionaries," critics of what any healthy mind would recognize as common decency. As the economist Joan Robinson once remarked, ideology is like breath: one does not smell one's own.

Political correctness has thus come to be regarded as the spontaneous conduct of everyone not suffering from false and evil ideas such as racism, sexism and homophobia. But it is a spontaneity that has been ruthlessly imposed upon those for whom it does not come naturally. One prominent instrument for the imposition of this emerging orthodoxy is the "role model," a descriptive term invented by the sociologist Robert Merton, and one that has come increasingly to describe any set of people whom the young are believed to imitate. We thus have a symbiotic relationship between the young on the one hand, and role models (such as pop stars, television celebrities, sporting heroes and models) on the other, and the relationship works both ways. Each may be controlled in terms of the other. Teachers are told (by governmental agencies, for example) that they must not smoke in public for fear of influencing their pupils, and cigarettes have been removed from contemporary images of famous figures such as Franklin Delano Roosevelt and Jackson Pollock.

The familiar versions of totalitarianism did not hesitate to purge unsuitable "matter" from the state. Our contemporary civil morality does just the opposite: it insists on including everyone in the benefits of society—but only on its own terms. Where sensitivity does not exist, people will be publicly instructed in it, and there will be no nonsense about volunteering. Indeed, by putting together the apparently separate developments that are transpiring in many corners of contemporary Western life, one can begin to recognize some of the agents of homogenization. They are to be found in a highly dispersed network of lawyers, civil servants, counselors, social workers, teachers and other agents of government, each of whom is performing one small part of this grand task, each part having its own highly specific justification. Therapy and public instruction are much nicer than liquidation. But we may invert Mandeville's famous parable of the hive: while every part is full of virtue, yet the whole is very far from being a paradise.

THE BOLSHEVIK ILLUSION

The totalitarian drift is largely composed of specific responses to changing circumstances, but there is perhaps one shared central idea that makes the totality of moves coherent. We might call it "the Bolshevik illusion," because the Bolsheviks were the first people to act on it. They had acquired from Marx the view that history was the story of a hitherto blundering humanity that had finally arrived at an understanding of its own real character. At last mankind was learning how to take its destiny into its own hands, and the Marxists themselves were the ones who had the knowledge of how to do it. Modern societies were defective in that the riches of human skill and culture were still limited to small groups in society. Such specialization had hitherto been necessary for progress, but we now had come to know, among other things, the secret of economic productivity and cultural creativity. In the new society, everyone would at last enter into the full human heritage. Redistribution was not merely of material things, but embraced the entire culture.

Unfortunately, the Bolsheviks believed that the ultimate in productivity was the assembly line and the blast furnaces of heavy industry. They went overboard for the time and motion approach of Taylorism. And their culture slowly collapsed into propaganda. Before long, the capitalist world had cut the ground from under their feet with a variety of dazzling new technologies.

We may well fail to learn from this interesting episode, because endemic to Western thought is a belief in the all-conquering virtues of instrumental rationality, what Michael Oakeshott called "rationalism." It is hard to keep before our eyes the fact that most of the turning points of our civilization did not happen because we planned them, and that many things we did plan proved self-defeating. Christianity seemed so full of mysticism and confusion to some early modern thinkers that some of them maintained that Islam was a far more rational religion. Who in the West would now agree? Again, the religion of a crucified God hardly seemed to qualify (especially to pagan Romans) as the basis of a militarily dominant civilization, yet that was how it turned out. Max Weber has plausibly argued that much in capitalism emerged from the activities of Calvinists whose eyes were focused on heaven. The intellectual power of the modern West partly results from the academic activities of thinkers who had no interest in power at all; much of its creativity accords with Hamlet's "by indirections find directions out." Intrusive governments, however, leave no indirection undirected.

The fact that modern technology has made so much of our culture instantly available tempts us to think that the world is now our oyster. In fact, all that is available to us is our culture *as formulated*, which is a small and insignificant part of what we are. The Bolshevik illusion involves the belief that everything that impels us toward a total and inclusive society is creative, even adventurous. The reality is that cultural exhaustion is passing itself off as *le dernier cri*. Fortunately, because of the plurality of the West, we may still have the resources to find our freedom anew. But it is important that we should know what is happening to us.

NOTE

1. See Jasper Becker, *Hungry Ghosts, China's Secret Famine* (London: John Murray, 1996).

Some Doubts About Democracy
How the Modern State Is Evolving

2002

Since I am not familiar with Turkey, nor Turkey with me, let me devote this first paragraph to personal remarks. I am a conservative, a liberal, a democrat, and a philosopher. I am a conservative because I believe that initiative in society should generally rest with the people rather than the state, and this is also the reason I am a democrat. I am a liberal because I believe that freedom—responsible freedom—is a value in itself, quite apart from its advantages. But today I am here as a philosopher.

Philosophy is the intellectual discipline that searches for the coherence in things, and today I want to engage this intellectual discipline in order to make some sense out of the idea of democracy. And my particular method is to begin by taking my bearings from the changes I see around me.

(1) DEMOCRATIC SALVATIONISM

The way democracy works depends largely on the ideas we have about it, and the dominant idea at the moment is that the more per-

Gazi University, Turkey. Kenneth Minogue, "Some Doubts About Democracy: How the Modern State Is Evolving." This article is reprinted with permission from the publisher of *G.U. İ.İ.B.F. Özel Sayisi*, Special Issue (2002): 141–154. Licensing under Creative Commons. iibfdergisi.gazi.edu.tr.

fectly democratic we become, the better our civil and social life will be. In other words, many and perhaps most problems in politics are ultimately problems of democracy, or more precisely, of imperfect democratisation. We may call this idea "democratic salvationism," as long as we remember that we are here dealing with rhetoric and justification rather than the realities of politics. One interesting—and indeed rather odd—implication of democratic salvationism is the historical thesis that mankind has for many thousands of years been blundering around (except perhaps for a brief episode in Athens) in search of the proper way of conducting its public business, and only in the last two centuries have we discovered the one true political system. It does sound rather unlikely; it certainly exhibits the arrogance of our epoch.

Democracy is thus thought to solve most if not all problems, especially the problem of war and other forms of conflict. A belief has spread among political scientists that democracy is, for example, the key to peace, because (so it is said) there is no need of democracies ever going to war with each other. In *Time* of Sept. 11, 2002, John McCain (p. 98) argues that "The only way to defeat terrorism is to fight for democracy everywhere, including in Iraq." McCain's argument poses a causal relationship: "The more countries are governed with the consent of the governed, the fewer there will be where resentment caused by corrupt rulers can be misdirected towards the U.S." Here in journalistic form is the idea that democracy brings peace. The general idea, however, can be found at all levels of articulation. In the work of Amartya Sen, for example, we find in highly technical guise the parallel argument that democracy prevents famine, and it may be that Africa is currently a confirmation of this view. Sen belongs in the company of normative political philosophers ranging from Jurgen Habermas and Seyla Benhabib who search for the democratic norms that could create a better, or even perhaps a perfect society. For Professor Ben Barber, democracy is the way to a better community, understood in terms of an active citizenry. Normative political philosophy, then, presents democracy as the criterion of a better society, and this idea has filtered down, as philosophical ideas do, to practical life. It is a belief in the wisdom of deciding public issues by public debate. The more we talk, it seems, the more democratic our politics will be.

One issue raised by democratic salvationism is one logical. The classic political wisdom of the West identified a good constitution with balance between the various powers in a constitution. The English constitution was from early days regarded as a historical development which happened to correspond to the classical idea that politics was a balance between the one (usually the king) the few (the aristocracy) and the many (the people, or in English politics, the Commons). Each element contributed its own value to the process of deciding what should be done. The later theory of the separation of powers was a version of political wisdom understood as a balance between the elements in the state. Today, in modern salvationism, we have the very different idea that it is not a balance of principles but the universalisation of one principle which will provide wisdom and justice in the state.

Democratic salvationism is a version of the wider doctrine that constitutions determine policy. Philosophers will remember that Immanuel Kant laid down the principle that monarchy was the cause of war, because kings were the owners of the state and could go to war without any threat to their own lives, their banquets, or their courtly pleasures. In a republic, however, where everyone was a citizen, and a decision for war would threaten all with loss of property and prospect of death. The project of abolishing war thus required that every state should become a republic. Kant was no friend of democracy, but the current optimism about the effects of wider democracy in the world is recognizably a descendent of Kantian thinking. Republics will deal peaceably with each other for the same reason as today political scientists think democracies will be peaceful.

Kant was writing in 1795, and his doctrine was at that very moment being refuted by the ferocity of the revolutionary wars in the next two centuries. One remembers the Paris mob at the end of Emile Zola's novel *Nana* rushing through the streets unwisely shouting "A Berlin. A Berlin!" The people are by no means immune to bellicose enthusiasms. And the Americans were pretty enthusiastic about fighting Spain in 1898, the British about fighting the Boers in 1899.

We may perhaps universalise this point by saying that no constitutional settlement entails any particular public policy. Constitutions are abstract things, and how they work will depend on circumstances as much as on formal structures. This is an important point, but for our present argument, it merely shifts the question back to what we mean by "democracy." The terms refers in the first place to a specific type of constitution in which the ruled are somehow involved in government, but there can be immense variation in the details. Do we then simply mean by "democracy" a set of fundamental laws, or are we suggesting that once the people have been accorded some rights in determining how they are ruled, a new social and moral as well as a new political situation comes into being. This was certainly the view Alexis de Tocqueville took as far back as the 1830s as he analysed the customs and practices of those he called the "Anglo-Americans."

There are, then, two versions of the doctrine we are considering. In the old Kantian version of the doctrine, a constitutional change (the movement to a republic, or to a democracy) would change the terms of politics, but this would require no essential change in human nature. It would still be "men as they are, and laws as they ought to be" as Rousseau once put it. The second version invokes a causal chain in which democracy changes human nature, which then causes an aversion to war. In Kant's version, the causal relation between republicanism and peace was a priori. The modern doctrine is largely based on the inductive observation that we don't (so far) have much experience of democracies going to war with each other. The old doctrine (constitutions determine policy) was false, but the new doctrine verges of tautology. It is no doubt

true that good tolerant wise peoples will only go to war against others when some dire necessity forces them to do so. The problem is
how to get people to be wise and tolerant.

And the answer would have to be, I think, that if it can be done
at all, it certainly cannot be done quickly. It is true that democracies don't go to war with each other, but some countries that have
recently been democracies can certainly be very warlike indeed.
Germany before 1933 and Italy before 1922 were technically democracies, but both turned into dictatorships (with it seems wide
popular approval) and both turned into bellicose monsters. The
idea that democracy prevents war, then, has as one of its minimal
conditions, that the democratic constitution has operated over a
long period of time. Democracy makes demands on people. It requires tolerance of other ways of life. It requires a society in which
any person will cooperate with any other citizen on the basis of
the other's personal qualities, not his or her social status, tribal allegiance, religious affiliation or any other divisive test. It requires
habits of self control that allow passionate issues to be discussed
without coming to blows. These are characteristics without which
democratic constitutions will clearly soon fail, and which democratic constitutions encourage. They are immensely difficult, and
countries, or parts of them, often slip back into old bad habits—as
has happened in Britain with the long-standing problem in Ireland.
Democratic stability is never to be taken for granted.

Indeed, even more dangerous than taking it for granted is imagining that we know what it is. The external tests of democracy require some kind of constitution, elections, freedom of association
and speech and vigorous public discussion. Few countries in the
world currently lack some of these external marks of democracy,
but the inner reality is often very different. That a practice is called
an "election," or an institution a "parliament" is a very poor guide
to politics. In any case, democratic salvationism assumes that democracy is something fixed and known. But as we also know, nothing in human affairs is immune to change.

The central problem in a democratic constitution is that of getting government to respond to the will of the people. This is a problem so intractable that new ideas about it, and new demands on democracy will in each generation have the consequence of changing, often quite radically, the way the thing we call "democracy" actually works. And if we grasp this point fully, we shall find, I suggest, that democracy over the last two centuries in Europe has been a transitional phase between monarchy at the beginning, and some new form of liberal oligarchy in the present period. The paradox is that democratic salvationism is putting all its faith in a political form that no longer corresponds to political reality.

(2) ACTUALISING THE POPULAR

Democracy is government by the will of the people, with the implication that the people in a democracy ought to get what they want, and that this is what in fact happens. This definition, however, is less part of the essence of democracy than part of its public relations. For one thing, the definition is merely formal. The people are very various and modern states are full of different ideas about how we ought to live. There has to be some way by which the will of the people (by contrast with the discordant clamour of what is called "public opinion") can be revealed. The entire theory of democracy consists in giving some account of how we might move from "the people" as a rather inchoate mass to "the government" which articulates rational public policies. *E pluribus unum*, as the Americans optimistically put it.

One popular mistake used to be the belief that ideally the people should assemble together in the agora, discuss issues and perhaps vote, as they may have done in classical Athens. On this view, representative democracy is a second-best system resulting from the size and complexity of modern states. The dream of Athens inspires theorists of participatory democracy who hope that getting people together to discuss things leads to popular consensus. Even in this simple model, majority rule can become a problem, and so also can the changeable character of the demos—as for example when the Athenians voted differently on different days about how to treat the city of Mytilene which had risen in revolt against them.

We today have representative democracy, in which the people vote for a parliament of representatives to do the public business for them. But again, by what electoral system can we transmit the will of the people so that it becomes the will of the government? There are many competing views and practices. One of them is the British "first past the post system," which works well in Britain but has the disadvantage that an opinion that has no more than a minimal level of support will not be represented in parliament. This is a system that forces parties to compromise their principles in order to gain wide support. No such party corresponds precisely to what anybody wants, but those policies that are supported at least have reasonably wide support. This system has the further problem that it can hardly work except in reasonably homogeneous societies.

Alternatively, democracies may solve this problem by making provision for the representation of quite small bodies of opinion—those which can in aggregate command about 5% of the vote are often in Europe accorded parliamentary recognition. This seems preferable, and is certainly often advanced as being more democratic on the ground that more popular opinion will find expression in parliament. Alas, at this point we are forced to recognise that we are dealing with a field in which every solution turns into another problem. If there are many parties in a legislature, no government can be formed without extensive post-electoral negotiations, and the result is that the policy of the emerging coalition may bear very little resemblance to what the electorate thought it was voting for. And there is a further shadow over even this democratic advantage, since it is often the case that small extremist groups will benefit from this system of election. This is the kind of politics often called "populist." Populism is democracy you don't like.

In federal states, these problems can to some extent be finessed by having one governing body elected by individuals and the other

by provinces or states. This solves problems resulting from antago-
nisms between elements in a dispersed population, but can result
in deadlock when the two assemblies disagree, as happens every so
often in Australian federalism.

The mechanics of popular representation are a familiar problem to game theorists aware, for example, that an electoral system
will not preserve the transitivity of preferences found among rational voters (the Condorcet problem, for example). These technical
questions amuse specialists, but they have little light to shed on
much more fundamental questions such as whether it is possible to
discover a firm line distinguishing those things that governments
ought legitimately to regulate (concerning public goods, for example) and those things which ought to belong in the discretion of the
individuals themselves. This problem, which in one of its forms
might be solved by a system of entrenched rights, is itself a political question, likely to be solved politically in terms of the interests
of assemblies and bureaucrats rather than any direct declaration
of the popular will. The dilemma of democracy thus surfaces in
a new form. Either the people speak directly, which is impossible
in large modern states, or they speak through representatives, in
which case the representatives (and the bureaucrats through whom
they often work) may develop interests and ideas at variance with
the popular will.

And to reinforce the point that democracy is not a single constitutional model to be copied, but a constantly changing historical
experience, we may cite a new version of the problem of actualizing
the democratic will. As with many changes of political consciousness, it can first be detected in a shift of vocabulary, according to
which the term representation comes to signify less a process by
which an elected person speaks for constituents than a doctrine
that the composition of parliaments ought to correspond to the
composition of the population at large—as indicated by gender,
ethnic identity and whatever other natural characteristic should
make a bid to this kind of status as a kind of constituency. The

political process of elections is overshadowed by an insistence on distorting the terms of the election so as to ensure that rainbow societies should generate rainbow parliaments.

The emergence of this new theory of representation brings into even clearer focus one of the many things that democratic theory cannot help but take for granted: namely, what do we mean by speaking of "the will of the people?" The will itself is a psychological organ more or less constructed out of Christian doctrine by Saint Augustine, and adapted by mediaeval jurists to a world of corporations. The will was the choosing branch of the self, and the self in modern Europe was no longer the rational entity theorised by the Greeks, but a coherence of thoughts and passions by which the individual responded to the changing world. Theologically speaking, the will revealed the moral character of the individual. Thomas Hobbes in *Leviathan* (1651) argued that the will was simply the last appetite following deliberation, but this reductive account was rejected, especially by French and German philosophers. Rousseau's general will (in *The Social Contract*, 1761) was a collective judgement resulting from citizens deliberating patriotically about the common good, and in Hegel's *Philosophy of Right* (1821) we find an attempt to combine reason and the will, in the idea of a rational will, as a progressive judgment emerging from the processes of history.

Democratic theorists have seldom risen to these heights, but they certainly regard the will of the people as more than the fragmented thing that Rousseau called "the will of all." The reason is that popular opinion today emerges from discussion in which an educated electorate participates, and whatever form public policy takes in response to such discussion will have been formalized by politicians and civil servants who as a group have a generally superior understanding of the realities of politics. Thus the theory of deliberative democracy offers debate as an answer to the question of where political wisdom will be found—not in philosophy, as Plato perhaps suggested in *The Republic* but in a rhetorical process.

Here then is a familiar account of the terrain theorised by democrats. Does it correspond to any reality? Is it perhaps merely a dream emerging from normative theory of desirabilities? The answer depends on which local and historical passages of democratic politics we are studying. Too much idealizing of democracy is foolish; democracy does not allow human beings to transcend the human condition. Too much cynicism fails to explain the enormous popularity of democracy today. But to understand the problems of democracy today one must understand a paradox: that while democracy is "about" actualizing the will of the people, wise government is in many ways about frustrating them. One should never forget Churchill's remark: democracy is the worst of all forms of government—except for all the rest.

(3) FRUSTRATING THE WILL OF THE PEOPLE

The problem with democracy is not merely that it is impossible to formulate any satisfactory way of actualizing the will of the people, but that many people actively want to be able to frustrate that will. No one quite puts the matter in this way, but it certainly corresponds to the facts. Frustrating the will of the people sounds undemocratic, and indeed it is, but it responds to a real problem in politics. Let me explain.

A federal constitution, for example, is a device for making sure that the interests of various minorities—territorial or ethnic—cannot be overridden by a contingent, or especially, by an entrenched majority. Federalism protects the interest of the Quebequois in Canada, for example, just as the Senate in the United States protects small states against majorities in the more populous. This is the most elementary example of how and why the will of the people might be frustrated.

Again, the history of democracy suggests a steady decline in the sophistication of how elections are conducted. In American elections, the thousands of citizens who used in the nineteenth century to listen for hours to Lincoln and Douglas debating the issues

of the day have now become the consumers of brief television com-
mercials puffing one candidate or (more commonly) denigrating
an opponent. In the German elections of 2002, according to *The
Times*, the parties are vying for the youth vote with sexually suggestive posters—one for the current Chancellor's Party shows two
lips pursed in a kiss, with the slogan: "That was just foreplay. The
climax is yet to come." In Britain in the middle 1990s voters were
asked, among many other questions, how they had voted in the
1992 election which had been won by the Conservatives. A majority said they had voted Labour! Voters are, in other words, no more
reliable about the past than they are in judging the future. In any
case, it has long been observed that popular opinion changes dramatically in response to recent newspaper stories: a dramatic murder will have a notable effect on opinions about the death penalty.
Indeed, the death penalty is a celebrated issue on which the opinions of the demos can differ dramatically from those of the elite. An
Indonesian journal called "Tempo" reported a recent poll according to which 60% of the respondents favoured the introduction of
the Sharia, yet only 30% approved stoning as the punishment for
adultery (though rather more approved of the Sharia punishment
for theft). In other words, popular opinion is often a logic free zone.
We might also note that some millions of electors suffer from problems of mental health, yet the British government not so long ago
took steps to give the vote to those who had voluntarily entered
homes for the psychiatric patients. In other words there is abundant evidence that might lead one to consider the demos a wild and
irrational entity. Its wisdom often seems severely limited.

These points exemplify something that has long been known
and discussed: namely that political opinion is subject to powerful
irrational forces. No doubt the general will, or the rational will,
are definitionally free of such blemishes, but they exist in a world
of definitions, not in the world of empirical politics. And, as we
have seen, it is virtually impossible to elicit such a will with any
certainty. Part of the problem is that most of the time, politics is a

special taste, like an interest in ice hockey or opera; most people most of the time find it boring, and even more know little about it. This means that we must distinguish, as realists in political theory from Machiavelli to Schumpeter always have, between a minority of political enthusiasts (call them the "elite") and very many people largely indifferent (call them "masses").

This might seem to solve the problem of political wisdom. Should not politics be left to the elite, except for the periodic elections, which are like consumer tests of products, in which the people can vote for a different product? It may indeed be the case that this is what democracies are actually like, but it certainly does not deal with the rhetorical problem. For the elite itself will contain some lunatics, some who are mentally ill, some fanatics, some profoundly stupid, some who use the theatre of politics as a stage on which to strike postures. Here is a problem about democracy on which nearly everybody will agree, whatever political tendency they belong to. Believers in the free market are inclined to regard socialists as dangerous, while liberals and socialists worry about xenophobia and nationalism on what it is conventional to call "the right." And many countries have their own specific version of this problem. Thus modern Turkey was based upon a rejection of the entire Ottoman system and was established, forcefully, by Kemal Attaturk who could not have operated in terms of what the people wanted, and who certainly did not for a moment think of doing so.

The result of this democratic reality is that modern democratic governments (rightly called "liberal democracies" in testimony to their dual character) are in many respects strikingly oligarchic. And to understand this, one needs to look at characteristic devices of modern governments.

(4) HOW TO FRUSTRATE THE WILL OF THE PEOPLE

The first of these is the practice of elevating those beliefs currently thought to be so fundamental that no one would reject them into unchangeable rules beyond the possibility of change through the ordinary political process. These are called "human rights." They are often presented as an extension of the freedom of citizens, since they are often formulated as limitations on government. On closer inspection, they will often be found, paradoxically, to have the general effect of extending, rather than diminishing, the power of the state. Some rights, for example, demand additional taxation, many of them require the establishment of inspectorates to enforce them. They always involve more work for lawyers and judges.

A second device is for democratic governments to align themselves with grandiose international projects by signing up to international treaties. On such issues as environmental protection and international jurisdiction, states will often sign up to vague ethical desirabilities whose detailed implications can include decisions that a government could not have got through its own parliament. International agreements about modernization (for example on trade unions, or on health) have a powerful attraction in many countries.

Each of these examples is an instance of a general principle at work. To be politically active in the modern world is commonly to support a modernizing programme often hostile to nationalist projects, religious traditions, local customs and the situational responses of peoples in the third world. The place of women in different cultures is an important example. In one form or another, it can be possible for governments to establish regulatory agencies as the custodians of these policies, with powers to enforce social change going far beyond what would be approved by any elected parliament. This is certainly the case with many anti-discrimination agencies in the West. Whether such independence of parliament is good or bad no doubt depends on many questions. What is much less arguable is that this kind of "blue sky" policy is a way of frustrating the will of the people.

A further aspect of the ways in which governments frustrate the will of the people is by managing the public perception of events—what is currently called "spin." Spin is a managerial technique relevant to the fact that modern states are constituted by the propensity of its people, or many of them, to focus their attention, day to day, on the events that get into the news. These range from sporting events to political projects and other national events. The movement of political support depends to a large extent on the value placed on these events. Indeed, it often depends on the extent to which they are known and understood, which makes managing the media central to politics. Governments and newspapers have their own judgements of newsworthiness, and the working of democracy is powerfully influenced by it. In the world of advertising, public relations and politics, releasing news at the right moment and getting it interpreted in the right way is often thought to be a matter of life and death.

We might sum these tendencies up by saying that the quality of public deliberation in modern democracies has become increasing verbal or pseudo-intellectual. To put it more brutally, modern politics facilitates persuasion by the glib, those who have plausible reasons for whatever they recommend. It is no place for the slow thinking person who has doubts about a policy but can't quite see how to formulate those doubts. Modern politics is thus a good world for liberals, but not a good world for conservatives, or indeed for believers in religious doctrines, such as Islam, which constitute a complete and exclusive form of life.

(5) THE EVOLUTION OF DEMOCRACY

Modern Western states are commonly called "liberal democracies" and both words point to important features of political reality. What is not often realised is that they conflict with each other. A modern state is indeed genuinely democratic, and that is genuinely important, but democracy is, and perhaps must in some respects, be modified and frustrated. I am not concerned, of course, with arguing whether this is good or bad—merely to advance a hypothesis about the way in which the modern state is actually evolving. And for that purpose, I wish to suggest a three stage view of what is happening.

In doing so, I come into direct conflict with what I have called "democratic salvationism." This doctrine assumes that democracy is the last stage of historical evolution, and that the more democratic we become, the better our institutions will work. My view, on the other hand, is that democracy, like everything else in human affairs, is part of a process of continual change, and that the modern state is democratic in its justificatory rhetoric and oligarchic in its actual operation.

What we must remember is that democracy emerged in Western Europe as a powerful movement as late as the end of the eighteenth century. In the remaking of European institutions at the time of the French revolution and Napoleon, the sovereign powers that had largely been in the hands of kings came increasingly into the hands of parliaments. Democracy was, one might say, an optional extra for modern constitutions. Citizens acquired the right to vote, and traditional institutions adapted as best they could. Fashions change, as fashions will, even in politics. Balkan nationalists in the later nineteenth century commonly thought that independent statehood required a monarch, and Serbia and Greece and others imported such figures. But the First World War destroyed many monarchies, and few were left after 1945.

We may therefore identify the first stage of democracy as that in which it modified the essentially monarchical institutions of Europe. The franchise was extended, the executive of most countries became, to some extent responsible to elected parliaments and much of politics revolved around extending citizenship to all. But even by the beginning of the twentieth century, authority remained royal and aristocratic. When Germany and France went to war in 1914, both had parliaments and indeed strong socialist parties with pacifist and internationalist inclinations, but it made no difference to the outcome. And the fragility of democratic institutions was further illustrated by the collapse of democracy in Italy in 1922 and Germany in 1933.

Nevertheless, one implication of democracy was that "the social question" came increasingly to dominate politics. What should be done about the urban poor? Bismarck in Germany between about 1870 and 1890 has sometimes been seen as the originator of the welfare state, but a similar movement for spending public money to equalise in some degree the condition of the poor was spreading over Europe and after 1945 it had become almost universal. Hence we may distinguish a second stage of democratic evolution, in which the arrival of a democratic constitution created a democratic society. It had taken time, indeed, but the coming of democracy in the end followed the developmental trajectory that would have been expected by Aristotle and other political philosophers reflecting on the experience of democratic Athens. The spearhead of this impulse was, of course, socialism, but the point is that egalitarian policies and egalitarian doctrines came increasingly to be universally current. In the second half of the twentieth century they were everywhere dominant, and the European Union has given them a new lease of life.

One might well think that this was the path to the future. You might almost call it an "end of history." And political philosophers have commonly taken this view. Impressed by realist theories of democracy which emphasised the irrationality of democratic practices, they have emphasised that democracy as a system must involve everyone in public debate and deliberation. The general will as the achievement of a rational public interest in which all citizens have been involved beckoned before them. But it will be evident that there are important barriers blocking this happy fulfilment, and that leads me to suggest, tentatively, that we are moving into a third stage of political transition.

(6) A NEW OLIGARCHY?

To understand what is happening, we must observe certain constitutional problems. I shall illustrate the position in terms of Britain, but the broad picture is similar everywhere. In 1800, the British constitution was essentially monarchical, and over several previous centuries, much attention had been given to the problem of preventing the monarch from engaging in any form of absolutist rule. The British constitution was understood in terms of balance: the power of the king was balanced by that of parliament, the power of parliament by free elections, the executive by the independence of judges, and all authority was subject to legal supervision. In other words, the dangers of tyranny and despotism were well understood so long as the formal government of Britain was monarchical. But what happens when, over a long period of time, the will of the sovereign monarchy gives way to the sovereign will of the people? Those who love freedom will oppose any king who oversteps his power, but how can we, the people, oppose the will of the people? As the Communists used to say, "the people cannot oppress the people." Nothing so gross as that slogan surfaced in Britain, but there is no doubt that democratic fundamentalism has weakened the restraints on power which long centuries of experience had built in to Western constitutions. When rulers are clearly distinct from the people (and many of them are aristocratic) the danger to freedom is well understood in political circles; when the dominant theory is that the people are the rulers, we have a new situation, and one in which freedom is a good deal less secure.

We thus enter a period of constitutional decline, by which I mean that most people tend to judge the validity of a public policy in terms of what they take to be its desirability rather than its formal constitutionality. The question they ask is: is this a good thing? They are much less concerned to ask: "does the agency have authority to do this thing?" and this utilitarian impatience with formal restraints is common throughout Europe. A current example: the European Court of Justice has just validated a directive banning the manufacture in Europe of high-tar cigarettes. The real reason is that high tar cigarettes have bad effects on health, but the ground of the decision argued before the Court was that health issues can sometimes be used as barriers to trade, and therefore the Community has jurisdiction. Yet the national states of the E.U.

have not so far given the Commission authority to regulate health. Constitutionality thus gives way before (supposed) desirability. Over the last century, European governments have used their authority to validate the discretion of the Executive over a wide range of subjects, while from the demos have come increasing demands that government should use its money and its authority to supply benefits that would in earlier times have been the responsibility of individuals and families. One major engine of this extension of governmental power has been the subsidy. Governments have found many reasons to pay for benefits to the people—in the form of education, cultural support, health care and so on—and very soon after the subsidy comes the control. As the familiar feminist slogan has it, "the personal is the political," a slogan that invites the government into the living room, the bedroom, the kitchen and the nursery. Governments have not been slow to accept the invitation.

Hence it is that Ferdinand Mount, in a notable discussion of the British constitution quotes the Oxford political scientist Nevil Johnson: "there has over a fairly long period been a retreat from constitutional ways of thinking in Britain." The suggestion is that even our language of constitutional discussion has atrophied. Mount also quotes with disapproval a former Conservative Minister of Education, John Patten. Patten invoked the traditional idea of balance. But what was the balance between? On Patten's view, it was between effectiveness—the capacity of government to govern—and consent, maintaining popular support for the political system. Mount finds this "a bizarre conception of balance" and no doubt in traditional terms it is. "Balance" used to refer to constitutional powers that blocked each other's tendency to tyrannise. But what Patten's remark reveals is that he is recognizing the fact that no government that seeks to manage the lives of its subjects can possibly hope to have the approval of the whole people. It just needs to make sure, by a variety of means, that most people will at least accept whatever is being done. What in fact this observation brings out clearly is that Britain has become what Michael Oakeshott calls an enterprise rather than a civil association. A "civil association" means, in Oakeshott's argument, an association of individuals living within a framework of law and pursuing their own individual and cooperative enterprises. In an enterprise association, by contrast, the whole state has become an enterprise in which all the members are coercively managed so that they support whatever ends the entrepreneurs have chosen.

I have, then, identified two stages in the spread of democracy in Europe. In the first stage, democratic elections were merely modifications of political practice in states which had long been evolving a monarchical structure, and this means that democracy was largely foreign to their customs and conventions. This stage is an analytic idea, but it roughly corresponds to Europe in the nineteenth century. In the second stage, democracy began to exhibit those equalising tendencies in which a dominant majority, being poor, uses political power to change economic outcomes. States take into their hands ever increasing powers to appropriate the resources of society and to distribute those resources in accordance with principles such as equality and social justice. The effect has been a profound modification in the moral, social and constitutional condition of Western states.

I now want to conclude from this analysis that the modern state is turning into a new form of association (a third stage in terms of my schema), in which an emerging elite based upon an educated skill in deploying legal and rhetorical instruments of persuasion acquires the power to manage the people rather than merely rule them. This is a kind of utilitarian project whose aim corresponds in one way or another with trying to secure the greatest happiness of the greatest number. The objective is peace and harmony both within the state, and between states. One important aim of this new order of things is to obliterate the gap, or to seem to have obliterated the gap, between the government and the governed. That, I think, is one reason why people these days are learning to talk about "governance" rather than government, for governance is a word suggesting that rules and regulations materialize, as it were, out of thin air. There is always a tension between rulers and ruled, but the high art of management is to persuade the managed that they are all involved in the same enterprise. Here then is a new oligarchy in which democratic salvationism supplies the justification while endless negotiation and moral concepts such as rights supply the means of constructing this new order.

Such is my hypothesis, and it is, of course, highly arguable. That democracy is evolving into oligarchy is a logically peculiar doctrine. It combines the argument that democracy has given way to oligarchy, with the prediction that this tendency will continue. Both propositions are no doubt contestable, but I think it is important to bring them out into the light of discussion.

Two Concepts of the Moral Life

SEPTEMBER 2005

Britain Today: Part VII. Kenneth Minogue explores the moral life, or lack thereof, of modern Britain, and how it differs from that of past generations.

One way of tracking the movement of a civilization is to follow the evolution of thought and sentiment in the moral life. The moral life is not, of course, any particular moral system, but the daily flow of thoughts and desires we experience as we respond to a sense that there is some right thing we ought to be doing. People have very different ideas, of course, about what the right thing is, and that is my theme. The situation is further complicated by the fact that very few styles of morality ever disappear entirely, so that Britain (for example) is morally a vast patchwork of responses to the world, responses that are constantly changing. Such changes can to some extent be tracked in public discussion and actual conduct over the generations. And my argument here is that by the end of the twen-

Kenneth Minogue, "Two Concepts of the Moral Life." This article is reprinted with permission from the publisher of *New Criterion* 24 (September 2005). © 2014, *The New Criterion*, www.newcriterion.com.

tieth century, a striking new style of moral response to the world had come into being.

Let me indicate the kind of change I mean by sketching elements of the historical movement of the moral life in recent times. We commonly observe that in the later part of the nineteenth century, the more educated Britons were often struggling with religious doubt aroused by Darwin's evolutionary theories. A widespread response among Queen Victoria's subjects to the "melancholy, long, withdrawing roar" of the Christian faith was to absolutize a morality of Duty detached from its religious moorings. In the novels of Henry James and a little later of Joseph Conrad we have the most exquisite imaginable sensibilities of a purely moral kind. But within a generation, these upright Victorians looked repressed and stultifying to (for example) D. H. Lawrence and the Bloomsbury circle. Sexual freedom and an accommodation with natural impulses—that was the thing! The history of twentieth-century morality is one of elite freedoms seeping down to the more respectable classes, partly as a result of experiences such as that of war, and partly from the implications of political radicalism. Out in the expanding suburbs of Britain, things changed slowly, but the young were always convinced that they lived in a more liberated world than had their elders. The upper crust may have been as morally adrift as Evelyn Waugh portrayed them, but the wider world valued respectability, and pregnancy generally led to marriage.

The Second World War continued the process of liberation, partly by detaching so many people from norm-reinforcing communities, and partly by continuing to undermine popular respect for authority as such. The reputation of the 1950s seems strange to the historian: moral attitudes had strikingly liberalized, yet later generations have locked them into legend as dull and restrictive. The reason, one may guess, is that the young were already looking forward to making an even grander bonfire of accepted conventions than actually occurred. Just such a bonfire soon came as the 1960s experience of popular tertiary education created dreams of new liberations. Heterosexuality and monogamy crumbled as absolutes, or even as dominant standards, and the vogue for moral and political satire made defenders of "morality" look as if they were the fossils of an earlier time. Ethical relativism, long familiar in the universities, drifted into the advanced chatter of the sophisticated.

The period since the 1960s has largely developed the themes already evident earlier in the century. It has been a time in which ideas accepted as radical and liberated have spread to all corners of society, and some of their implications have begun to be explored. The main agents of change have been the government on the one hand, and commerce on the other. The consequence has been a rather dramatic "transvaluation of values." The virtue of chastity, for example, has been left for dead, and a Roman Catholic priesthood demanding celibacy has barely survived, so dominant has become the idea that sexuality is a natural expression of human wholeness whose denial must be in some degree unhealthy or pathological. Again, loyalty has been notably downgraded in moral terms. The rich and the royal have great difficulty in finding employees who will not soon cash out their intimacy with the famous for the benefit of a tabloid readership. Loyalty to employers has been weakened partly by economic and political changes, but perhaps most obviously by the emergence of a kind of counter-morality in which the citizen or the employee has a higher loyalty to truth. The "whistleblower" is admired for an integrity that transcends mere loyalty. Loyalty to one's own country has also changed. Mere patriotism was reclassified as an unthinking prejudice especially by many who had been to universities and there picked up the idea that morality was adherence to abstract principles, preferably principles in conflict with one's own apparent interest. Peace and justice were higher values than merely loyalty to one's country.

And what of thrift as a virtue? A few children still have piggy banks, but saving up to buy something for which we yearn began to disappear in the 1950s. Partly this was a function of rising wealth, and partly of the credit policies of such banks as the National Westminster, which famously offered to "take the waiting out of wanting." In the slogan "we want it now," the radicals of the 1960s tried to turn anger and impatience into virtues serving politico-moral causes. Inherited morality had regarded the suppression of these tendencies as part of self-mastery, but the newly popular sentiment of impatience diffused itself throughout society. It is thus one of the arenas in which moral conflict has been fought out. A capacity to "defer gratification" had long been identified by economic and social historians as an element in the success of rising capitalism, but capitalism itself was the subject of politico-moral critique. Thrift thus began to disappear, partly because wealth and commerce combined to make it easier for people to buy things. There was another powerful force that led in the same direction. The British Government diminished the incentive to save. In the past, people had feared being unable to pay the doctor, the hospital, or even the undertaker. Losing one's job was also a serious matter in less flexible times. People saved for a "rainy day," but now the government has abolished rainy days. At the personal level, the balance between saving and expenditure changed dramatically.

It might seem as if these developments constituted nothing less than a bonfire of the virtues and that British society was sliding into a kind of moral chaos. Many people do indeed think this, and many changes in society would make such a conclusion plausible, but it is far from being the whole picture. Sexual liberation, for example, has been the most dramatic of the changes, but the restraints that were once recommended to the young on moral grounds have found a new life in arguments of prudence about the dangers of unwanted pregnancy and sexually transmitted diseases—AIDS, of course, most notably. Abortion as a form of birth control remains an area of hot dispute, though a glance at the moral history of the

Soviet Union would make it clear that the long-term effects of large-scale abortion as a form of birth control can be serious. Thrift again has disappeared from morality, only to resurface in the pensions crisis, in which the present generation finds itself facing massive financial commitments for which no serious provision has been made. Loyalty has not been a beneficiary of this widespread transposition of the moral into the prudential, and for the moment, the posture of being "above the battle" in national disputes, even indeed "above" cultural or civilizational partisanship, remains the dominant attitude of those who have been to universities. Even that judgment minimizes the change: many people are almost viscerally hostile to the West and all it stands for. It may be, however, that this attitude will change as a result of the crisis over Islamic terrorism.

Replacing moral obligations by prudential ones might well seem to be merely a change of vocabulary. Surely, it might be argued, conduct remains the same, even if the ideas sustaining it are different. In fact, those sustaining ideas have lost a significant amount of their force. In sexual matters, for example, the decline of marriage and the emergence of units consisting of a mother and her children have large social consequences. But in any case, the thought that goes into a moral act is itself a part of that act. The reasons we act in one way rather than another reflect back on our conception of ourselves, and these reasons have a variety of "hooks" or implications that have important effects on the development of individual character. A prudent act is much less fixed in place, and much more susceptible to circumstantial variability, than an act done from the moral conviction that it is right. In other words, the moral situation has certainly changed, even though many of its appearances have not.

The collapse of some of the virtues into prudence is therefore significant, but it leaves one question open. Assuming as I do that human beings are irredeemably moral creatures, and that thinking morally is an essential element of their psychological furniture, what has happened? We have observed a pretty clean sweep of important moral convictions in the collapse of the virtues of chastity, loyalty, and thrift. Is this merely to be recognized as a case of moral decline? Or have these virtues been replaced by something else? And if so, what? The moral life has clearly evolved—but where has it gone?

The evident answer, I think, is that moral sentiments now focus on benevolence, philanthropy, and charitable causes. In the dynamic market of moral responses, some virtues are always losing value and others gaining it. Benevolence is a seventeenth-century virtue developed as a counterweight in an individualist society to the vice of self-partiality or self-love. It emerges from Christian precepts about loving thy neighbor. Philanthropy in modern times described the way in which the benevolent rich have used their resources to improve the condition of society or some people in it. But should it be only rich people who benefit their fellows by good works? The idea has spread that we all have something to contribute to others, and that "giving something back to society" is perhaps our most important duty. The ideal goal of philanthropy is to make itself redundant, but there are suggestions that it may serve the purpose of cultivating character. Philanthropy is an important duty recommended in courses about "citizenship and values" in British schools, and in the United States there is instruction in the administration of charity. Is this perhaps how the moral life has been evolving?

As a new morality, this development prides itself on releasing judgment from a narrow concern with sex in order to bring ethical standards to bear on the really serious decisions made in government and commerce. As one admirer of the new turn observed, it gets morality out of the bedroom and into the boardroom. It seeks to encompass corporations no less than individuals, and thus lies on the borderline between morals and politics. It finds expression in such enterprises as the "fair trade" movement or the spread of "ethical investment." It has been a great generator of Non-Governmental Organizations. It is deeply egalitarian in its rejection of any version of the sin of pride, and especially of any idea that we are superior to other peoples. The new morality thus incorporates both multiculturalism and "political correctness," in that both basically respond to a solicitude for the sensitivities of people different from "us." This sentiment extends to the view that it is merely good fortune that allows some of us to live prosperous and secure lives, while others live in poverty and insecurity.

Ethics and politics thus come together in what we might well call "the politico-moral" arena, and the consequences are dramatic. In this explosion of charitable endeavors, people of all kinds set themselves tasks whose point is to be "sponsored" by others who will make a financial contribution to the enterprise that will be given to good causes. The fashion among the young for a "gap year" between school and university has generated schemes by which the young will be funded to go and perform good deeds in the underdeveloped world. The British government has a multi-million pound scheme to enroll "volunteers" for good causes, while an alternative to punishment by prison has been "community service," in which the delinquent performs useful non-paying work.

Nothing, however, has been as dramatic an expression of the new morality as the response of the British public to the financial appeal for the victims of the Asian tsunami in 2005—unless it be the Live 8 concert whose point was not to encourage the giving of money, but the taking of it from the public budgets of rich countries so that we should "make poverty history," especially in Africa. Spending other people's money is one of the favorite occupations of modern democracies, but here was this ambition on quite a new scale. All these endeavors are promoted on impeccably moral grounds, but prudence has not been entirely left behind. Government ministers are often to be found saying how such charity teaches the philanthropic new skills, and how good it will look on the *curriculum vitae.*

✦ ✦ ✦

Here then, we seem to have the materials for advancing a long way towards the dominant aspiration of our contemporaries: namely, perfecting society. Morality has broken out of the confines in which it linked the duty of integrity to oneself with the good of those we actually encountered. It has now become the moral and metaphysical condition on which we relate to the rest of the world. It has above all identified the people who need help, both those victimized by disease or misfortune in our own society and those afflicted in other parts of the world. Morality has thus liberated itself from the merely personal element of being true to oneself and become a program for perfecting the world. We would seem to have the materials here for a radical leap forward.

Alas, the imperfections of the human condition are not so easily removed. In considering the moral evolution of British society, our attention to the vast and perfectly real benevolence toward outsiders has been only one side of the picture, and the other side is all too familiar. It largely comes under the heading of social disorder but it has to be understood as a form of moral collapse. Schools have trouble keeping order and bullying is a major problem. Vandalism distorts the visual aspects of British cities, and arson sometimes results from disgruntled pupils, some of whom merely think it a good way of securing a holiday. Doctors in casualty departments and firemen fighting blazes find that they are abused and assaulted as they try to help people, while the transport services threaten strike action unless they are protected from the gratuitous violence of angry customers. Intimidation is so rife on council estates that the new device of the Anti-Social Behaviour Order has been invented in order to deal with it. Intimidation, which threatens the role of witnesses in courts, has also reached nasty levels in some ethnic communities, particularly among those that have come to specialize in some criminal activities, such as Albanians in sexual exploitation and Jamaican "yardies" in drugs. The aesthetics of intimidation have recently been enriched by the practice among teenagers of wearing the hoods of their jackets up, partly, it seems, so that they may indulge in low-level thieving without being easily recognized. Young people have problems making commitments, even commitments short of marriage, while the welfare state is surrogate father to the many women without resources who become pregnant. The rising number of single-person households is exacerbating the housing shortage, while polls suggest that lots of couples are locked together unhappily because they don't have the resources to separate. The government has recently invested millions in the training of debt counselors to help people who cannot be trusted with plastic credit cards. Admittedly, there are elements of this litany that can only provoke sardonic amusement, but we have said enough to make the point that British life is dramatically different from what it was a less than century ago, when George Orwell, the benchmark authority on this question, described the peaceable, orderly, and disciplined character of the British.

Here then is the paradox: Britain is an improving society with very high levels of virtue, and Britain is in a condition of near social collapse. The moral lives of Europeans were in earlier times more or less all of a piece. The rich may have been louche, but they were usually discreet. Most of those in employment were middle or respectable working class and they respected the moral pieties of the time. This kind of orderliness required a fair amount of self-conquest, and this was a virtue that had generally been acquired in childhood, often as a result of religious belief. And then on the edges of "society" could be found a marginal group of ne'er-do-wells, criminals, casual workers, immigrants, people with mental problems, and others who scratched along in and out of official care, but who threatened the moral order only at times of high political tension.

Today, however, we have a remarkable dissonance between a vast public allegiance to the betterment of our fellows, on the one hand, and a vicious incapacity to behave morally to those who are closest to us, on the other. Part of the paradox is that we seem to hate people who are trying to do us some good, as with teachers, doctors, and firemen. This contrast is at the level of practice. At the level of public utterance, pious expressions of tolerance and love of diversity collide with a rather violent hatred of what is taken to be prejudice, bigotry, racism, and other forms of intolerance. At the level of manners, we may certainly see a decline in civility—more jostling in public places, children who sit contentedly in seats while women and the elderly are standing. And at a theoretical level, there is a notable gap between a general skepticism about morality, and bureaucratic dogmatism in the enforcement of the strictures of political correctness.

The paradox has, then, many aspects. Some of its features but not others are replicated in other Western states. And there are, of course, wide variations within states; Britain itself is far from homogeneous. The puzzle is how to make sense of the contradictory ways in which people behave. Let me finish by making a few suggestions.

It might be that the benevolent and the delinquent Britons are two entirely separate parts of the population. Perhaps the antisocial might be Ferdinand Mount's recently discovered "downers," or Charles Murray's "underclass." But if so, we might well ask the simple question: What makes the delinquents behave as they do? Could it perhaps be that the one moral impulse actually feeds off the others—that the very philanthropic desire that seeks to improve and to understand better the conduct of the delinquent (its "root causes," as people confusedly put it)—might create perverse incentives to its worsening? It may be that "anti-social conduct" has its own rewards in eliciting attention and other benefits from the rest of society. Children now have rights and many of their delinquencies are costless amusements. The British Government even has a Minister for Children whose latest idea for dealing with delinquency is to supply the young with plastic cards on which they may earn rewards for good behavior—a misjudgment of human nature that will certainly rank high in the annals of fatuity. But perhaps the basic point here is that the transposition of bad moral conduct into the language of social acceptability and social capital removes it entirely from the innerness of the moral life. It misunderstands human beings by treating them as mere organisms mechanically responding to the conditions in which they live.

But no human society is neatly divided into its good and its bad lots. Let us focus on something else: it is difficult to imagine that this so-called "anti-social behavior" greatly increases the happiness of its practitioners. Indiscipline in class has its amusements, but only as a bit of Saturnalia. As standard behavior, it becomes sour and boring. Can it be, perhaps, that much of this problem is to be explained in terms of a vulgar error in moral understanding, an error that has been especially influential in the period since 1945? The error I refer to starts from the premise that Morality with a capital M is forbidding stuff that stands in the way of our pleasures and desires. It is merely the arid disapprovals of the old and the dull. Morality frowns on drinking, smoking, sex, and a good deal of other forms of merrymaking. It seems to demand that we approach life with a solemn humility. The conclusion that might be drawn is that the less of it we have, the happier we'll be. Hence the program of sloughing off the inherited prohibitions of past times—particularly in such areas as sex, where technology has changed the terms and conditions—looks like liberation into a jollier form of life. The point is, of course, that the moral sentiments of the very young are significantly different from those of the wider world, and lack the advantage of a basis in experience of the real world. This foolish view of Morality as merely repressive fails to understand that (in any of its many varieties) morality is an education in self-mastery. Without some such element of self-control, human beings are vulnerable to every idiocy that impulse might suggest.

✦ ✦ ✦

We often describe any qualifications of our desires as "moral restraints," which suggests that they are merely inhibitions, but they
are, of course, more subtle than that. They canalize and redirect
our desires in ways that offer more fecund satisfactions over the
long term. If therefore moral agents forsake these inner complexities of the moral life in favor of the simplicities of "anything goes,"
they are left with nothing to sustain order except the brutishness
of regulation or the pains of shipwreck. It is significant that polling data, for what it might be worth, does suggest that people are
less happy today than they were in earlier decades. Critics have
seen another type of paradox here—that prosperity (contrary to
supposed popular belief) is negatively correlated with happiness.
Perhaps. But at a more profound level, we would have to diagnose
moral confusion.

Perhaps the most striking feature of the new morality is the way
in which it turns inherited morality upside down. Our basic moral
duties today are owned not to those we encounter daily but to those
who on a utilitarian calculus are in most need of them. The new
politico-moral order imposes on us duties to strangers, people we
have never met, and for the most part never will. Particular duties
to family and friends, much less that central duty of integrity to
ourselves on which the older moralists laid so much stress, hardly
enter the picture. Indeed, it is worse than that: doing good things
for our friends is at best doing what comes naturally (and therefore
is hardly morally significant) and at worst exercising our virtue on
those who probably need it much less than others. In these concerns, we may merely be adding to the injustices of society. Sending one's children to a good and expensive school, for example,
may well be caricatured as the selfishness of "pushy parents."

A paradox, of course, lies in how a situation is described. Reality knows no paradoxes. Our problem is therefore to find some
structure of understanding that can make sense of the way in which

public policy and moral evolution in modern Britain has created a Jekyll and Hyde society. There can be little doubt that this is a central issue in our civilization.

A notable oddity of our situation is that past generations differed from us in accepting the imperfections of human life, partly because they doubted much could be done about them, and partly because many thought in Christian terms. Today a generation of secularists has higher aims. To every imperfection there now corresponds the aspiration to set up machinery to make sure that such things will never happen again. We seek, in other words, nothing less than perfection. Could it be, however, that our very greed for social perfection has destroyed our grip on the real moorings of human life? Perhaps our sentimental addiction to the superficialities of social perfection has eroded our capacity for the hard and demanding work of moral integrity. Certainly, tolerance and benevolence are often shallow virtues. But it may well be that this personal loss of integrity merely reflects a similar collapse of integrity in the institutions of civil society as they respond to the sickly embrace of government and of projects of social perfection. Our judges have been less concerned with the dry and limited technicalities of the law since they have been given all those delicious rights with which to make a just society. The universities are less and less concerned with scholarship because they dream that their research will solve the problems of society. The churches have abandoned otherworldliness in order to become the public relations branch of an improving government. Industrial firms are hounded by activists into giving up their basic business of making good things at a decent price; they now want to be respected for their "social responsibility." And I have not even begun to mention our police, now focused on communal relations, or our prison service, which is no longer content with punishment but wants to improve its charges as well. Nor have I been able to mention teachers and journalists, subjects in their own right. Such wonders of improving benevolence we all enjoy! But can it be that all of these cooks with their muddled ideas about improving the world are just spoiling our social broth?

This then is the world we have made, wittingly or not. It is a world that corresponds—for better or worse—to what we want. Will it still be what we want as we experience the way it will develop in the longer term? The fundamental problem is that that very question, like any suggestion for improvement, exhibits precisely the cast of mind in which we currently live.

Aesop tells the story of a bird with a worm, who saw its image in a pond, and dropped the worm in its desire to have that other reflected worm, as well. What a foolish creature!

Seduction & Politics

NOVEMBER 2006

THE MORAL AND POLITICAL HISTORY OF SEDUCTION

The original meaning of "seduction" was "to persuade a vassal, servant, soldier, etc. to desert his allegiances or service." The OED dates that first usage from 1477, and it was only in 1560 that "seduction" came to be used also as inducing a woman to surrender her chastity. As usage evolved, "seduction" was generalized to mean "being persuaded to abandon, or betray, a commitment." And also from early on, the term came to be used to cover "a cause of error; an allurement." By 1782 we have "seductive" as "tending to lead astray," and a decent gender balance was restored in 1803 with the appearance of "seductress."

Seduction is thus a central, indeed in certain respects, *the* central, idea, in political life. It signifies a course of action deliberately designed by one or more interested agents to undermine and replace some established loyalty—moral, political, sexual—and to substitute for it a different rule of conduct. The outcome of seduction in medieval times was clearly treason: the follower betrayed

Kenneth Minogue, "Seduction & Politics." This article is reprinted with permission from the publisher of *New Criterion* 25 (November 2006). © 2014, *The New Criterion*, www.newcriterion.com.

the leader. He became a traitor. Such conduct threatened the moral dissolution of society. Modern Western societies are not based on such loyalties, and they have little place for the moral machinery of oaths of allegiance. A commitment or a promise is, with us, a much looser affair than in earlier times. Nevertheless, loyalty remains a central part in our lives. We are loyal to our friends, our lovers, and our families, and in some areas loyal as well to our employers and other associates, and we take it for granted that they are loyal to us. Most would think that their very world had crumbled if they found that a friend or a lover was covertly doing them mischief.

Political loyalties have survived less well: many of the rights of citizenship in Western states have now been extended to everyone, and that has diluted the corresponding sense of duty. Few educated people would now be disposed to take the line of "my country right or wrong," and many have detached themselves from national loyalty so far as to contemplate international issues from some floating region of outer space. This view from a kind of nowhere—actually a Platonic world of ideas—takes off from the *prima facie* judgment that one's own country, far from always being right, is more likely than others to be wrong. Such a position demonstrates rational detachment from local prejudice—a mechanical test of such rationality, indeed, but we are not here dealing with very sophisticated people. Nonetheless, where the safety of a country is at stake, subverting loyalty to it is treason, the paradigm of all forms of betrayal. In past times, before regimes could rely on bureaucratic organization, loyalty was often the cardinal virtue; it defined one's worth, and disloyalty brought with it the threat of anarchy and collapse.

Still, even in our more relaxed modern world, integrity remains a matter of doing the right thing in relation to husband, wife, friend, employer or employee, and other such elements of our world. Such integrity is a limitation on the impulses we might otherwise indulge. To be morally serious is to be firm in commitments of this kind. To seduce someone is thus to make him or her, in a moral sense, worse. But here two problems evidently arise that explain the strange thing, emphasized by an early anthologist of literary seduction: "The fact is," wrote Robert Meister in 1962, "that while the literature of nearly all ages and cultures abounds in seduction scenes, the concept, the theory of seduction has been universally ignored." There are at least two reasons for this, and let us point to the frivolous one first. The whole idea of seduction today has an archaic air about it. In the era of "Sex and the City," the idea of female virtue being overcome by lust and deceit belongs to an age of lost innocence. The supposed victim may well be into the bedroom several steps ahead of the seducer. The whole strange metaphor of "conquest" in these matters has lost all credibility.

There is, however, a more complicated and serious reason why the idea of seduction has been overtaken by a certain desuetude. It is that our moral sentiments have largely abandoned loyalty as a fundamental virtue, and embraced an abstract standard of rectitude. The criminal who "grasses" on his fellows is no doubt regarded with contempt, but the dissident, the whistleblower, and the man of principle believe, rightly or wrongly, that "doing the right thing" trumps loyalty. There are in some countries organizations, partly funded by governments, whose actual business it is to facilitate the whistleblower. Again, in ideological politics, loyalty to one's associates was no more than an element of bourgeois morality easily trumped by the necessities of the struggle. Like all political sectarians, Bolsheviks, for example, turned on each other with enthusiasm. Here was a world of such high-minded and moralistic opportunism that no one could rely on anyone's loyalty.

But the most dramatic case was that of Nazism, in which a large and more or less sophisticated population—certainly an educated one—was seduced by Hitlerian rhetoric. The result was that they could be induced to behave with an insane arrogance in most ways directly contradictory to their inherited moral sense. Here was a mass that came to be imbued with a whole new conception of themselves as members of the Aryan race, people with a higher duty to humanity, charged with a mission to save the world from corruption. It was almost as if Germans had resented being locked into a set of moral inhibitions that were a burden to them, and were here being offered a public world in which was licensed any kind of willfulness. They could shed their shames and guilts and enjoy a kind of liberation.

One element of seduction is thus that the person being seduced is liberated from some restraint in order to do what he or she often finds desirable anyway. The seducer is someone who for his own purposes undermines the integrity of another by encouraging the betrayal of a basic commitment. We have the word "seducer" to cover the active term in this interesting relationship, but what shall we call the other term? "Seducee" is convenient but sounds absurd, while "victim" suggests that the person seduced is merely passive. Nonetheless, I shall use "victim" because it most vividly covers the point I want to make.

Seduction in romantic affairs may be located between love and courtship on the one hand, and rape and violence on the other. The seducer characteristically pretends love, but his real purpose is power or lust or some other self-interested passion. The political sense of seduction fits into a similar schema. Seduction in politics is to be distinguished from the ordinary political techniques of persuasion leading to consent on the one hand, and intimidation and violence on the other. It is the technique of inducing the victim to betray a commitment. The real explanation for the betrayal must be found in the ulterior motive of the seducer, but the victim's moral understanding must be recalibrated so as to make his betrayal seem like something different. In politics and social life, the real purpose of a seducer is sometimes easy to recognize. Bribery seduces because the person bribed abandons duty in exchange for some benefit, usually financial. The corrupt official commonly rationalizes his conduct with elementary bits of moral defensiveness—"everybody does it," "I'm not being properly paid anyway," etc.

The substance of the seduction may cover anything from a change of political opinion to the explicit violation of a commitment. In times of revolution or political turmoil, all manner of temptations become available to people who might otherwise have led relatively blameless lives. The dramatic cases are familiar to us. We have mentioned the Nazi example. In contemporary terms, the average jihadist may know perfectly well that it is wrong deliberately to kill bystanders, but he has been seduced into believing that divine command requires it. And what these examples reveal is that seduction may result, according to situation, from low temptation or from perverse high-mindedness. The moral world is complicated enough, of course, for occasions to happen when abandoning a loyalty is the right thing to do. And hard choices may well arise, as they did in mid-century America over Communist affiliations. The English novelist E. M. Forster wrote in 1951, "if I had to choose between betraying my country and betraying my friend, I hope I should have the guts to betray my country." Such abstraction, of course, merely betrays moral obtuseness.

Why not treat this complex phenomenon as merely cases of political rhetoric, in which (in the Nazi case for example) an evil orator played upon the gullibility of his victims? Why invoke a fancy term such as "seduction"? The reason is that rhetoric and intimidation are standard features of political life, but they do not normally involve the kind of moral betrayal to which the idea of seduction alerts us. Persuasion is one thing, but a complete somersault of moral convictions, as sometimes achieved in ideological conversion, is not at all the same thing. What then are the elements that make it plausible to talk of seduction rather than mere persuasion? The first element to be noted is the clear distinction between seducer and victim. In standard political rhetoric, the persuader genuinely shares the position he is recommending to his audience.

With politicians, of course, there is always some element of ulterior motive relating to the distribution of power, but it is not the point of the process.

Shakespeare's treatment of the plot to assassinate Caesar points up the ambiguity of these situations. "None so strong that cannot be seduced," observes Cassius and wins over Brutus partly by the power of his argument, but also by such deceits as faking a public opinion demanding that Brutus should move against Caesar. It is not merely that Cassius wants to recruit Brutus, but that without Brutus the conspiracy could not succeed. Here then is a case in which much of the seduction is conducted on high-minded grounds, and the seducer and his victim are both sincerely involved in the same project. And that is why, as sometimes happens in seductions, the victim here comes to hold the upper hand over the seducer.

The most significant seduction in our civilization exhibits all the characteristic traits of such an event. There is cleverness on one side, and simplicity of mind on the other. Satan in the guise of the serpent creeps up on Eve and with much flattery induces her to eat forbidden fruit from the Tree of Knowledge. Eve is understandably surprised to be addressed by a beast: "What may this mean? Language of man pronounced / By tongue of brute, and human sense expressed?," as Milton has her reflecting in *Paradise Lost*. The "guileful Tempter" presents such an alluring picture of the delights of eating the fruit of the fatal tree that poor Eve is overborne, and persuaded that the disobedience is trivial and the consequence— death—not to be feared. To eat of the tree, explains the serpent, has had delightful consequences in his own case. He then provides an argument of moral revaluation.

> Shall that be shut to man, which to the beast
> Is open? Or will God incense his ire

For such a petty trespass, and not praise
Rather your dauntless virtue, whom the pain
Of death denounced, whatever thing death be . . .
Be real, why not known, since easier shunned?
God therefore cannot hurt ye, and be just . . .

Here is Satan in his Nietzschean mode as the promoter of an ethic of risk and adventure—a rationalist, too, in his assumption that virtue results from knowledge and experience, rather than from innocence and protection. Eve is accorded an equality with God as a moral reasoner, and persuaded that the very fact that God is just must exclude the possibility of punishment for disobedience.

It is striking that Milton the poet (writing many years afterwards) takes a different line from the young Milton writing as the exponent of freedom of the press. This later Milton stands by the sin of Eve as the source of woe in the world, but the younger Milton could never praise "a cloistered virtue." To be human was to wrestle with temptation. It is this rather revisionist cast of mind that leads intellectual historians to construe Eve's transgression as a "fortunate fall" in the theodicy of the moral life, for it leads on to man's becoming what Nietzsche called "an interesting animal." Without it, we would be as sinless as organic creation, and no more morally significant.

The art of seduction involves the practice of moral argumentation. It would be surprising if seducers were entirely lacking in plausible arguments to support their persuasiveness. The essence of moral persuasion—it is the central problem of the human condition—is that it cuts both ways. Consider for example why we admire dissidents in totalitarian countries. They have rejected the basic political loyalty available to them in favor of some higher moral idea. This abstract principle may itself be generalized as morally admirable, so that it becomes the contingent fact of rejecting national loyalty that constitutes the virtue of the dissident rather than opposition to the moral character of the regime being opposed.

Sustaining national loyalty, understood as a merely inherited commitment, may thus be rejected as the betrayal of some higher critical vocation. In this way, the moral issue can become extremely complex, with traditional loyalty to country or religion being written out of our moral admirations as being a kind of conformity. Is our loyalty merely a case of being unthinkingly bribed by a comfortable life? Surely, runs this morally athletic program, our duty is to stand by the right against the seductions of conformity. We should all be dissidents, for we live in an imperfect society and an imperfect world. And here, of course, the force of moral argument depends on its connection with the psychology of self-regard.

In this form, a collectivist version of the technique of seduction swept over Europe as one component of the politics of Romanticism. Nationalists juxtaposed the abstract principle of cultural essence against inherited legitimacies. Should the Irishman be loyal to the British crown, the Czech to Austria Hungary, the Sicilian to his Bourbon oppressor, or the Basque to remote capitals in Spain and France? The greatest of moral virtues was struggle for a righteous cause, and a merely inherited political loyalty was a form of cultural betrayal. Early Marxism was virtually a primer in how to seduce whole classes of people away from their inherited allegiance. The idea of seduction had been turned into the abstract virtue of something called struggle, the appropriate response to an oppressive world. In creating revolutionary movements, many of which became in time oppressive regimes, this creed was a moral twist that did indeed turn the world upside down, and its consequences are with us still.

Here, in the ideological doctrines of the nineteenth century, we find a technique by which clever intellectuals seeking power could turn unsophisticated populations into instruments of their ambitions. But to isolate the pure form of seduction—its underlying dynamic, as it were—we cannot do better than look to the eighteenth century, which was deeply preoccupied with the experience. The classic elements are brilliantly explored by Mozart and Da Ponte in *Così fan Tutte*, alternatively titled *The School for Lovers*. It poses the entire problem in the most brutally direct way. Two young men, Gugliamo and Ferrando, enter into a bet with the cynical Don Alfonso—a kind of devil masquerading as a scientist—that their sweethearts will not remain faithful to them even for a day.

The sweethearts in *Così*, two enchanting creatures called Fiordiligi and Dorabella, are deeply cast down as they say goodbye to lovers supposedly off to the Balkan wars. Our heroes promptly reappear disguised as a couple of Albanians, and immediately declare themselves enslaved to love for the two girls. This provokes nothing but derision. The "Albanians" are gleeful, thinking that they will soon have won their bet, but they must remain in character by moping around, and Don Alfonso keeps commending them to the girls as old friends. They resist all such blandishments. Then Alfonso enlists the help of their maid Despina, who supplies a cynical chorus on the proceedings throughout the opera. The "Albanians" now declare themselves so devastated by rejection that they prefer death, and they pretend to swallow arsenic. They collapse on the stage, the doctor is summoned—it is Despina in drag—and the new Galvanic technology saves (as it seems) their lives.

This event supplies two of the essentials of seduction in concentrated form: drama and flattery. The next stage in the seduction requires an entirely general doctrine to undermine the established significance of the fidelity in question. It is supplied by Despina, who is a proto-feminist. What do you think your lovers are doing? she asks her mistresses. Obviously, they are doing what all soldiers do—looking to the local talent. Pining away, as Fiordiligi and Dorabella are doing, is merely the result of having been deceived by romantic illusions. In any case, can the girls even be sure that their lovers will return? They may be killed in battle, and women must look to other opportunities.

Our heroines also treat this doctrine with derision, but Despina has opened up a new moral arena in which the issue may be considered. The girls now have two contrasting ways of understanding their fidelity. Are they supremely moral and faithful, or are they dupes? It is always dangerous to consider how other people behave, because you are likely to find that they have looser standards and mores than you do. This two-pronged attack on Mozart's heroines—by dramatic consequences and by abstract doctrine—illustrates central mechanisms of seduction. Those to be seduced must be persuaded that their fidelity is causing disastrous results that can only be avoided by falling in with the seduction.

On the margins of understanding lies a consideration of the pain and boredom that results from exercising moral integrity. Virtue comes to seem a dull and boring option. Soon Dorabella is being seduced by a rich gift, and even Fiordiligi is won over, even while despising herself, by the passionate asseverations of Ferrando. The two girls thus succumb, supposedly demonstrating that "they're all like that"—until the original lovers make their surprising return. The ultimate moral is to insist that wisdom lies in accepting human beings as they are. And that means to recognize the limits of loyalty.

The technique of seduction, then, requires both a powerful temptation on the one hand, and an alternative moral doctrine that will show that the supposed betrayal no longer counts as a betrayal at all. The moral doctrine might be an appeal to some supposedly higher duty (as with Brutus) or it might be a kind of realistic reductionism showing that nobody takes seriously the inhibiting considerations, as with Despina. In both cases, the victim must be flattered. Seducers, like politicians, are great flatterers. The theory of seduction is a belief in the realistic doctrine that everyone has his—or her—price. And there are two aspects of this realism.

The first concerns the way in which the temptation to betrayal must be kept constantly before the mind of the victim. The seducer must block off any possibility of the victim making the right decision, and moving on to other things. The situation must be incessantly chewed over. The point here is that given enough discussion about the rights and wrongs of some situation, more and more possible actions will come to seem morally defensible. Our modern liberal view is that the more we open moral questions to informed discussion, the more rational will be the decision. That may often be the case. Yet abstract discussion of moral issues cannot help but make the participants in such discussions increasingly aware, as poor Eve became, of the possible satisfactions to be enjoyed by the forbidden courses of action, alternatives which the victim had previously not seriously considered. In other words, a great deal of what we construe as virtue depends on the inheritance of a stable identity, and too much discussion of the principles constituting that identity may well weaken it. The Victorians, who thought it wise to avoid what they called "occasions of sin," admired many feminine virtues as being the result of "innocence," something that today would often be taken as an instrument of oppression. It has to be recognized that virtue and rationality do not always cohere.

The second point needing explanation is the doctrine that no one is so strong as to be safe from seduction. Modern systems of justice have strict rules arising from this presumption, so that policemen must not get convictions in the courts by the device of "entrapment," which is setting the suspects up by tempting them to do the kinds of things the police think they know they have long been doing. The reason for these rules is clearly summed up in *Hamlet*: "Give every man his deserts and which of us would 'scape whipping?" And as for positive temptations, we assume that most people have their price. By way of *Nineteen Eighty-four*'s "Room 101," Orwell argued that we all have some aversion so powerful that they would make any betrayal rather than suffer it. Correspondingly, we may well suggest that most people have some temptation to which they would succumb. As Cassius remarked, "none so strong as cannot be seduced." This indeed is a common literary theme, from

Faust to *Murder in the Cathedral.* In Eliot's play, the tempters try wealth and power, but their most dangerous temptation is pride, for (as Beckett realizes) "The last temptation is the worst treason / To do the right thing for the wrong reason."

The moral of *Così* might seem to be that we ought not to concern ourselves with seduction, because moral absolutes and fixed commitments are "against nature": They will not stand against temptation, and perhaps they ought not to. The world cannot become a romantic arena of fidelity because the contemporary world requires that we should adjust our principles to our situation. We not only refuse to praise a cloistered virtue, we hardly recognize such a life as virtuous at all. The very attempt to seduce may well be seen today as a virtuous act in its own right, opening up possibilities of choice that ought to be frankly discussed and explored.

This is, indeed, for better and worse, the way we live, and what people have said of democracy, we may say of Western moral practices: namely, that they are the worst of all possible lives—except perhaps for all the rest. In our form of life, everything is permanently up for revision. Liberalism, in other words, is the death of romance, because romance is based on limit. The hero or heroine is someone who has taken a stand. Our problem is that we find it difficult to distinguish limit from frustration. Romance is based upon determinate identities, and that means, unavoidably, that the committed may have to suffer. We are torn in other words between recognizing the fidelities of romance as illusions, and yet deeply yearning for them. We want a world of infinite possibility but we seldom reflect on its costs—which include romance. The idea of seduction seems quaint today for many reasons, but the most profound is that it has been eaten up by the idea of liberation and choice.

The idea of seduction thus opens up notable contradictions in the way in which we understand the moral world today. Our cur-

rent preoccupation with what it is to have an "identity" is one arena
of this conflict. The whole point of an identity is that it must be a
limitation. Husbands, wives, priests, Hindus, judges, and so on no
doubt all have positive duties, but they are essentially constituted
by the things they will not do. In our world, however, no identity
should stand in the way of circumstantial modification. Our ambivalence about religious commitment is another arena in which
this question bites, for the pieties of religion, if taken seriously,
block off a life guided by nothing else but the drifting utilities of
contemporary opportunism. No less dramatic than these tensions
is our indecision between two views of the value of Western civilization. On the one hand, we explore a *topos* according to which
our civilization is an evil thing and that the basic imperative of life
must be to change it for the better. We do not hesitate to recognize,
indeed we often insist upon our own selfishness and decadence.
On the other hand, we present its distilled essence, in the form of
declarations of rights, as small candles of goodness in an essentially
evil world. We demand that the rest of the world should live as we
do, and that it should recognize our pieties dressed up as rights.
And the irony is that both the manichean and the imperialist versions of our self-understanding are equally hostile to integrity in
the form of concrete loyalty. Whichever way we go, we find ourselves sinking knee-deep into abstractions.

These issues cannot be avoided in exploring the idea of seduction, but they evidently go beyond our present scope. They point
to confusions that clearly result from the overweening ambition
of contemporary rationalism. We are no longer content to live
decent moral lives according to our lights. We want instead to
abolish world poverty, atone for the sins of our forefathers, bring
social justice to the world, save the planet—little things like that.
It is a remarkable moral sensitivity, as shallow as it is ambitious. It
is shallow because the righteous proponents of these imperatives

demand that we recognize in the very ambition of the aim a proof
of the seriousness of the endeavor. It is a moral and political project
("ethical" is often today's preferred word) bound to induce des-
peration as we contemplate inevitable failure. In this strange cast
of mind, our civilization can be deplored because we have not succeeded in o'erleaping the human condition. The pursuit of such an
insane perfectionism constitutes a moral mania that can only be
self-destructive. It can also be destructive of other cultures, which
do indeed change, but usually slowly and seldom in accordance
with our desires.

Mozart's lovers were expected to learn the lesson of not demanding absolute perfection. The derangement that Mozart was
satirizing has always had deep roots in our civilization. Mozart's
opera may be read as a warning against pushing any absolute too
far. And it is by exploring the idea of seduction—especially in its
political forms—that we may in some degree take the measure of
our current moral disorientation.

Conservatism & the Morality of Impulse

JANUARY 2008

ON THE CHALLENGES OF RESPONDING
TO MODERNIST MORALITY

Conservatism is a form of political wisdom that consists in thinking that the present can best be understood through what the past reveals. It is a way of "accessing" political reality, often obscured beneath confusing talk, the chatter and "noise" of the moment. That is why the historian Maurice Cowling thought that conservatism was a kind of historical method, a discovery procedure. Conventional academics may find this view absurd. How can a practical, value-laden idea like conservatism play an explanatory role? The answer is that it can help us avoid falling into at least some illusions. I propose to follow this thought in asking: What is the reality of early twenty-first-century Anglophone life?

I take my bearing from the last decade of the nineteenth century—from Victoria's Diamond Jubilee in 1897, or perhaps in American terms from the Spanish-American War of 1898. Queen Victoria and Teddy Roosevelt might thus be taken as symbols of

Kenneth Minogue, "Conservatism & the Morality of Impulse." This article is reprinted with permission from the publisher of *New Criterion* 26 (January 2008). © 2014, *The New Criterion*, www.newcriterion.com.

that period—the one absolutely confident of her own probity, the other vibrant and ebullient. They believed in Western civilization as a wave of progress, and that they were on top of the wave.

The late nineteenth century is three or four generations back, a little beyond most direct contact, even for older people. I choose it because it was (in Britain at least) the last period in which a British government did little more for its people than govern them. Welfare was on the horizon, and was to begin arriving with Lloyd George's 1909 budget. By contrast, our own period is one in which welfare rights have vastly expanded, and the state spends a large proportion of the national wealth on being good to us—providing us with free medicine, money if we fall on hard times, pensions for the aged and the disabled, advice and succor for those who drift into drugs or debt.

By any ordinary test, nineteenth-century governments ought to have been rather unpopular, because they made no attempt to improve our lives, whereas in our own time, governments ought to be objects of admiration from a grateful electorate. As we know, the opposite is the case. Britain in 1897 was vibrant with enthusiasm for Victoria's Diamond Jubilee, and before long World War I was to demand vast sacrifices from the people. Their volunteering in 1914 showed that the public enthusiasm for the Jubilee was no superficial thing. The striking contrast today is that politicians as a class find few admirers, and they can no longer call upon a united national effort. Some people actually hold them in derision. These facts remarkably contradict every conventional assumption about human nature in politics. Politicians try to win elections by showering gifts (of a kind!) upon us in the hope of a grateful response. Yet in the past, we admired those who reminded us of our duties, and today we rather despise those who shower us with rights.

I believe that this contrast has profound lessons for understanding the condition of our civilization, but in these remarks I want merely to consider one aspect of this change. My argument requires understanding that there are two basic types of human relationship, and modern societies have got themselves into a terrible tangle because one of them has tended to collapse into the other.

Most social relationships between adults are equal, and can be terminated at will, but certain relationships, especially involving the young, may be described as "tutorial." In these cases, superiors teach and train inferiors. Their point is to form young people in preparation for adult life, and more generally, to teach them the arts of controlling impulse and doing their duty. It will be obvious that the family is the model of a tutorial relationship, because the children are under the discipline of mothers and fathers. And it is important not to fall too quickly into running together these two sets of people—mothers and fathers—as being the abstract thing called "parents" because, within the vast differences between one family and another, they play significantly different roles. No single parent can provide the full range of influences that come from the combination of both mothers and fathers.

The family is, then, the model of a tutorial relationship, but there are many others. A teacher in a school shares tutorial responsibilities in guiding a child towards the ways of learning and the achievement of knowledge. Here again, the point is that educational discipline must suppress impulsive distractions by teaching the child how to concentrate on tasks that may not be immediately appealing. Again, supervisors and matrons in hospitals have, or used to have, tutorial responsibilities and the power to enforce them. Employment law has, however, taken away much of the power such people exercised in the past. Some element of the tutorial is to be found in the policeman/bystander relation.

The power to enforce these responsibilities is essential, because we are here talking about authority. Tutorial authority is the power to impose whatever is the appropriate discipline, and it may well involve passages of conflict between the "tutor" as it were, and the "child." The most extreme account of a tutorial relationship was the stuff of many movies made in the 1939–1945 period. In this version, a tough sergeant (sometimes played by John Wayne) had to lick a set of raw recruits into shape for the coming conditions of battle. The recruits hated him—until they were tested in battle, and recognized the value of the training he had so roughly imposed on them. And the roughness was a necessary part of the training.

One might think that the government/subject relationship would also be tutorial, but this judgment is not quite right. The point of the criminal law is indeed to discourage subjects from solving their immediate problems by killing, raping, or stealing from others. Strictly speaking, however, criminal law is a set of hypothetical propositions specifying certain kinds of conduct that will attract sanctions if their occurrence should be proved in a court of law. The law does not command us to do anything.

Modern governments do indeed have a powerful—and increasing—tendency to behave tutorially in relation to their subjects. They employ the techniques of public relations in so-called educational campaigns (e.g. about smoking, diet, sex) and they often throw out hints about what they want, and against which they will legislate if they do not get it. This, however, merely reflects the drift in modern states towards despotism. A state is not a family, and no one today looking at the rulers of his country is likely to think that those rulers are supremely wise.

A tutorial relationship is, then, different from all the free and equal relationships that constitute civil society. Our relations with friends, employers, fellow enthusiasts, lovers, and all the rest are transactions. Both sides benefit from them, and if that ceases to be true, the relationship will fade. It is of course this free and easy character of most social relationships that distinguishes them from the tutorial kind. We do not volunteer for most tutorial relationships, and they are essentially hierarchical.

And that is the point at which our analysis must begin. In the egalitarian atmosphere that has prevailed since the late nineteenth century, hierarchy is the one type of human relationship that makes people uncomfortable. In much economic and social life, of course, hierarchical relationships are unavoidable, but these situations are all functional, and often the subordinate may look forward to rising up to the higher levels of a career structure. We tolerate this, though we often find semantic and moral ways of turning some kinds of hierarchy into equalities.

What used to distinguish tutorial relationships from the egalitarian kind is that the tutor normally disposed of forms of discipline that the "child" feared. Families used occasionally to be kept in order by the prospect of a good belting by the father, though a telling off by the mother might be just as effective. Teachers might have recourse to the strap or the cane. Matrons in hospitals could dismiss the nurse who did not measure up to standard, and sergeants certainly had ways of making the recruits obey. The essence of a tutorial relationship was respect, and parents and teachers were respected, parents for their love and wisdom, teachers for their erudition. But in the tutorial encounters of the past, fear was an almost indistinguishable element of respect. The child generally shrank from displeasing the parent. It is a large subject to understand the transformation of the place of fear in the social and moral life of our time.

The problem with dispersed authority in social life is that, even more than any other kind of authority, it may be abused. Families are based on love, schools on a shared purpose to instruct. To recognize authority of this kind depends on trusting to the love of parents, and the common sense of teachers. Such things may be lacking, and brutal and bullying "tutors" may become a scandal. Such monsters have certainly been an enduring theme of novels and plays in our time.

It is with this nexus that we encounter one of the great problems of all modern politics, a problem to which there cannot be a perfect solution. If we trust the tutors, some abuses will occur. And yet, if "we" (i.e. the state) step in to control abuses, we destroy trust and codify the "rights" and duties of tutor and child. The result is to transform the vocational calling of mothers, fathers, teachers, matrons, etc. into a form of public employment that corrupts the whole relationship. A more or less professional (which is to say, disinterested) relationship has become a matter of organizational obedience. In the worst cases, parents may be held responsible for the conduct of their children while also being regulated about how they control them.

It is thus hardly surprising that tutorial relationships have tended to become more and more egalitarian. The point of a tutorial relationship is to exercise a discipline that teaches the subordinates to control mere impulse and behave rationally. This task has become more difficult with every recent generation. Engines of distraction such as radio, television, computers, mobile phones, canned music, and the rest have multiplied. We live, it has been said, in an era of continuous partial attention. The parental tutor has a hard task trying to control these influences, and an impossible one from that early age in which the child spends more time with his or her peer group. In any case, many modern parents are uncomfortable with the hierarchical aspect of the tutorial relationship because it inevitably distances them from their children. The philosopher Locke thought that only when the children became adult could they become the friends of parents, but today's parents hate the distance that authority requires. They want to be friends from the toddler stage onwards.

The significance of tutorial relationships was, we observed, to teach the "child" to internalize rational and thoughtful conduct as against the natural tendency to follow impulse. Modern wealth and technology tend, however, to encourage impulsiveness, and so do many social and political developments. Advertising presents tempting images beyond the pocket of most people, and the temptations of credit card debt are hard to resist. State provision of welfare payments and services tends to make some of the prudential virtues valued in the past less pressing. Between the 1890s and today, there has been a vast change in the moral culture.

That the recipients of tutorial discipline might find themselves resenting its pains, as the raw recruits to the army hated the sergeant, would be an understandable human response. The odd thing, however, is that in family life, the pressure to turn a tutorial association into an egalitarian one has come as much from the parents as from the children. Some of this is no doubt the familiar guilt of working parents who compensate for lacking time with their children by giving in to whatever they ask for. No less important is the appearance of a strange new moral doctrine that understands authority itself as a form of violence that ought to be replaced by negotiation and persuasion. In the past authority sustained its disciplines by an adroit use of sticks and carrots, and in the past the stick did not need to be used excessively; its background role sustained a whole structure of life. In this new atmosphere, sticks have been abandoned as being forms of aggression, and only carrots are left. Carrots without sticks are merely a form of bribery. In other words, the basic moral category is no long reward and punishment, but attitudinal manipulation. To punish, runs the doctrine, is to send the wrong message: that violence pays.

This is, then, the new world we have created in which everyone ("tutors" and "children" alike) slides towards egalitarian relations. Informality rules, and we have given up those special conventions that used to dictate how we talk to those we respect, by contrast with the way we talk to our peers. It is a world we greatly prefer to that of our forefathers, because we abominate the prejudices of times past. We accept as an inevitable misfortune of our new mores such things as the rise of single-parenthood, but we luxuriate in our tolerance, or perhaps merely in our self-admired niceness. Pupils like the conversion of tutorial authority into egalitarian informality. They no doubt approve of no longer being subject to corporal punishment. And we are here describing a tendency that has by no means exhausted itself. Activists wanting to change the world seek to punish parents who slap their little ones, and governments love to extend their power. Meanwhile parents are happy to relinquish a burdensome responsibility.

Against this, we need to remember the problem from which we started. It was that people now get (from the state in particular) just what they say they want, yet they despise the people who give it to them. In part, this is no doubt a rejection of what must be recognized as the side-effects of our getting the egalitarian world that we seem to want. The lesson taught by tutorial authority was that impulses must be controlled and that a certain disinterested pleasure was to be found in doing one's duty, however demanding or painful it might at times be. The decline of the tutorial would seem, on these terms, to result in a rise in impulsiveness and a decline in the virtue of individual self-control.

Such consequences are not far to seek in our world. Levels of debt, drugs, and addictions of various kinds are rising. Our contemporaries do not take easily to the experience of frustration, and take it out in physical and verbal abuse (for example directed at medical attendants in accident and emergency wards), or in "road rage." It is part of this new understanding of ourselves that much that used to be thought matter for moral judgment has become construed as a form of pathology. Psychiatrists, never willingly letting a bandwagon pass them by, have turned road rage into "Intermittent Explosive Disorder." Impulsiveness of the mind has become a deficit of attention, to be fixed by medication. Children have become subject to strange behavioral disorders (relating to eating, or self-harm) that were hardly recognized before. And new crises keep surfacing, such as obesity. Crime, delinquency, and vandalism are certainly not decreasing. And there is a worrying tendency among the young for the kind of low-level dishonesty found in such acts as plagiarizing homework from the internet.

A conservative analysis of the current condition thus leads us into a familiar paradox. The demos gets what it wants, but doesn't like it very much. Egalitarianism is a kind of ideal. It banishes tutorial authority as being something repressive, but all such perfections have a price. Personal impulsiveness soon aggregates into a set of social problems. And once a collection of personal problems has turned into the thing called a "social problem," the government steps in, and supplies by regulation what virtue no longer sustains.

The issue is, ultimately, our way of life as a free people. Individual self-control is an indispensable condition of freedom. Without it, we become the puppets of governments. Many people not only realize this, but also feel a slight sense of disgust at the way in which they have been seduced into easy options by politicians on the quest for votes. As in all forms of seduction, what we lose—our independence and self-reliance—is more important than what the seducer gets. We may think we like it, but we feel that it is repugnant to have the responsibility for our own lives taken out of our hands by the state. I suspect that there is, under our surface attitudes, a profound desire to return to a world in which duty and responsibility play a larger part in our lives. The question is: how may people respond to these problems? They make no easy appeal in contemporary democracy.

It would obviously be no use taking a poll of the desires of the spoiled child. Would he or she demand that parents should control their television viewing and curb their desires? Even focus groups would be little help. Would pupils favor increasing the punitive sanctions to the teacher? Would turkeys vote for Christmas! We have, therefore, a political system that has evolved over the century into a machine for actualizing the most superficial tendencies of contemporary Western life. No political solution is in sight, but we do at least retain some power over our own lives.

Marriage in Our Time

JUNE 2009

ON MATRIMONY IN A CULTURE OF CONVENIENCE

One of the excitements of growing older in the contemporary West is the recognition that the moral basis of life has flipped. It happens in every generation. Consider the position of Lord Melbourne in 1837, kissing hands as prime minister with that delightful but formidable girl who had just been crowned Queen Victoria. This Regency rake, a real swinger in his time, suddenly had to recognize that he had blundered by longevity into a very serious and engaged moral environment. It was to be called "Victorian." He adapted very well, especially to the Queen, but he knew he was in a different world.

Think again of those same Victorians at the end of the nineteenth century, when Oscar Wilde and the Café Royal set were just beginning to attach a sneer to the very idea of respectability, an attachment that became increasingly explicit as the twentieth century wore on. Respectability is, no doubt, an ambiguous expression. It means being respected, being worthy of respect, and

Kenneth Minogue, "Marriage in Our Time." This article is reprinted with permission from the publishers of *New Criterion* 27 (June 2009).
© 2014, *The New Criterion*, www.newcriterion.com.

also (pejoratively) conforming one's life to external standards so as to sustain reputation with others. The sneer comprehended all three meanings and undermined the importance of the whole idea of reputation, which had hitherto kept many people on the straight and narrow.

Again, from the 1960s to the present day, our own time has witnessed moral somersaults no less dramatic than before. Censorship hardly survives, art has been politicized, and a whole range of previously criminal sexual activities has been not merely legitimized but made entirely—well—respectable! Even the mechanics of morality have been transformed. The idea of human rights has revolutionized the way we conceive of decent conduct, and these rights are enforced in new legalistic ways. This is a large area, and all I propose to do here is to explore the consequences of this revolution in the dull old subject of sex.

The basics are familiar. In the first half of the twentieth century, sex went with marriage (sometimes at the point of a shotgun), and marriage was for life. Bernard Shaw suggested that the advantage of marriage lay in simultaneously maximizing both the temptation and the fulfillment, but others think that Zsa Zsa Gabor hit the nail on the head: "I don't know anything about sex. I've always been married."

Divorce had indeed become possible, even a little before the twentieth century, but for a long time it required money, lawyers, and often some fake dramatics about matrimonial fault. It was out of the reach of most people; they could hardly conceive of it. In more recent times, divorce has become vastly easier, and about a quarter of cohabiting couples no longer even bother with marriage at all. The reasons for this are as familiar as the facts themselves. Contraceptive technology has broken the link between sex and procreation; people live a good deal longer; and while divorce is now much easier, it can also lead to the most astonishing financial settlements. The magnitude of those financial settlements has largely been a response to feminist agitation. Indeed, feminist theories of the relations between men and women have been central to all the moral changes in this area of life.

My question is: What do these changes tell us about the moral world in general? And one simple clue lies in the balance between pleasure and pain. The utilitarian imperative to maximize pleasure and minimize pain has never been absent from human affairs, but today it is virtually our only principle of public policy. The basic fact about marriage has been that most people do it when young, and the young are notoriously the victims of their impulses. At any moment subsequent to marriage, sometimes even as soon as walking back down the aisle, one or other member of the couple may be starting to think that the rest of life in this company is going to be very far from joyous. To be stuck for life with a spouse one can no longer stand is profoundly inconvenient, and the drive of modern morality is to remove every inconvenience that seems to us unnecessary. We now judge that the point of marriage (as of any other act in life) is to find happiness. Why not, then, liberate unhappy couples from their married bondage and let them find more compatible companions? This is the essence of liberation. Easier divorce is one solution, avoidance of marriage an even more effective one. But that merely dances around the question. It helps explain the increasing rarity of lifelong marriages, but tells us nothing much about the new moral order.

We must therefore distinguish two occasions of marriage down the ages. In the first, marriage is an arrangement made between families, often involving considerations of property, politics, wealth, status, or other benefits, an arrangement in which the affections of the proposed couple might well be entirely marginal. In the second, which is our own European alternative, these practical considerations were seldom absent, but marriage also depended in some degree on the emotions of the couple intending to tie the knot. The troubles this alternative type of arrangement can create are famously dramatized in Romeo and Juliet, lovers whose individualist view of their relationship violated every communal norm and led to a great deal of social disruption. In contemporary societies, the contrast may be seen in the difference between our free and easy Western ways and the communal practices that can lead to the so-called "honor" killings that occasionally occur in Muslim circles.

In the individualist culture of modern Europe, then, marriage is an act of will made by two individuals, and it has, for all its dependence on such unstable foundations as human affection, been able in the past to generate stable family bonds no less reliable than the communal practices of other civilizations. Marriage thus stood in the morality of individualist commitment as one of those bonds on which the entire coherence of a life depends, and many things from the stability of property to the welfare of children depended upon it. Until recent times, the theory of marriage was therefore entangled not only with the morality of individuals but also with the romantic conception of human love.

Marriage in this traditional sense was the emblem of individualist, indeed even of chivalric, morality. The point is of the first importance. The moral lives of most people at all times, and of our own people at some times, have been characterized by conformity to moral rules. Those rules were known and shared in society. But in European marriage we find something new and different. Moral conduct is understood as fidelity to *self-chosen commitments*. It was society ordering itself in terms of the coherence of commitments rather than "obedience" to the rules of some notional right form of life. Few people today understand this distinction with any clarity, and what survives of it is largely in the popular notion that holds morality to be a matter of individual choice. We must not, according to this "echo," be judgmental. But in the real individualist moral life, these choices had to be serious and binding, not mere responses to the impulse of the moment. When people said of others in Victorian times that a gentleman's word was his bond, they were referring to the full dimensions of this complex moral form of life.

The alternative conception of morality is much more familiar to us because we all grow up under its tutelage and it never ceases to play a part in our lives. Morality here is a set of rules to be "obeyed." The moral theory of Immanuel Kant (which today competes among political philosophers with utilitarianism) incorporates individualist moral sentiments by insisting on the *autonomy of right action*. In acting morally, we must be responding to a rule, but one we have chosen for ourselves on rational grounds. Rules are, however, abstractions that must be interpreted according to circumstances, and the fact that our moral understanding has become corrupted may be found in the common belief that rules are commands. They are in fact very different things. You *respond* to rules, you must *obey* commands. In the past, of course, rules did in fact approach the character of commands: indeed, one of the most famous summaries of good conduct is known to us as the Ten Commandments. But moral rules are not actually commandments because, today, they usually have no authoritative commander, and because they always require circumstantial interpretation. As moral agents, we may only allow them to shape our behavior because it is logically impossible that we could actually obey them.

It is this contrast that shows us the wider significance revealed in the fate of marriage in our time. Marriage has, to a degree, lost the element of self-chosen commitment, and, if affection should wane, little is left except a collection of restrictive prohibitions on choice, and thus as an impediment to future happiness. This development seriously weakens the whole individualist imperative of living by self-binding commitments. Such binding commitments are currently being eroded in both large and small things. Punctuality, which used to be the courtesy of kings, is now less necessary because of the adjustments to timing that can be made on a mobile phone. In other words, the stable and reliable moral world of the classic individualist is giving way to a new condition in which individuals manage their relationships in terms of mutual convenience. Everything is up for adjustment.

The consequence is to liberate the sorts of impulse that societies in earlier times were keen to control. It is a move from morality to manageability in the calculations of moral agents. Individuals are reduced to being calculators of their own convenience. The most common form of the moral life, from time immemorial, has involved suppressing impulse by conforming to custom, or by obeying priests and magistrates.

The unique feature of modern European states, however, has been the emergence of a certain detachment from community in which the individual may claim a sphere of autonomy of his own. Individuality is a characteristic of all human beings, indeed of all organic creatures, but individualism is a different kind of thing. It is individuality recognized as having certain rights of choice within a wider moral framework. Superficially, individualism looks remarkably permissive, but, in actual practice among our forefathers, it was strict and demanding. Individual judgment could generate, beneath the rough and tumble of civility, a robust kind of social order and cohesion at which other civilizations, ordering their societies by doctrine from above, could only wonder. And because our moral and social life has been opened up to choice, modern societies have been vastly more inventive and enterprising than traditional societies. Our morality of coherence, rather than mere obedience to authorities or conformity to custom, is the essence of what we mean by freedom.

Freedom in this form of life is a moral commitment not merely because we have *chosen* a course of action but because that course of action has *duties* attached to it. It is the conjunction of these two features—choice and dutifulness—that constitutes the morality of individualism. This point should be emphasized, because the collapse of much moral understanding in our time has resulted in the vulgarization that makes the moral life entirely a matter of the chosen at the expense of the dutiful. It is this vulgarization that makes non-Europeans fearful that individualism merely means following one's impulses and trafficking only in selfishness and disorder. In earlier modern times, when these things were better understood, individualism was far from being a liberating practice. On the contrary, individualists had the highest of moral standards because they were themselves the essential judges and spectators of their own conduct. In 1861, when Sir Henry Maine gave an account of this new form of life in *Ancient Law*, he characterized the modern world in terms of the move from status to contract: a contract incorporates the essential element of reciprocity in moral agency.

My account of modern individualism is, of course, a formal one, and the moral reality of European life obviously included many who fell very far short of it. As the work of such writers as Gertrude Himmelfarb and Christie Davies has shown, however, the low level of criminality and corruption in the nineteenth and early twentieth century in European states was a notable contrast with the disorder and corruption of much in the customary life of other cultures, as well as with the moral disorientation of our own times.

Our problem thus becomes one of understanding the move from a world of fixed moral commitments to one characterized by convenience, adjustment, and manageability. One key change is the vulgarization of our civilizational self-characterization as free. Individual freedom has always with us depended on individual self-reliance and self-restraint, but in the twentieth century freedom was widely understood as that quite different phenomenon that is more properly called "liberation." This particular corruption of moral agency happened in two distinct ways. The first stage, which has already been discussed, was to misunderstand good conduct as mere obedience to moral rules, taken as commands. These supposed "commands" were further taken to emanate from an alien and inappropriate source: namely, the outmoded beliefs of our ancestors. The virtues—chastity, thrift, courage, etc.—were construed as *merely* inherited from the past. The second stage in freedom's collapse into liberation resulted from focusing a utilitarian apparatus of rational criticism on the set of rules constituting late-Victorian and early-twentieth-century respectability. These conventions often blocked our desires. Our contemporaries are impatient when their desires are frustrated. Are these conventions still necessary, they ask. What is their point? Freedom thus suffers a semantic slide: It no longer means being bound only by self-chosen commitments. It means a liberation from any unnecessary convention where each person serves as his or her own judge of necessity.

The implications of this moral evolution for marriage will now be apparent. Liberation and choice as the essential contemporary values are likely to collide directly with the restrictions stemming from one unfortunate marital choice, often a choice made when the choosers were young and inexperienced. Marriage forecloses future choices over a large range of desires for the rest of a natural life. A powerful, slightly irritable, conviction arose among us that society required a radical rethinking of the supposed necessity of conventions that no longer made much sense. If the point of chastity, for example, was to control procreation, technology had now allowed us to achieve the same effect without the pains of frustration. Chastity seemed, in these terms, to have become pointless. Analogously, the idea of punishment lost its salience: if its point was to rid society of criminal conduct, it had clearly failed because the criminals, no less than the poor, were always with us. New ideas and greater understanding of the real motors of human conduct were clearly needed.

This point of view deprived marriage of its character as a self-chosen life-long commitment, and turned it into a potential threat to freedom. Social and personal predictability is no doubt necessary in human life (especially for the benefit of the children of a marriage), but it is painful not to be free to do as one chooses. Our contemporaries approach this problem as one of balancing the advantages of stability against the pains of restraint. Current moral and social life is the endless process of squaring these interesting circles, and the result has, in some areas, been a great shedding of the virtues as superfluous to the requirements of contemporary life. No one should be "punished" (as the emerging moral semantics has it) for the rest of life as the result of an unwise decision made when young. The overriding imperative of the new morality is the abolition of unnecessary pain, and, if a marriage has irretrievably broken down, it is irrational that people should be indefinitely trapped in it.

My concern is to explore the meaning of these two moral practices, for we have all encountered them both in theory and in practice. Novels and news stories alike force the issues on our attention. Moralities of commitment are to be found throughout history, but they usually derive from the obligations entailed in status and rank. *Individualist* commitment seems to have been a modern emergence. It is striking that when Henry V conquered Harfleur in 1415, he captured many prisoners who could be profitably ransomed, but had to release them on his desperate march back to Calais. On that march, of course, the English won the battle of Agincourt. A few days later when the English arrived in Calais, their prisoners, who had been released on their honor to return, all turned up. They all faced the expense and the prospect of a long captivity in England. Yet they came back! This is a remarkable example of the knightly ethos of chivalry, a sensibility which led directly into the modern idea of individualism.

As it happens, I have just been rereading *Portrait of a Lady* by Henry James, one of the great explorations of the moral world. Our heroine, Isabel Archer, is married to a soul-shriveling pedant. She lives with him in Rome, but comes back to England because her cousin is dying, and the last chapter of the book concerns her taking up threads of a life that had earlier been elaborated in this superbly subtle novel. We are in suspense to know what she will do. Will she abandon this husband and return to her earlier happiness, as almost all of the readers fervently hope? Or will she return to lovelessness in Rome? The clue to what she will do, implicit in the account of her character throughout the novel, is tossed away in a few sentences: "He was not the best of husbands, but that didn't alter the case. Certain obligations were involved in the very fact of marriage and were quite independent of the quantity of enjoyment extracted from it."

We are likely to respond, I think, by feeling that there is something heroic about the decision, and horrible about its consequences. Here is a potentially dazzling life immolated on the altar of a commitment that was the result of an earlier misjudgment, one that we can only regard as essentially formal. It is not merely that her husband is a pedantic bully—he also married her for her money. And yet she returns. One would have to say, I think, that this is a moral grandeur unlikely to be exhibited by many people at any time, but, in less grandiose terms, this sense of dutifulness actually corresponds to what very large numbers of people in those earlier times actually did. The novel is set in the 1870s, and if one were in 1900 to come across an elderly lady, probably a widow, and wonder at her situation, it would not at all be obvious that her life had turned upon a sense of obligation resulting from a commitment so contrary to what we today would think sensible.

What sense can we make of her decision? It was not, I think, a case of a grinding sense of duty overcoming inclination such as we often experience in the course of everyday life. It could only be explained, I suggest, from a kind of moral exhilaration in which a commitment illuminates and dramatizes the very moral character in which the individual's pride is invested. A kind of self-understanding here demands, beyond all other satisfactions of desire, that one must be true to oneself, whatever that may cost.

To choose duty over so evident a temptation to happiness is, in our eyes, such a strange judgment that one may hypothesize that it requires a certain almost perverse moral exhilaration, something we might well recognize as a form of the moral life in which duty itself becomes a kind of self-oriented romance.

It is romantic because, like all romance, it transcends, or seems to transcend, the everyday habits, routines, and choices that we make, and the feelings we enjoy. Such exhilaration about moral pain is unusual, but far from unknown. Martyrdoms in the past often had this character, as among Christians did the agonies of approaching death, which were sometimes interpreted as divine reminders of a human fallibility soon to be translated to a higher plane. But it could, indeed can, also appear as a feature of everyday life. The famous film *Brief Encounter*, based on the Noel Coward play, is an example of this clash between a romantic passion and the duties of the everyday, and it is romantic precisely because the heroine returns to the duties of her marriage rather than running away with her doctor to South Africa. Had she done this, the story would have involved a certain commonplace banality. Romance involves suffering.

The *romance of duty* is, of course, the essential element of romance itself. There is no romance unless there is a commitment that transcends, or seems to transcend, the flexibilities of everyday life, for as the Bard reminds us, love is not love that alters when it alteration finds. We often cynically suspect that the practical problems of the human humdrum explain why most romantic stories end at the point of marriage. The late nineteenth century seems to have been a notable period exhibiting what I have called "the romance of duty"—or it might just be that this theme is misleadingly prominent in writers such as James and Conrad. Perhaps it is no coincidence that both were immigrants to England. In public fashion, such moral connoisseurship, always fragile, was soon to be replaced by the exploration of sex as the great adventure of life. Adventurers such as D. H. Lawrence and the Bloomsbury Group turned out to be the pioneers of our own moral world.

How then, may we characterize our own moral world? The first thing to be said about it is that the avoidance of pain, and especially any frustration of impulse, is central to our concerns. The astonishing success of medical technology has generated the hope that we might be able to create an almost pain-free world. Pain has ceased to be an important element of the human condition, something to be considered as part of the economy of experience. It has become a problem to be solved. Like Bentham we comprehend our options in terms of cost-benefit. Most of us have now become devout and pious utilitarians.

Convenience generates, of course, a dangerous cast of mind, because we may wrongly dispose of restraints, the necessity of which can only emerge several generations down the line. Some critics diagnose our condition as "presentism," the illusion that the way things are now is the way they naturally are, and will always be. Presentism is, of course, the mistake we have made in transposing our moral culture into the language of universal rights. Such abstractions are useful in exporting our way of life to people of other civilizations, but they also transfer the custodianship of how we live away from religious and moral judgment into the hands of lawyers. Presentism is a kind of moral arrogance in which we imagine ourselves to be the culmination of human progress. Hegel was misunderstood by Francis Fukuyama to have argued that history had come to an end. In the presentism of the moment, we may recognize a shallow version of that same conviction. But we still have to characterize how this moral conviction may be understood.

It is clearly a moral world in which the problems of life are estimated in terms of the disposition to minimize pain and (what is thought to follow) maximize happiness. We might well call it a *culture of convenience*. And "convenience" here means getting what we want without delay or impediment. Impulses must move swiftly to their satisfaction. No longer having to wait for horse or sailing ship to get us to our destination, we prefer the supermarket that saves us the bother of going from shop to shop, the credit card which allows us to acquire without having to exercise thrift, and the pills that will often abbreviate the irritations of convalescence. We assume that there is no pain for which there is no solution.

The "romance of duty" was thus part of an old-fashioned world, in which events and distractions did not come upon us so thick and fast as to remove the time for reflection. The evolution of the romance of duty into the cultivation of convenience did not happen rapidly. Indeed, we live as always in a world in which many forms of the moral life are cultivated, but there is a sense in which the railways largely put paid to moral rigor. I suspect that fast transport began that irritation with having to wait that facilitates the value of convenience. Duty as a central conception of conducting one's life was the world we encounter in the novels of Jane Austen. Romance is inextricably bound up with suffering, and the suffering, one might paradoxically say, must sometimes be its own reward. This is a morality that borrowed some of its serious-mindedness from religion, but (as we may see in the novels of Conrad, James, and others), it was essentially free-standing: a moral exhilaration with its own sources in reason and the passions. And it was, of course, a romantic world, because romance is about commitment and suffering. We today are characterized more by a wariness about commitment than a readiness to be reckless.

The romance of duty could not, of course, avoid creating a world in which many people found themselves in terrible situations about which there was nothing to be done except endure them. Given that one's situation must be understood as inevitable, of course, one usually knuckles down to living through it. Some in the past, no doubt, looked forward to release in early death, but others could find a few mitigating pleasures, because the revulsions of after-marriage were in themselves no more reliable than the intoxications leading to the marriage itself. The total quantum of happiness and misery in that earlier time was probably not very different from our own. But it would not be an option for us: the romance of duty had costs that we are certainly unwilling to bear. We value a different distribution of costs and benefits; indeed, the essence of our situation is precisely that we do think in terms of costs and benefits.

By contrast with the romance of duty, the culture of convenience allows us to find happiness with vastly less restriction. That does not mean that it is any more likely than any other moral system to cure the ills of the human condition. But we like its informality, its looseness, its openness to all possibilities, indeed a certain banality, and we do not miss that fact that we have, in some degree, bought our happiness at the cost of the romance we so much enjoy in fictions. The danger, of course, is that we have miscalculated human life, and that the institutionalization of those pains, in punishment and in lifelong marriage, an institutionalization we have abandoned, may, in the long run, prove essential to social and moral order. All human life is shot through with illusion. The illusion constituting the romance of duty was the grandeur of the will to duty in all its purity. The illusion of our cultivation of convenience is that the world can always be managed so that it conforms to the way we like it. That seems to me, as illusions go, a rather precarious one.

Morals & the Servile Mind

JUNE 2010

ON THE DIMINISHING MORAL LIFE
OF OUR DEMOCRATIC AGE

I am in two minds about democracy, and so is everybody else. We all agree that it is the sovereign remedy for corruption, tyranny, war, and poverty in the Third World. We would certainly tolerate no different system in our own states. Yet most people are disenchanted with the way it works. One reason is that our rulers now manage so much of our lives that they cannot help but do it badly. They have overreached. Blunder follows blunder, and we come to regard them with the same derision as those who interview them on radio and television. We love it that our rulers are—up to a point—our agents. They must account to us for what they do. And we certainly don't live in fear, because democracy involves the rule of law. Internationally, democracies are by and large a peaceful lot. They don't like war, and try to behave like "global citizens." There is much to cherish.

Yet it is hard to understand what is actually happening in our

Kenneth Minogue, "Morals & the Servile Mind." This article is reprinted with permission from the publisher of *New Criterion* 28 (June 2010).
© 2014, *The New Criterion*, www.newcriterion.com.

public life under the surface of public discussion. An endless flow of statistics, policies, gossip, and public relations gives us a bad case of informational overload. How does one tell what is important from what is trivial? The sheer abundance of politics—federal, state, and local—obscures as much as it illuminates. The first clarifying step must be to recognize that "democracy" in the abstract misleads us. Living in a democracy—and it is lived experience that must be our theme—becomes a different thing in each generation. Something that benefits us in one generation may no longer be a benefit in the next. Experiencing twenty-first-century democracy is radically different from what our ancestors cherished in 1901. Rising levels of prosperity, for example, change many responses. For, as Plato noted, constitutions are made out of human beings: as the generations change, so will the system.

My concern with democracy is highly specific. It begins in observing the remarkable fact that, while democracy means a government accountable to the electorate, our rulers now make *us* accountable to *them*. Most Western governments hate me smoking, or eating the wrong kind of food, or hunting foxes, or drinking too much, and these are merely the surface disapprovals, the ones that provoke legislation or public campaigns. We also borrow too much money for our personal pleasures, and many of us are very bad parents. Ministers of state have been known to instruct us in elementary matters, such as the importance of reading stories to our children. Again, many of us have unsound views about people of other races, cultures, or religions, and the distribution of our friends does not always correspond, as governments think that it ought, to the cultural diversity of our society. We must face up to the grim fact that the rulers we elect are losing patience with us.

No philosopher can contemplate this interesting situation without beginning to reflect on what it can mean. The gap between political realities and their public face is so great that the term "paradox" tends to crop up from sentence to sentence. Our rulers are theoretically "our" representatives, but they are busy turning us into the instruments of the projects *they* keep dreaming up. The business of governments, one might think, is to supply the framework of law within which we may pursue happiness on our own account. Instead, we are constantly being summoned to reform ourselves. Debt, intemperance, and incompetence in rearing our children are no doubt regrettable, but they are vices, and left alone, they will soon lead to the pain that corrects. Life is a better teacher of virtue than politicians, and most sensible governments in the past left moral faults to the churches. But democratic citizenship in the twenty-first century means receiving a stream of improving "messages" from politicians. Some may forgive these intrusions because they are so well intentioned. Who would defend prejudice, debt, or excessive drinking? The point, however, is that our rulers have no business telling us how to live. They are tiresome enough in their exercise of authority—they are intolerable when they mount the pulpit. Nor should we be in any doubt that nationalizing the moral life is the first step towards totalitarianism.

We might perhaps be more tolerant of rulers turning preachers if they were moral giants. But what citizen looks at the government today thinking how wise and virtuous it is? Public respect for politicians has long been declining, even as the population at large has been seduced into demanding political solutions to social problems. To demand help from officials we rather despise argues for a notable lack of logic in the *demos*. The statesmen of eras past have been replaced by a set of barely competent social workers eager to take over the risks of our everyday life. The electorates of earlier times would have responded to politicians seeking to bribe us with such promises with derision. Today, the *demos* votes for them.

Our rulers, then, increasingly deliberate on our behalf, and decide for us what is the right thing to do. The philosopher Socrates argued that the most important activity of a human being was reflecting on how one ought to live. Most people are not philosophers, but they cannot avoid encountering moral issues. The evident problem with democracy today is that the state is pre-empting—or "crowding out," as the economists say—our moral judgments. Nor does the state limit itself to mere principle. It instructs us on highly specific activities, ranging from health provision to sexual practices. Yet decisions about how we live are what we mean by "freedom," and freedom is incompatible with a moralizing state. That is why I am provoked to ask the question: can the moral life survive democracy?

By "the moral life," I simply mean that dimension of our inner experience in which we deliberate about our obligations to parents, children, employers, strangers, charities, sporting associations, and all the other elements of our world. We may not always devote much conscious thought to these matters, but thinking about them makes up the substance of our lives. It also constitutes the conditions of our happiness. In deliberating, and in acting on what we have decided, we discover who we are and we reveal ourselves to the world. This kind of self-management emerges from the inner life and is the stream of thoughts and decisions that make us human. To the extent that this element of our humanity has been appropriated by authority, we are all diminished, and our civilization loses the special character that has made it the dynamic animator of so much hope and happiness in modern times.

It is this element of dehumanization that has produced what I am calling "the servile mind." The charge of servility or slavishness is a serious one. It emerges from the Classical view that slaves lacked the capacity for self-movement and had to be animated by the superior class of masters. They were creatures of impulse and passion rather than of reason. Aristotle thought that some people were "natural slaves." In our democratic world, by contrast, we recognize at least some element of the "master" (which means, of course, self-managing autonomy) in everyone. Indeed, in our entirely justified hatred of slavery, we sometimes think that the passion for freedom is a constitutive drive of all human beings. Such a judgment can hardly survive the most elementary inspection of history. The experience of both traditional societies and totalitarian states in the twentieth century suggests that many people are, in most circumstances, happy to sink themselves in some collective enterprise that guides their lives and guarantees them security. It is the emergence of freedom rather than the extent of servility that needs explanation.

Servility is not an easy idea with which to operate, and it should be clear that the world we live in, being human, cannot be fully captured in ideal structures. But in understanding Western life, it is difficult to avoid contrasting courage and freedom on the one hand with servility and submission on the other. We think of freedom as being able to do what we merely want to do, but this is a condition cherished no less by the slave than by the master. When the cat's away, the mice will play! Here is the illusion that freedom is merely having a lot of options available. What freedom actually means is the capacity not only to choose but also to face the consequences of one's choice. To accept employment, to marry, to join a cause, to sustain a family, and so on, all involve responsibilities, and it is in the capacity to sustain self-chosen responsibilities, the steadiness to face up to the risks and inevitable *ennui* inseparable from a settled life, that we exhibit our freedom. And its essence is that each individual life is determined by this set of chosen commitments and virtues (whatever they may be) rather than by some set of external determinants or regulations. Independence of mind requires thinking one's own thoughts: poor things many of them may be, but they are our own, and we have found some reasons for thinking them.

The problem about identifying servility in our modern Western societies results from the assumption that freedom and independence are admirable, and their opposites not. Hence the strong human tendency to trade off freedom for some other condition of things—

money, security, approval—must take on the appearance of a virtue. A further problem with servility is that its opposite might
seem to be a swaggering parade of one's own independence, but
this is just as likely to be a cover for a servile spirit. Since the essence of servility is dependence of mind, independence is compatible with situational caution, as in the case of the assistant to Lord
Copper in Evelyn Waugh's *Scoop*, who responds to whatever idi-
otic remark his press baron employer might make with the words
"Up to a point, Lord Copper." Wariness, tact, and hypocrisy are
inevitable elements in the comic conditions of modern bourgeois
life, and their significance is never obvious, even to those indulging
them.

The real opposite of servility is individualism, as it has long
been understood in European thought. But the very word "individuality" itself is often confused with egoistic self-interest and the
pursuit of mere impulse. One needs to tread with delicacy in using
any of the common words in this area. In our time, the structural ri-
gidities that have emerged from the basic ideas of social justice and
of vulnerability in contemporary society constitute a new world of
servility, but the essentials of the condition were recognized nearly
a century ago by Hilaire Belloc. His slightly eccentric diagnosis of
the condition remains acute even in our time. The issue is how we
judge the character of society. As he writes: "Society is recognized
as no longer consisting of free men bargaining freely for their labor
or any other commodity in their possession, but of two contrasting
statuses, owners and non-owners." It is a world in which the servile
seek security in avoiding the risks of life, even at the sacrifice of
their freedom. And it cannot easily be recognized in action.

The social conditions of the servile mind are much less elusive
than the personal. That they consist in welfare dependency has
been widely recognized—even governments themselves find the
resulting costs, crime, and apathy of such programs intolerable.
But servility is also evident in the state's concern to protect any set
of people from prejudice, offense, or danger to self-esteem. Immi-

grants in earlier times did not need, and many would have regarded as demeaning, the current apparatus designed to protect supposedly vulnerable people. Courage and resilience did for these people what the state now does for their successors. Such legislation, in protecting people from victimhood is, paradoxically, simultaneously an education in how to be a victim.

One of the collateral corruptions of this situation is that control must often be exercised not against those who commit whatever offense is in question, but against those who might, at the convenience of lawyers and the state, be made accountable. An employer, for example, may become accountable for sexual harassment committed by an employee because he has not provided what appears to be known as a "safe environment" for women. Employers are much more satisfactory targets for legislation and litigation, a version of the idea of "deep pockets." More generally, the duty not to offend the vulnerable classes in speech has been codified as the amorphous thing called "political correctness." As disposing of the power not only to rebuke, but also to enforce by penalties, such codification makes the codifiers our masters. We must obey less in deference to the law than from the demand to regard "correctness" as a moral virtue. To legislate opinion is itself to create a servile relationship. Codification of this kind destroys the freedom to respond to each other (within the law) as we choose.

And if it should seem that invoking servility as characterizing some of the conduct of modern Westerners is excessively dramatic, let me observe that we do actually have a vocabulary that recognizes slavishness in the everyday life of our societies. It happens, for example, when we call someone a toady, creep, wimp, careerist, or some other such denigration. Indeed, our vocabulary reveals a variety of ways in which we recognize tendencies which are quite precisely servile. Any failure to perform a public duty unless some private benefit is given, for example, is an exercise in corruption, and such corruption is a derogation of the moral life characteristic of the slave. Again, our common moral disapproval of "greed" characterizes those who go beyond the capitalist drive for the best deal, in order to gain something to which they are not entitled. This judgment implicitly invokes the charge of allowing reason to be overpowered by impulse. But of course, servility has much more evident characteristics. Let us bring them out by a contrast.

The European societies that became democracies in the course of the last two centuries understood themselves as associations of self-moving individuals. Rich and poor alike made their own arrangements within a civil society containing a large and increasing range of associations: social, charitable, religious, mutually supportive, unionized. These associations expressed that capacity for spontaneous institutional creativity which so impressed visitors to Europe, and especially to Anglophone countries. The crucial mark of independence was the ability to generate the resources needed for life without dependence on governmental subsidy, and it constituted "respectability." No doubt it was sometimes easier for the rich to sustain such independence, but moral character was the crucial point. The respectable poor in the nineteenth century recognized themselves, and were recognized by others, as having a proud sense of their independence.

The major change from the late nineteenth and early twentieth century is thus one in our very conception of society itself. In Europe, and even to some extent in the United States, it has become less an association of independent self-moving individuals than an association of vulnerable people whose needs must be met and sufferings mitigated by the power of the state. The idea of "vulnerability" has become such a cannibal of meanings that it has now acquired a remarkable range. The victims of crime were evidently vulnerable; in modern usage, however, the perpetrators of crime have also become vulnerable. The reason underlying this remarkable semantic development is that "society itself" has failed in its duty to instill decency and integrity in those who have turned to violence and crime. Here we have the most direct possible challenge to the basic idea of moral agency.

It is considerations of this sort that lead me to assimilate the moral order of Western societies in some degree to that of the slaves of the ancient world. We must today as citizens accommodate ourselves to increasing regulation and dependence on authority even to the point of falling in with the correct opinions. The moral world of the classical individualist emerged from the coherence of self-chosen commitments. His basic duty was to his own conception of himself. Contemporary moral life by contrast is marked by a greater involvement of external elements. It is not only that states regulate ever wider areas of life so that even family life becomes subject to demands for compliance. It is also that we have learned to pick up signals about respectable opinion from the responses of others—a feature of modern life that the sociologist David Riesman (in *The Lonely Crowd*) called "other directed."

"Democracy" is central to this change in our condition not because it "causes" the change, but because most changes in our moral and political sentiments will sooner or later be recommended and justified as some form of democracy. What causes what in social life is so complicated that we can hardly be sure of any particular connection; we only ever grasp parts of it. Technology and economic enterprise, the secularization of life, changing opinions, new moral tastes—many such things are implicated in these changes. But the drive to equalize the conditions of a population, to institute something called "social justice," to make society a model of "inclusion"—all such things will eventually be advanced as an element of "democracy." Household democracy is men and women equally sharing the burdens of running the household. It may also involve granting children a vote on family matters. Educational democracy consists in switching resources to the pupils currently less capable of getting good results. No remnants of hereditary constitutions are safe from this homogenizing steamroller: Democratization is the most dramatic of all the corruptions of constitutionality in which separation and balance are to be replaced by a single ideal believed to solve all problems. The moral life can no more be isolated from this drive than anything else. It too must be democratized. And the result is to destroy individual agency.

Our inherited moral idiom is thus being challenged by another, in which individuals find their identifying essence in supporting public policies that are both morally obligatory and politically imperative. Such policies are, I suggest, "politico-moral." Such an attitude dramatically moralizes politics, and politicizes the moral life. It feeds on our instinctive support for good causes. Yet it also suggests that the most important sign of moral integrity, of decency and goodness, is not found in facing up to one's responsibilities, but in holding the right opinions, generally about grand abstractions such as poverty and war. This illusion might well be fingered as the ultimate servility.

Some might think that morality is of little significance, because it is merely the subjective values people adopt. No doubt sexual mores in our times are in a state of massive confusion, but no one believes that doctors can choose about putting the interests of the patient first, or accountants may legitimately make up the figures, or friends betray us. The current muddle between subjectivism about morals and dogmatism about rights, for example, merely conceals the semantic changes by which the moral is being transposed into the manipulable, leading to a gullible acquiescence in the projects of governments. These semantics cannot help but attract philosophical interest. And the philosopher had better start by observing that what we recognize as our "culture" is merely the surface of our lives, the debris left behind from our moral responses in times past. It is out of date even as it is recognized. We never step into the same culture twice.

✦   ✦   ✦

At the end of a period of civil strife, as Tacitus tells us, Augustus Caesar established peace and security in Rome during the long period in which he ruled, ending in A.D. 14. Augustus carefully preserved the constitutional structures inherited from the republican period. Rome was still, in a sense, at the height of its power. When he died, however, the Romans discovered that a new system had quietly come into being: they had acquired a master. And what they also learned was that almost insensibly, over the long reign of Augustus, they had learned the moral practices needed for a sycophantic submission to such a figure.

The fate of the Romans under Tiberius, who followed Augustus, was alarming beyond anything even imaginable in our time, but we should not forget the broader lesson: that over long stretches of time, the moral changes that take place only become evident in the light of some unexpected crisis. It is a lesson that ought to make us wary of our easy-going and liberated ways. Our world is infinitely benign, and we are in no immediate danger of falling into the distractions and treacheries that afflicted the early days of Rome under the Principate. But we should never forget that moral change never ceases, and it takes place below, and often deeply below, the surface of a culture.

The Irresponsibility of Rights

NOVEMBER 2010

OVERTHROWING *ANCIENS RÉGIMES*

European thinkers have often indulged in a flirtation with classical republicanism. It was a doctrine particularly vibrant in the so-called Radical Enlightenment. Modern European states are essentially monarchies, and largely remain so even though their kings and queens may not survive in institutional form. The reason these states are monarchical is that they derive from feudal conditions, and feudal monarchies have generated, through complicated chains of development, an individualist version of the rule of law. Being Christian states, they construed human beings as fallen creatures of limited rationality. Recognising such fallibility, they created tolerant commercial societies based on what Gibbon called "science and taste." And they inherited, of course, the Christian distinction between God and Caesar, public and private life. In this form, though shaken by many forms of political folly, they have, over many generations, fought off various forms of the totalitarian temptation.

Kenneth Minogue, "The Irresponsibility of Rights." This article is reprinted with permission from the publisher of *Quadrant* (November 2010). © 2010, *Quadrant* Magazine Ltd., Suite 2/5 Roseberry Place, Balmain, NSW, 2041, www.quadrant.org.au.

Now this combination of characteristics—monarchy, Christianity and a certain stubborn conservative resistance to extreme radicalism—constitutes (if abstractly considered) a kind of *ancien régime*, as it featured in the rejections of the revolutionaries in France. Monarchies were understood, in the manner of Roman republicans, as centres of autocracy and tyranny, surrounded by flunkeys. They were identified with servility. The Christian religion was obviously a set of outmoded beliefs picked up from a long-vanished Jewish tribal past. And the conservatism was clearly a dumb aversion among the ignorant to the changes needed to create a better society. Here was a set of imperfections for which a radical package of perfections lay to hand: republicanism, secularism and radicalism. They could plausibly be packaged as the formula for freedom. In the imaginative version of it supplied by Rousseau (in one of his moods), it was the discovery that although we think we are free, we are still in chains. Perfection thus became in some degree the overthrow of real or notional *"anciens régimes."*

It is worth pursuing this current form of perfectionism a little further. What does it involve? At one level, an *ancien régime* might be understood as an image of the oppressions of capitalist life, in the United States for example. But in Britain, more obvious targets are easy to find. The abolition of monarchy and the House of Lords are plausible versions of any project of democratisation. Getting rid of monarchy today, however, is largely a recessive ambition because the political power of the monarchy is slight, and there are powerful reserves of reverence for an institution that stands above politics and represents the unity of the British. Nevertheless, some classical republicans take a close interest in polling data that may register the popularity of the monarchy going up and down. Every decline provokes republican muttering. And as with all radical aspirations, a successful negative popular vote could destroy an institution leading to an oblivion from which no positive vote could restore it. Meanwhile, the House of Lords in Britain has led a strange half life, as projects of reforming it or transforming it hiss and splutter to little purpose.

Then there is the issue of Christianity regarded in this context as the constitutive superstition of the West. The first decade of the twenty-first century was marked by an evident push for a final triumphant secularisation. Evidence-based science should at last be the recognised foundation of our lives rather than superstition.

And then (along with monarchy and Christianity) there was conservatism, often taken by its enemies as no more than an irrational resistance to improvement, a falsity of consciousness generated by no more significant a source than the interests of the rich. Here in the abolition of these elements of European life is a progressive program for building a democratic and secular radicalism that could at last begin to grapple with the real problems of perfecting our society.

I suppose that the best description of this kind of program would be to understand it as constitutional fundamentalism. The problems of human folly are attributed to bad institutions, especially monarchy. The program might alternatively be regarded as an instance of "the Kantian Fallacy," after the philosopher who thought, in the 1790s, that a Europe of republics could be nothing else but a Europe at peace. How can we be free, asks the progressive, when we are subject to monarchical rulers (even notionally) and dominated by unscientific and outmoded ideas? Monarchy is associated with servility, Christianity with a population on its knees before an imaginary ruler of the universe. And both of these institutions prevent us from taking our destiny into our own hands, standing on our own two feet, and—democratically no doubt—engaging with our real problems, which turn out to be oppressions and inequalities.

As perfectionist aspirations go, this one is not currently distinguished by any great vitality, but the remarkable thing is that it has survived at all. The unavoidable defect of real classical republics is that they spend so much energy being anxious about moral decline. As Montesquieu analysed them, republics depended on civic virtue, and even the noble Catos of Rome failed to avert such a moral collapse. In European monarchies, by contrast, a certain sort of moral corruption is recognised as inevitable. It is to be found, for example, in commercial incentives to virtue, but its real habitat is the sentiment of honour by which Europeans do the right thing not because it is the right thing, but because they would be dishonoured if they did not. This may be, as classical republicans generally think, an "indirect" and inferior form of virtue but it is certainly a form of virtue, and in a world massively given over to corruptions of every kind, it is not negligible.

Among the unrealities of this version of perfectionism is its historical perversity. Without monarchy, no liberal democracies would have come into being. Monarchies in Europe have long been the notional sources of honour, and as a focus of national unity, they enabled party disputes to develop institutionally into a distinction between government and opposition without degenerating into civil war. Certainly no classical state generated our kind of conversational politics. As for servility and dependence of mind, European monarchies (and America of course belongs to this class) are pretty obviously the least servile of societies in the modern world. North European monarchies are the most free and stable states as well as the least corrupt democracies in Europe, and that means the world. It is significant that the overthrow of monarchy in Russia, Spain and Germany in the twentieth century led on to very bad times indeed.

Monarchy, Christianity and conservatism are three institutions that virtually define what all forms of Western radicalism find imperfect in human nature, and in the attacks upon them, we may sniff the curious sense that those who want to overthrow these supposed elements of *ancien régime* seek a final solution to the basic source of history as a Voltairean story of crimes and follies. This "final solution"—abolishing monarchy, refuting Christianity and overcoming conservatism—is no doubt benign and only marginally to be compared to the famous Final Solution of Nazi dreams, but it has the same mad sense of human megalomania about it. That Christianity, taken abstractly as a belief system, has problems may be easily conceded, but it is also the source of the traditions on which Western openness has been created. And intellectually speaking, setting up Augustine and Christian theology against Marx and his modern successors is to match giants with dwarfs. Again, if the issue is conservative thought, then Burke, Salisbury and their successors need hardly fear being unmasked as bearers of false consciousness. But there is a more substantial point.

It concerns freedom. Perfectionism doctrinally can exist in no other context than that of a dialogue about imperfections. The deepest source of the radical drive in Western states is the conviction that we suffer from concealed forms of oppression which destroy our freedom unless they are unmasked. Rousseau's idea that we are enslaved was taken up by many radicals of later generations, and (as we shall see) by all intellectuals who had the mobilising ambitions of totalitarianism. What, then, is it that makes a slave? Chains and commands, no doubt, but also the slave's own recognition that he or she is a slave. To think oneself oppressed is to think of oneself as a slave. It is a step on the way to releasing in oneself that element of servility that lurks in all human nature. And it was this idea of being oppressed that seduced the Russians into Bolshevism, the Germans into Nazism. They wanted to throw off bourgeois chains in the one case, and the oppressions of the worldwide Jewish conspiracy on the other. Neither Russians nor Germans had been notably servile populations before they succumbed to ideological enthusiasm—but they certainly became so.

The mistake of identifying freedom with liberation is evidently a mark of pretty unsophisticated peoples, and it has been a happy distinction of Anglophones that they have usually managed to avoid its nastier consequences. They did not however entirely escape this confusion in universities during the 1960s, which were a textbook example of the destruction of real institutional independence by liberation movements. Suddenly becoming available to unsophisticated and uneducated people, universities succumbed to democratic and liberatory slogans and lost the academic authority that made them distinctive. In succumbing to such servility of mind, they were unprotected against governments bidding to take power over them.

All servility is dangerous. To be even a little servile is to think that whatever is frustrating must be a form of oppression, from which liberation alone will provide release. Often, however, one is frustrated not by "oppression" but by reality, or an instinct for self-restraint. It is a feature of life to which some kind of "rage" is not an appropriate response. Servility is a personality structure with little protection against the temptations of impulse. The search for liberation is a rejection of the responsibilities of freedom in favour of a release into the irresponsibility of rights. And a right is irresponsible because it is a legally entrenched liberty that does not contain within itself the limitations instinctive in a free society. That is why there is a constant moral fussing in current societies about the necessity to match rights with responsibilities. As Jack Straw, a British Minister of Justice, has remarked, human rights are being treated like consumer goods for selfish ends by some people in Britain. "I am really worried about the commoditisation of rights, and the sense that people should see their rights as consumer goods," he said.

I cite constitutional fundamentalism merely as one familiar form of contemporary perfectionism, one that lurks a little below the surface of our current politics. While not being particularly sophisticated, it has a certain cachet in universities, because it is likely to give less sophisticated academics the pleasing sense that they are being "socially critical." In this context it is in part a component of the wider doctrine of the intellect as essentially critical, and in part an instance of the politico-moral rejection of our civilisation as failing to confront the evils of the world.

IGNORANCE, POVERTY AND WAR

The politico-moral cast of mind is happy to ally itself with other versions of perfectionism, but its own central focus is to destroy ignorance, war and poverty, both in our own societies and in the world more at large. No small ambition, one might say. These problems have always been with us. Solving them would certainly be a transformation of the human condition. But they clearly raise the most difficult and controversial moral questions. What is to count as ignorance? How is it related to war? The politico-moral transcends the complexities and mobilises our *political* sentiments for a *moral* crusade. As always, the question becomes: how can this problem-solution nexus be made plausible? Given that moral integrity and political prudence seldom coincide, how can the politico-moral present itself as *both* an imperative moral crusade and as *politically* compelling?

The answer is that the crusade presents itself as both abstract and figurative at the same time, a concept and an image fused together. If we construe these grand problems at the right level of abstraction, then policies become thinkable and imperative in a way that would not survive examination either at the brute level of particular reality, or that of philosophical universality. And it is only by falling into line with a conviction in this form that we can be persuaded to bend all our efforts towards solving these problems as the real expression of our real humanity.

The perfectionist program to conquer poverty is perhaps most plausibly presented in the form of the view that poverty is ipso facto an indicator of injustice. As Thomas Pogge puts it in *Freedom from Poverty as a Human Right*: the "massive persistence of severe poverty is the great scandal of this globalised civilisation and threatens its promised gains in peace, stability and prosperity." Pogge argues that the poor half of humankind consumes under 2 per cent of the global product. Statistically, we are in the world of the poor living on a dollar a day, a proposition hard to make sense of since it depends so much on conditions and currencies, but nothing much rests on this basic feature of the rhetoric of perfection. No one doubts that there are millions of people living in dreadful conditions, doomed to drinking unclean water and poor food in small quantities, living on the edge of survival so that a military conflict, a bad harvest or governmental caprice can kill. Of the facts of the case, there is certainly no doubt.

The moral case for the duties we owe to the poor is analysed by Pogge in terms of the negative duty of avoiding harm, and the positive duty of creating at least some elements of material adequacy to replace the impoverished conditions of the chronically poor. The negative duty is enough for him to suggest that the causes of such poverty lie in the foreseeable consequences of economic arrangements that have been structured by interlocking national and international arrangements set up by Western states. It thus becomes our duty to modify these arrangements so that "everyone has real opportunities to escape and avoid extreme poverty."

Pogge has little patience with the argument that poverty results from local causes. This is an argument made plausible by the fact that so many states in the Third World have actually learned how to generate wealth. How have Japan, Thailand, Taiwan and other non-Western areas escaped from being doomed by those "interlocking national and international institutional arrangements"? Social scientists, he tells us, feel "emotionally more comfortable" with tracing persistent world poverty back to "national and local causes" rather than to "global institutional arrangements." This kind of remark is just a bit of *ad hominem* flim-flam, and need not be taken seriously.

Mark Fleurbaey, one of Pogge's contributors, also judges the responsibility for global poverty as lying with Western states, because he thinks that poverty results from oppression. Economic constraint and physical violence both reduce real freedom, he argues, taking as "real freedom" a situation of resource equality between those entering into a transaction—a situation so unusual in the world that it would generate very few transactions at all. People exchange precisely because they are unequal in resources. That is how work, for example, turns into cash. The conclusion Fleurbaey draws is that unequal trade is a form of coercion like physical violence. Poverty, like physical aggression, violates the integrity of the person. Here we have an explosion of analogies designed to reduce all the complexities of economic relationships to versions of the one key concept, oppression.

This sounds like a powerful moral case in terms of rights, and it tempts various writers in this field to suggest some system of global dividends drawn from rich countries and given to poor. Such a global tax would (so the argument runs) begin to deal with global poverty. The thesis is that the poor are poor because they have no money: an irresistible conclusion, indeed. No less irresistible, however, is the judgment that any vast sum of money likely to be accumulated for this purpose would be a magnet for the corrupt, the greedy, bureaucrats on the make and many other undesirables. Large funds of money for good purposes have a way of producing very disappointing benefits, and that has been precisely the history of much Western aid to the underdeveloped world.

Nor need we take too seriously the idea that poverty results from the way the international economy works, rather than from the culture involved. It would hardly be surprising if some cultures were very much more effective at creating wealth than others. Cultural difference has to do with moral probity, corruption, work ethics and similar considerations. Some cultures are undoubtedly less successful than others. Africans seem to find it hard to organise themselves in states in which wealth flows to those who work rather than to those with guns or licences. The Islamic world is another arena of such global poverty such that, like Africans, Muslims are very keen to get out of Islamic states and migrate to richer Western pastures. Indigenous peoples in the Pacific and in parts of Latin America are also notably dependent on money provided by others. Somehow, Mexicans never seem to manage their economy well enough to discourage thousands of their number from trying the desperate expedient of walking across the border into the USA.

The idea that severe poverty is caused by structural arrangements that suit the Western states but are disastrous to others is clearly refuted by the success of Asian states. The positive case that bad government is a serious cause of poverty may be illustrated currently from the Zimbabwe case, in which starvation is a direct result of the folly of rulers and not at all from structural conditions of any kind.

The converse evidence supporting the same principle is that the Chinese, who have all the talents and lack nothing of the enthusiasm to grow richer, could over long stretches of the twentieth century succeed only when ruled by the British in Hong Kong and in Singapore, but not in China. The madness of Maoism was a marvellous stimulus to poverty. These elementary considerations are enough to dispose of the simple view that severe poverty is a violation of a human right, and especially one for which we in the West are responsible. Global poverty is certainly terrible, and it would be good to alleviate it, but making its alleviation a right is merely a form of megalomania among normative theorists.

That we may have a duty to suffering individuals is easily granted; that we have a duty to entire peoples who suffer is also pretty plausible. But here again we face the problem of morality versus the national interest. For one thing, any Western responsibility for feeding the world runs into the difficulty that we embrace an open-ended commitment to deal with a problem largely out of our control. One reason for poverty in the Third World is that the starving populations get bigger generation by generation. A great deal of aid already goes to impoverished countries, but they multiply faster than we can deal with their needs. Some European cultures used in earlier times to adapt to changing Malthusian pressures by adjustments in the average age of marriage: in good times, people married earlier, in bad times later. Third World countries benefit from medical advantages that have reduced infant mortal-ity, but have no cultural mechanisms to deal responsibly with these problems themselves.

Western difficulties in responding wisely to the problems of ignorance, poverty and war take on an even darker complexion if we contemplate a future world in which (unlikely as it seems) these problems would have been solved. We may well envisage a future in which impoverished states become prosperous, and hence active players in the already complicated and conflict-ridden world of international politics. The West is demographically shrinking, and there are vastly increasing populations in Africa, Asia and South America. We would then find ourselves in an international world in which we would be small, weak and probably still richer than these countries.

You hardly need a crystal ball to predict that such nations would be in all likelihood highly aggressive in their claims and demands on us. Whatever we might have done for them in the past would generate no permanent source of gratitude or even of consideration. International relations have no place for the gratitude one might expect in the world of individuals. Britain abolished slavery, but this notably virtuous act exhibited in past times is no barrier to its being the object of many resentful claims by those descended from the slaves.

The Intellectual Left's
Treason of the Heart

SEPTEMBER 2011

It is a striking fact that throughout the Anglophone world, most academics have left-wing political views. In the United States, for example, eight or nine professors out of ten in Arts and Social Sciences will be Democrats. This fact is striking because the actual politics of the United States oscillates between Democrat and Republican, both in the presidency and in Congress. We thus have the interesting problem of a conflict between academic and popular opinion. How might we explain it?

Given that since professors are in some sense to be considered the most intelligent people in any modern society, left-wing politics might be the most intelligent way of dealing with the public business of liberal democracies. On the other hand, it is far from obvious that left-wing administrations have been better for any country than so-called right-wing governments. Australians have been able to get along no less under Howard than under Keating. For good or bad reasons, electorates choose different parties at different mo-

Kenneth Minogue, "The Intellectual Left's Treason of the Heart." This article is reprinted with permission from the publisher of *Quadrant* (August/September 2011). © 2011, *Quadrant* Magazine Ltd., Suite 2/5 Roseberry Place, Balmain, NSW, 2041, www.quadrant.org.au.

ments. Hence it might be that we need to distinguish between theoretical and practical intelligence. In the spirit of *1066 and All That*,
we might suggest that academics are right but impractical, and that
ordinary electors are wrong but pragmatic. We might ring many
changes on this formulation, but first we should ask: does it matter
that professors lean to the left?

Part of the answer is that in our opinionated times, many people
are impressed by those they imagine might know better than they
do. In the middle of the twentieth century, communists invented
an interesting new figure in politics, generally called a "fellow trav-
eller" (and by Lenin a "useful idiot"). Such a person supported
many of the high-toned aspirations of communist doctrine without actually being a communist. Professors were often trumps in
this propaganda contest—not indeed as important as actors and
other entertainment celebrities, but still significant, especially in
bulk. And academics still occasionally, in bulk, bring their wisdom
to bear upon current affairs by signing up to collective positions.
Back in 1982, Margaret Thatcher's stiff medicine for the travails
of welfarist Britain was attacked by a cohort of no fewer than 364
economists. Who could stand against such massed ranks of intelligence? Fortunately Thatcher did, and she was right to do so.

And this, I think, is where the problem becomes interesting. If
it is the case that academics often get practical matters wrong, we
are confronted with a remarkable juxtaposition of—to put the matter brutally—intelligence and stupidity. One sub-set of academic
opinion, for example, goes by the name of "intellectuals." These
are people who have read a lot of books and take up positions on
public affairs. Their opinions are often interesting, but inevitably
look superficial when illuminated by hindsight. In particular, intellectuals have often exhibited an undiscriminating passion for the
idealism (or even worse, the realism) attaching to the political fashions of the moment.

Sometimes, illusion leading to superficiality results from a
rhetorical game in which intellectuals must exhibit their identity

as above all "critical" thinkers, and this is done by indulging in a merciless view of what has been set up as "conventional wisdom." "Conventional" is the academic opposite of critical, and is basically instantiated by anything that might locally in Western states be seen as patriotic or "ethnocentric." In a recent book, *Heaven on Earth: The Varieties of the Millennial Experience*, Richard Landes, whose theme is the down-playing of apocalyptic and millennial experiences in Western understanding, considers that the postmodern rejection of local loyalties is a transposition of millennial themes. As he remarks:

> Modern, and even more so, postmodern modes of interpretation emphasize both self-criticism and empathy with "the other." Whoever is right, my side or not, us *and* them, win-win, war is *not* the answer. "We can work it out . . ." Western progressives favor this essentially active transformational apocalyptic mode. . . . There is even a post-modern, post-colonial school of *alterity* that gives epistemological priority to the "other's" narrative. In its most extreme form it starts from the position: "their side right or wrong."

Misplaced enthusiasm is always a subject for comic treatment, and no one looking for comedies of misplaced enthusiasm could find better illustrations of it than in another recent book, *Treason of the Heart: From Thomas Paine to Kim Philby*, by David Pryce-Jones. His account of the strange propensity of some academics to salute the public relations of dodgy regimes, is certainly a notable exhibition of comic gullibility in politics. Foreign despotisms only have to declare their passion to improve the condition of the poor, and many an academic is lying with his back on the floor waving his paws in the air. A related academic mood is less comic: the bold embrace of murderous methods if they are wrapped up as "necessary" for achieving the greater good. The ideal academic moral posture, in other words, often combines a besotted political idealism with an ability to swallow some pretty gritty realism about method. It is this combination of folly and insight, stupidity and intelligence, which makes this phenomenon so interesting.

Pryce-Jones's account of British enthusiasm for foreign causes stretches over two centuries, from the American War of Independence to the collapse of the Soviet Union. Very many of those in his vast cast of the foolish are notably intelligent people. Here we have an abundance of empirical materials for looking into the foolishness of the bright. Pryce-Jones's archetypal "traitor of the heart" is Tom Paine, who supported the American colonists against England. Paine would not be my choice of the iconically foolish, nor was his support for American independence especially remarkable. Supporting the Americans against George III hardly counted as an eccentric foreign enthusiasm because many Britons did the same thing, but Paine gets his place in this gallery because he so clearly illustrates the point that enthusiasm for the foreign generally results from hatred of the local. I'm not sure even this is always true, but Paine's combination of alienation from the British and consistent support for the enemies of Britain was remarkably consistent.

Britain in the late eighteenth century does seem to have been experiencing what we might call "revolution envy." The excitements of Paris in the 1790s contrasted with boring Britain, stuck with a ghastly establishment that hardly seemed to have changed for a century. It was, of course, creating the modern industrial world, but that did not rate a headline. The real action was happening across the Channel where the world was being turned upside down. Many felt with Wordsworth, "Bliss was it in that dawn to be alive, But to be young was very heaven."

An advanced thinker like the anarchist Godwin (who had been married to Mary Wollstonecraft, the pioneer of women's rights) could dream of a world without the "rooted insolence" he detected in his fellows, and his friend Shelley (along with Leigh Hunt and other enthusiasts) came to advocate a radical doctrine of "sociability" which entailed sexual liberation. Much of it resembled our own dear 1960s, opening up an exciting sense of possibility. It took some time to taste the fruits of all this enthusiasm, but in the case of Shelley and the poetic liberation of that circle, the bitterness of those women who didn't commit suicide as a result was still being expressed decades after Shelley, Hunt and other plausible seducers of those days had died or moved on.

The French experience exerted a magic spell on the educated classes—and indeed not merely the educated—of England. The revolutionaries were creating a better society, and later Napoleon was the model of modern efficient administration—a kind of European Union with teeth. It was not only a bonfire of conventions, but was rationalising Europe by replacing the inherited tangle of dukes and monarchies with competent administration. And in the case of many of Pryce-Jones's cast, foreign enthusiasm unmistakably tottered over the line into treason: it was siding with the country's enemies. Virtually the whole class of English intellectual celebrities were affected in one way or another.

At the heart of the enthusiasm was a dream of social perfection. Lord Stanhope wanted to give up his title and be called "Citizen Stanhope," a step that goes rather beyond even champagne socialism. In *A Vindication of the Rights of Men*, Mary Wollstonecraft accused Edmund Burke of "contemptible hard-hearted sophistry" in his *Reflections*, and went on to dream:

> What salutary dews might not be shed to refresh this thirsty land if more were more enlightened! Smiles and premiums might encourage cleanliness, industry, and emulation— a garden more inviting than Eden would then meet the eye . . .

She was, of course, on more solid ground in moving to the rights of women, but she still lived long enough to learn of the heads dropping into baskets and the repression in La Vendee and other places. A generation later, the brewer Samuel Whitbread committed suicide after Waterloo, apparently from despair at the fate of his hero, while William Hazlitt famously went on a fortnight-long bender to deal with his unhappiness. These people took their politics to heart.

How, one might ask, did dreams of enlightenment lead to heads dropping into baskets? The answer is simply that the Jacobins faced up to one of the central problems of far-reaching social radicalism. It consists in the fact that many of the human beings inherited by the enlightened from earlier unjust regimes turn out to be unsuitable material for this new, improved society. The Jacobins responded with impressive revolutionary ruthlessness, and an understandable reaction against their methods quickly set in. Too many eggs were being broken for an omelette most people did not seem to want. The result is that the historical sequence of stages in the brief Jacobin adventure became the technical names for what later came to be seen as "revolutionary praxis"—from the Terror itself on to Thermidor.

There is a difference, of course, between sympathy for foreign developments on the one hand, and "treason of the heart" on the other. A great deal of European history is a creative dialogue between different nations each with its own distinct capacities in everything from culture to social institutions. But most of Pryce-Jones's subjects were irrational because they not only sympathised with foreign causes but did so *because* such foreign peoples and movements contrasted with those of Britain, and were generally thought superior.

Today, the idea of treason has been eviscerated so much that it almost counts as a claim to critical integrity. Loyalty is taken to be a servile characteristic, and self-respect depends on standing out from the crowd—or joining what has been cynically but appropriately called a "herd of independent minds." It happens, however, that on most of the grand conflicts of the last two centuries, the British position has generally coincided with one we might defend as enlightened—whether we are talking about the abolition of slavery or the rejection of totalitarian regimes. In these terms, then, we have a reformulation of our paradox: the unthinking, loyal patriots happen to have got it right, while many of the bold critical thinkers got it wrong.[1]

And that leads us to a deeper and more interesting question. Can we discover, in the follies of modern intellectuals and academics, a set of notable dispositions or mistakes that might be understood as disposing them towards folly? It is a line of inquiry worth taking up some of our attention.

The most obvious mistake has certainly been to believe that constitutions determine the happiness of peoples, or indeed determine any universal substantial outcome at all. And in this mistake, our enthusiasts were in good company. In the crucial year of 1790, the German philosopher Immanuel Kant published an essay arguing that the solution to the problem of war in Europe was to get rid of kings. People living in republics, he argued, had no interest in killing each other for a new bit of taxable territory. He was certainly in tune with the *zeitgeist*—indeed it has seemed at times that he was the *zeitgeist*—because Shelley, Godwin and the rest independently shared this progressive view. We may call this particular mistake "constitutional salvationism," and some element of it will be found in nearly every piece of nonsense from Bentham's utilitarianism to Marx's communism. Intellectuals with their lust for the new are much given to the belief that a new deal of the constitutional cards might give everybody a winning hand. This is not a fallacy, of course, because it is not a mistake of logic, but it is certainly a false understanding of political realities.

There is a further aspect of this particular mistake. It lies in the fact that the English Jacobins, and later the Napoleonists, had no direct personal interest in pushing their opinions. Like Lord Holland's Whigs, they clearly wished for the public good, even when it might seem to have been against their own personal interests. This is why we are dealing not only with an opinion, but with a moral posture. Those who affirm it can claim a certain disinterested superiority to others because they are above the vulgar clash of interests by which politics is often understood. Instead of self-seeking, or self-interest, we have an idealism seeking the good of all—or greatest happiness, as Bentham was later to promise. Today's version of this posture is sometimes expressed in the demand to think of "people" rather than "profit."

The "disinterestedness" often claimed as part of the idealist posturing of much intellectual opinion on politics is, in my view, a corruption of the idea of being disinterested. As it happens, the Australian philosopher David Stove in one of his posthumous essays just published by Encounter Books, *What's Wrong with Benevolence: Happiness, Private Property, and the Limits of Enlightenment*, features a claim to disinterestedness as among the postures popular among leading Enlightenment thinkers.[2] It was a claim to a higher idealism in promoting the projects of abstract benevolence that turned out to be so destructive in the ideological twentieth century. To pursue an interest is often wrongly thought to be inherently rather debased, whereas only good people support ideals, especially ones which they claim will benefit others.

We thus have here a complex of inducements to foolish enthusiasm. One of them is a simple mono-causal view that constitutions determine specific outcomes, and above all, that they determine the happiness of peoples. Related to that is a posture of disinterestedness which transposes the enthusiasm into the morally elevated realm of idealism. The reality claimed for such ideals, however, depends on nothing more substantial than the declarations of good intentions made by foreign radicals—what I have taken to be the "public relations" of radical idealism.

Perhaps the most astonished feature of the critical posture of many of Pryce-Jones's enthusiasts is an evident simplicity of mind. Many of them were simply starstruck! Thus Lord Holland might have been over the top, though not actually ridiculous, in thinking Napoleon "the greatest statesman and the ablest general of ancient or modern times," but Algernon Swinburne was certainly lost to reason in asking: "Is Garibaldi" (who had his suits made in Savile Row and energetically cultivated his own legend) "the greatest man since Adam, or is he not?" Well, if you insist, no. Garibaldi was the Che Guevara of his day, and focused the admiration many Britons had for the nationalists of Italy.

This version of the comedy of illusion however rather dies in the throat as we discover that Gertrude Stein in 1934 could think that Hitler should be awarded the Nobel Peace Prize, or we contemplate H.G. Wells describing Lenin as "the dreamer in the Kremlin." Even Bertrand Russell on meeting Lenin thought, "his strength comes, I imagine, from his honesty, courage and unwavering faith—religious faith in the Marxian gospel which takes the place of the Christian martyr's hope of paradise." The odd thing is that political enthusiasm has in some respects the strange frivolity of celebrity gossip. Mao, and even Pol Pot, were not safe from such remarkable adulation.

Pryce-Jones as we have seen emphasised that enthusiasts for foreign causes commonly also hate their own peoples. He cites R.N. Brailsford (described as "a scattergun intellectual of his day") who was widely thought to have loved humanity because he hardly loved anyone else. The fact is that one rubs up against one's own people all the time, and it is easy to find in them one or other defect. Australians are certainly familiar with this response to each other. The point is that we understand other peoples, abstractly, by signs, from a distance. Encountering them in limited circumstances makes it easy to get them wrong. Hence Byron admired the Greeks because he saw them through the filter of a classical education, while many later Britons became Italian nationalists from admiration of Garibaldi. Wagner was one source of admiration for German culture in a later generation. Even more Britons in the twentieth century supported the decolonisation of Africa because they admired African attitudes.

Illusion is a universal feature of human affairs, and its natural habitat is the future. This might explain the striking fact that the admirations of these British enthusiasts were not for the realities of the case, but were directed towards collective entities thought to be in the process of being born. Greeks, Italians and Africans were, for these enthusiasts, potentialities not yet actualised, and therefore suitable inhabitants of a vision. It is a notable economy of thought, of course, to be able to admire both a people and a cause as one package. The admiration for the Bedouin in the nineteenth century and after, for example, was sometimes based on a view that the English had lost their gentlemanly virtues and become corruptly commercial. Out in the sands of Arabia could be found simple authentic people uncorrupted by commerce. As Pryce-Jones points out, the famous explorer Richard Burton was really caught up in Rousseau's Noble Savage. Harry St John Philby (yes, father of the communist Kim) thought:

> the Arab is a democrat, and the greatest and most powerful Arab ruler of the present day is proof of it. Ibn Saud is not more than *primus inter pares*, his strength lies in the fact that he has for twenty years accurately interpreted the aspirations and will of his people.

Not much need for an "Arab Spring" in that fortunate land, then! Glubb Pasha wrote that "the Bedouin was every Englishman's idea of nature's gentleman."

My point in making these observations is to suggest that the occurrence of folly and illusion among the intelligent—where one might expect it least—is an under-explored aspect of the political life of our time. What universities seem to have developed is a new scholasticism. Medieval scholasticism resulted from a corruption of the idea of authority. This modern scholasticism emerges no less clearly from a corruption of the idea of criticism. Its source lies in the identification of academic excellence in terms of the idea of criticism, which is a half-truth. It has the useful benefit, however, of according the critic a form of moral as well as academic superiority.

The accolade of being critical, on the other hand, has the weakness of generally being self-ascribed. A scholasticism of this kind often generates the discovery of bad intentions underlying the policies of Western states. Some such policies may well be deplorable, but not usually because they fit into some postmodern stereotype.

My taxonomy of constitutive illusions, from constitutional salvationism onward, could easily be extended, and it could as easily be contracted into a complex account of the forms of rationalism that lose their grip on reality because they filter the world through a net of currently admired abstractions.

But whichever development of the idea might be chosen, this new scholasticism fits within the tradition Pryce-Jones has described. For as with the Jacobins down to the communists, the tradition satisfies its acolytes because it gives them a starring role in an exciting melodrama of victimhood, in which the business of life—life's meaning, as it were—is the struggle against oppression. And the moral self-satisfaction involved is best illustrated in the reflections of one late-repenting British communist who told an interviewer: indeed, we chose the wrong solution. But at least—we cared!

NOTES

1. Including, as we may now discover from David Bird in *Quadrant* (July–August 2011), the historian Manning Clark, who had a pro-German phase in the late thirties, and who fits into Pryce-Jones's thesis in that it seems to have been based on a pretty deep dislike of the British Empire.

2. It is, however, important to realize that "disinterestedness" is a good description of many human activities that are neither self-interested nor altruistic, and that disinterestedness is a central feature of modern Western culture.

Individualism and
Its Contemporary Fate

FALL 2012

My concern in this article is to explore what I take to be the essence of freedom and to locate it in the context of our civilization.
Described thus, the idea is insanely ambitious, and all I can do
is sketch a position. I shall identify freedom with individualism,
discuss first its emergence and then its established character in the
eighteenth century, and finally say something about its paradoxical
place in the world today.

Individuality is a universal characteristic of objects, but *individualism* is the practice that accords to some personal acts, beliefs, and utterances a legitimacy that may conflict with the dictates
of custom or authority. Today, this practice is usually formulated as
"self-interest," which makes it clear that individualism may liberate
some individual wants from customary controls. As self-interest,
individualism is often wrongly identified with the moral vice of
selfishness and gets a bad press. Sometimes it is foolishly attacked

Kenneth Minogue, "Individualism and Its Contemporary Fate." Sections of this
article are reprinted with permission from the publisher of *Independent Review:
A Journal of Political Economy* 17, no. 2 (Fall 2012): 257–269. © 2012, Independent
Institute, 100 Swan Way, Oakland, CA 94621-1428 USA; info@independent.org:
www.independent.org. This article was written originally for presentation at the
general meeting of the Mont Pelerin Society, Sydney, Australia, October 10–15, 2010.

as "consumerism" and described as "hyperindividualism" or the mania for accumulating material goods. These hostile characterizations are part of contemporary rhetoric to which we shall return. Let me begin, however, by sketching the emergence of freedom in its individualist form.

AMBIVALENCE AND THE COMING OF MODERNITY

We inherit various aspects of our freedom from the Greeks, the Romans, and the barons of the feudal period, but in the fifteenth and sixteenth centuries something new was beginning to appear. Urbanization and printing were its essential preconditions, and it took many forms, but in all cases the enterprise of individuals was at the heart of it. If the coming of freedom may be grasped in terms of any single formula, we might invoke that of Martin Luther writing on Christian freedom. Jesus came, Luther affirmed, to free us from the law into a higher dutifulness. These words make it clear why, whatever religious beliefs we may entertain, Christianity is and remains at the heart of our civilization. They also reveal why Luther's doctrines led to endless conflict. The question is: What might these terms—*law* and *higher dutifulness*—signify? For Luther, the law was clearly Judaic, and the higher dutifulness was Christian piety subject to divine grace. Luther was taking his followers back to what he understood to have been the pure origins of their faith. However, the "law" from which we might seek to be freed might in individualist terms be any restraint that a critical spirit encounters. Consider, for example, Montaigne's use of this structure of thought when he remarked: "Wherever I wish to turn, I have to break through some barrier of custom, so carefully has custom blocked all our approaches."[1] Such a formula might equally, however, become a dangerous incitement to any lunatic who wanted to shrug off all restraint or spread some rabble-rousing gospel of his own. What then makes this the insight that lies at the heart of individualism?

Human life is everywhere subject to customs, rules, and restraints, but in most cultures these things change more or less insensibly. In European cultures, by contrast, we have a world in which rising generations develop new enterprises and often challenge the assumptions by which their parents lived. Some old "laws" are rejected, and in general some new "dutifulness" emerges. Enterprise is the key, and competition is the result, and this pattern appears not only in economic endeavors, but in ideas, moral sentiments, science, religious convictions, and everywhere else. Human beings everywhere experience ambivalence about some area of life, and such feelings pose a serious danger to the settled order of things. Our evaluation of most things in our lives varies not only from person to person, but sometimes even from moment to moment. In Europe, however, we find the one civilization that found a way of combining ambivalence with social order. Ambivalence thus liberates the critical spirit, and it lies at the heart of many of the disagreements and conflicts among which we live. In our free societies, such attitudes can be entirely compatible with civility. The skill of combining ambivalence with civility did not come easily even to Europeans, however, and was especially difficult to practice in early modern times, when disputes about Christian theology and practice were at their most passionate. It took time before religious tolerance became a standard feature of European societies. In politics, centuries were to pass before we institutionalized the debate between government and opposition as the standard way of conducting public business. First religion and later socialism and nationalism subjected the harmony of European states to severe strains, but the eventual outcome was a societal condition not only remarkably free and tolerant, but also resilient and outstandingly prosperous. As modern European societies became prosperous and technologically inventive, even those who hated toleration and feared conflict had no alternative but to take notice. Everyone then wanted to understand the "secret" of European power and prosperity.

The basic "secret," one might say, is that modern European states differed from other cultures by the moral practice of individualism, in which the wants and beliefs of individuals are recognized not as disruptive, but as valuable in themselves. Intellectually speaking, individualism led to a revolution in the way in which Europeans thought about the world. The solid realities of traditional societies dissolved into subjective and objective components out of which Europeans could construct a world they found in some degree congenial. It was not at all irrelevant to this kind of pluralism that Europeans were divided into different cultural realms or states, each with its own language and traditions. These "national" variations stimulated each other. Custom, rank, and religion continued to be powerful elements in life, but alongside these universals of human experience something new had emerged: the recognition of difference as having a value of its own. The corresponding tendency at the level of the state was the appearance of sovereign rulers who could repeal laws without having to break them or ignore them. The right to repeal a law (whatever might be understood as "law" in this context) was essential in facilitating an unbroken moral legitimacy over the generations. The rule of law was thus to be distinguished from the commands of any ruler disposing of despotic powers; law must, of course, be distinguished from any sort of command, for law is not something we obey, but something to which we conform. Slaves may have to obey, but subjects conform to a law.

How did this new social and moral world differ from that of other cultures? The answer lies in the fact that in other cultures, custom and religion (along with the usual admixture of human caprice) determined the manner of life, subject to local variations. But whatever these variations, people in non-European societies lived according to what was believed to be the One Right Order of life, which supplied for each individual both a social location and a corresponding set of duties and expectations. Such orders in the most notably elaborated civilizations were the Hindu caste system, the Muslim sharia, and the hierarchies of the Middle Kingdom. And the basic point about these systems and of every other, down to tribal cultures, was that those living in such a world regarded their customs as the one right way of life. A consequence of this belief was a remarkable lack of curiosity about how other peoples lived. Lack of curiosity resulted from the belief that one need not take an interest in "error." Other ways of life were simply wrong! In fact, of course, most people in earlier times knew virtually nothing about the rest of the world. This contrast became one of the most conspicuous differences between European individualism and other cultures' traditional practices. Europeans were from an early period profoundly interested in how others lived, just as they were fascinated by other individuals' character. Shakespeare's creations—irresolutes such as Hamlet, lovers such as Romeo—expressed an attitude that corresponded to Montaigne's reflections on the parochialism of our judgments about how others live.

An interest in other ways of life fed the skepticism inseparable from the emergence of our individualist world. In this new world, even truth is subject to the bumps and bruises of competition. One typical figure was the poet John Milton, who believed that competition brought forth truth and challenged the doctrine of divorce on the basis of affirming the virtue of charity. In a world of printed books, the number of truths competing for the prize of recognition constantly multiplied. It was obvious from the very beginning, of course, that individualism causes conflict, and the same instinct that generates a dream of peaceful uniformity that ruled every other culture was also to be found in Europe. The price of such a dream is, of course, arbitrariness and repression. The passion for uniformity appeared in the early modern belief among European rulers that whatever other variations might be recognized, no state could be stable without a universal religious confession. It has taken a long time for this version of a basic homogeneity of belief to sink to the level of an abandoned superstition, but new forms of the one right order of belief keep appearing. They inspired, of course, the totalitarian projects of the previous century.

Here, then, in sixteenth-century Europe a quite new and remarkable moral practice appeared, and in a philosophically sophisticated civilization such as our own, it was soon theorized in a variety of different ways. In political thought, Hobbes, Locke, and Montesquieu were notable contributors to such understanding. Montesquieu was in a sense the Aristotle of modern political thought in that he supplied a taxonomy that recognizes the basic features of this new modernity. He recognized in most non-European states a form of rule based on fear, which he called "despotism." He also distinguished a heroic classical model of rule, based on virtue, something no longer possible for Europeans. This model was that of a republic. Modern Europe, however, had its own distinctive form. It was essentially monarchical, a condition in which people living under a rule of law enjoyed the citizenly freedom of personal security against the caprice of civil power. This security was part of what we understood by "freedom." Montesquieu identified the essence of the moral life practiced in monarchies as "honor," a term associated with high rank, but which we may understand as a recognition of individualism. In other words, the individualist as moral agent was concerned not only with the question of whether such-and-such an act was right or wrong, but also with what the act might reveal about his own character. In illustration, Montesquieu cited the case of the viscount of Orte, who was in charge of Bayonne when, after the massacre of St. Bartholemew in 1572, Charles IX ordered him to kill the Huguenots of the city. Orte refused, replying that his army did not consist of executioners. The right thing was to obey the king, the wrong thing was to massacre innocent people. In other words, individualism introduced into human life a significant moral complexity that was distinct from the custom and religion that determined the right thing in other cultures. Max Weber referred to one aspect of this complex movement of things as the "Protestant work ethic."

THE AUTONOMY OF ROBINSON CRUSOE

By the eighteenth century, the modern world had settled down, and religious conflict had become marginal in many areas, but the meaning of individualism remained a central preoccupation among Europeans. One of its great myths was the story of Robinson Crusoe as a remarkably self-sufficient individual creating his own world from scratch. Ernest Gellner identifies Crusoe with Descartes, who was in a sense the founder of modern philosophy and points out that other cultures could not generate a Crusoe figure. A Hindu Brahmin, for example, could not live a proper life as a Crusoe figure without the services of members of other castes, and similar forms of social dependence exist in most cultures. Indeed, even a Roman Catholic Crusoe, lacking a priest to administer the sacraments, would have a serious problem. Crusoe is a myth, of course, because he is not natural man in a wilderness, but a skilled creature generated by a culture with abundant knowledge and access to many artifacts contained in the vessel on which he was wrecked. But here is a heroic image of European man in all his individual resourcefulness, exhibiting dramatically the self-sufficiency of Europeans. To be an individualist in this sense meant that social relations (family, friends, associates, and so forth) were chosen rather than kin determined and were all the stronger for that. Crusoe's great adventure was that of a solitary, but he was certainly not a social atom, and, like Europeans in general, he was nested or embedded not only in a cultures, but normally in a social world of family, friends, and associates of many kinds.

The moral point of Crusoe lies in his independence of mind, and it reflects the fact that freedom in European societies is not an ideal or a mere value, but an element in these societies' practical life. It is the condition in which many of them live their lives. Hilaire Belloc claimed that Christianity had abolished slavery, and although both the acts and the opinions of some Christians over a long period were ambivalent on this question, one can see what he means. The barbarian kingdoms that arose out of the collapse of the Western Empire had slaves, but by the time we enter the modern world, slavery has gone. And at the end of the eighteenth century again, English reformers abolished the slavery that had arisen as an opportunistic and profitable trade. In the United States, an even more intractable form of slavery was painfully abolished through a civil war. The point is not only that Europeans themselves want to be free to manage their own lives according to their own judgments, but that they also have a taste for dealing with other people on the same terms.

This preference poses a moral problem because virtue is generally understood as a moral agent's subordination of his own desires to whatever is good for others. Each person's virtues in a traditional society, for example, are social because complementarity is the basis of such communities. To be "social" is to be part of a world of mutual dependence. But how are we to understand individualist societies in which each individual is seeking to advance his own interests? Such individuals would seem to be competitive or, in modern jargon, to be playing a zero-sum game. Abstractly (but not realistically), every gain to X is a loss to Y. Such a nexus has caused capitalism to be identified with selfishness. This identification continues to haunt our world.

The issue has deep roots in moral thought. For more than a century before Adam Smith's *Wealth of Nations*, philosophers and theologians had boldly toyed with the idea that a modern commercial society might in practice be possible on the basis of little virtue or, indeed, no virtue at all. It might be possible to have a tolerable society sustained by a collection of hypocrites doing the right thing merely because they feared punishment or loss of reputation. This line of thought in one sense culminated in Mandeville's satirical *Fable of the Bees*, in which prosperity was a function of vices such as vanity, self-indulgence, and legal quibbling. The traditional identification of goodness with the ideal society seemed to have been lost. "Morality" at its most demanding seemed directly contradictory to peace and prosperity. Commercial societies such as that of England seemed almost to find themselves in the uncomfortable position of resting on vice. This problem found one important resolution in a canonical statement by Adam Smith: a man intending his own gain, Smith wrote, "is in this, as in many other cases, led by an invisible hand to promote an end which was no part of his intention. Nor," he adds significantly, "is it always the worse for society that it was no part of it. . . . I have never known much good done by those who affected to trade for the public good."[2] The deep wisdom of that last remark must be clearly recognized. The point is that in a sense each person is an infallible judge of his or her own interests. We cannot, of course, exclude the ubiquity of human folly, but the point is that no outsider has as good a grasp of my interests as I do. But what does it mean to support "the public good"? Heads get broken and societies collapse from disagreement on that question.

Smith's famous remark is, then, a kind of revolution in moral sensibility. Something previously dismissed as a kind of vice was being admitted to a better class of moral standing. It was becoming clear that alongside the state, a legal order, and the broader thing called "society," a new and independent structure of things was coming into being, which we now call an "economy." It was based on production and consumption, and it had its own laws and processes as well as its own moral structure. A framework of social interdependence had been replaced by a dynamic division of labor that combined competitiveness with its own kind of complementarity. One enormous benefit was the generation of prosperity, yet commercial societies could never quite break free entirely from negative images. Christians worried about the idolatry of worshipping money—Mammon rather than God. Collectivists yearning for peace and uniformity pointed to the problems inseparable from freedom. Hostile images of what later came to be called "capitalism" soon generated a never-ceasing stream of proposals to replace the supposedly chaotic and selfish interests of individuals by central direction in the interests of all.

THE NEW CONTEXT OF INDIVIDUALITY

Individualism emerged unmistakably at the beginning of the modern world, and by the eighteenth century it was in its heyday. Let us now consider its fate in our post-1945 world. But before we revert to Luther's interesting formula, let me make a general point regarding something that has changed everything.

The moral and political issues raised in governing a modern European state have been complicated by the appearance of a new consideration: the social. Europeans, already in love with technology, began to think of society itself as a machine that might possibly become the object of managed improvement. Such a project merged with the millennial passions of Christianity, and the outcome was the project of social transformation. Needless to say, the project took many forms, but nearly all of them were collectivist. The aim was to turn an association into a community, with special definitions of both those terms. "Association" results from people's choosing to be together. It depends on will, whereas in a true "community" each person finds his identity in the good of the whole. Public policy in our time came increasingly to be judged in the light of its supposed consequences for bringing about a better society. The hope was that politicians would bring a bit of decent benevolence to the profit-driven calculations of economic enterprise. Such thinking revealed a remarkable simplicity of mind, but it was designed for simple people. The addition of democracy to the constitutional practices of European states gave this idea a great boost, for what else would the people want, politicians often thought, if not a better—notionally a more equal—society?

This passion for a better society, cultivated in churches, universities, nongovernmental organizations, and many other places, was not seriously compromised by the murderous careers of Nazis and fascists. Even the collapse of central direction in the USSR, long loved by intellectuals for its socially improving intentions, did not discourage people from thinking that there must be a better way of

managing our world than letting individuals seek their own betterment. European states, however successful, prosperous, tolerant,
and peace loving, could never escape some variant of the hostile
image of capitalism classically expressed by Marx and Engels in
The Communist Manifesto. Hence, public policy bifurcated: political wisdom sought to sustain a state whose business consisted of
providing such essentials as law and order, national security, the
suppression of corruption, and the control of power, while the
quest for a shadowy "social justice" justified policymakers' efforts
to advance social equality. In recent times, rulers even find themselves being seduced by a whole new technology that purports to
reveal the secrets of public happiness. Let us return, however, to
Luther's interesting formula.

One version of the "law" from which we have been released is
certainly that of personal commitment, above all in the form of mar-
rying and creating families. Men and women do indeed often live
together, and sometimes they have children, but fewer get married.
It is as if all those bold "experiments in living" that surfaced in Bo-
hemian circles early in the twentieth century—trial marriages, for
example—have become for many the wisdom of the moment. In
this area, two well-known developments are striking. The first is
the liberation of sexual morality from the many conventions that
even individualist societies had retained. Sex is so powerful a drive
that all societies seek to harness it to desirable ends, such as stability and the creation of new generations. Contemporary Europe
has marginalized these conventions, and stability and demography
have suffered accordingly. Worse, perhaps, the common identification of morality itself with sexual mores has diffused a widespread
opinion that all moral principles are merely a matter of taste.

The decline of serious commitment is also, of course, an en-
feeblement of identity because the individualist of past times found
his reality in his identification with family, disinterested pursuits,
and the nation to which he belonged. Commitment has eroded as a
result of subterranean shifts in moral sentiment, but not from them

alone. For in our time, the West's marvelous technological inventiveness has tipped us over into a form of life in which convenience trumps integrity. Punctuality is less pressing when one can rearrange matters by a quick message on the cell phone. Sex need no longer threaten us with procreation. Letters to friends have often given way to email messages, which reflect the impulses of the fingers rather more than the considered judgment of the mind. I generalize, of course, and we must remember that any Western society contains layers of sentiments and practices, some dating from quite remote pasts. These layers are what make us so interesting. The respectability cherished a century ago, for example, has now become an object of mockery—but not to everybody.

Our time has thus been a graveyard of inherited conventions. These now defunct conventions have been the "law" from which, in Luther's formula, we were released. Can we discover, then, a "higher dutifulness" into which we have evolved? I think we can. It is, I suggest, an admiration of compassionate feelings and of the virtue of benevolence toward abstract classes of people. We believe in a duty to respond to others' unsatisfied needs. The remarkable thing about this moral concern is that it has also become the most powerful *political* project of our time. It is now a generalized claim on the resources of both individuals and states, and these resources themselves reduce, of course, to the resources of individuals (and corporations) because states have no resources of their own. That junction of moral approval and political conviction resembles the early modern belief that the unity of a state required agreement on a single religious confession. Here in the idea of global benevolence is a moral sentiment that has progressed far beyond the judgment of Europeans themselves and found its most authoritative statement in universal declarations of rights, but it takes many forms. Feats of athletic derring-do, for example, are now often performed as incentives for sponsors to contribute to some deserving cause. Those who want to "make a difference" are thinking of the needy, and those keen to "give something back to society" seek to put their money or their energies behind some form of redistribution. We all are born, as it were, debtors to society, and we ought to work on repaying that debt. Business corporations are admired if they exhibit "social responsibility" by devoting some of their profits to good causes rather than to the shareholders who have staked them.

A standard form of politicomoral reproach has long been to condemn those who "put profit before people." In the higher reaches of philosophy, normative thinkers follow John Rawls in identifying justice with "fairness," an ideal nonetheless interesting because the concept of fairness can hardly be translated into any other language. The grand ideal of social policy turns out to be to maximize the equal consumption of goods and services without weakening the regrettable need to give an incentive to the self-interested, the workers and the entrepreneurs who must keep prosperity ticking. In an ideal society, we all would be egalitarians rather than profit maximizers. A whole new social sector has grown up composed of nongovernmental organizations devoted to charitable aid, both in the society itself and in the more impoverished parts of the world. These organizations in turn have extensive links with the broad international drive toward global equalization of consumption, and states act as good global citizens in conforming to a great variety of international commitments to implement human rights and aid the victims of bad fortune. Another large element of this abstract benevolence consists in the equal distribution of social respect. Both governments and private corporations employ officials to discourage and often to punish a variety of unsound responses to women, homosexuals, ethnic immigrants, the disabled, and many other classes of persons.

An ethic of abstract benevolence is obviously in need of a correlate: To whom must one be benevolent? The condition that philosophers long considered as the problem of the poor has been elaborated into terms such as *deprived, underprivileged, the unfortunate*, and, more generally, *the oppressed*, but the key term today has come to be *vulnerability*. There is a case for regarding feminists as the pioneers of this new move: women were vulnerable in a variety of ways—to violence, oppression, glass ceilings, sexual harassment, and no doubt other evils yet to be formulated. The feminist slogan that "the personal is the political" came to mean that personal security for women could be achieved only by state intervention. Women thus sought to escape the uncertainties of family protection by moving into the legally determined protections of the state. Vulnerability turned out to be a useful category, and other groups in society were soon claiming recognition as vulnerable—ethnic newcomers, homosexuals, transsexuals, children, problem families, drug users, old people, those with learning difficulties, the disabled, and so on.

Vulnerability also turned out to have the useful property of multiplying vulnerable classes of people. Thus, girls were thought to be disadvantaged at school but rapidly came to excel at examinations, thereby creating a new class of the vulnerable in the form of poorly performing boys, especially if working class. Victims of burglary were, as victims, evidently vulnerable and were commonly offered counseling by the police. The real, society-transforming character of this evolution of moral sentiments, however, is revealed in the fact that the burglars themselves, especially if young, were also thought to have been "vulnerable." Society had failed them. It is remarkably difficult to escape classification as vulnerable.

THE PARADOXES OF CONTEMPORARY
MORAL SENTIMENT

That victimizers are themselves victims might well alert us that this new moral world is a tangle of contradictions. Collective benevolence as we have been considering it may well seem to announce a society far kinder and gentler than that of a couple of generations ago. Out goes hanging and flogging, in comes counseling and "rehab," as it were. Physical pain, execution, indigence, derision, and lack of respect are just a few of the painful experiences we have now abolished. Are we therefore nicer people? Alas, we are not. For why are all these vulnerable people so vulnerable? They are because society is dominated by racists, sexists, pedophiles, exploiters, bullies, and many others whose destructive passions can be tempered and suppressed only by the enlightened elite who manage the state. In other words, the recessive side of this explosion of compassion is an insistence on our fellow citizens' nastiness.

A further paradox seems to me even more striking. It arises from those hostile images of "capitalism" (also known as a free society) that have been a constant expression of European critical self-understanding. No matter how much Western states have exceeded all others in tolerance and prosperity, the dream of an ideal society goes on revitalizing the idea of how awful we are. Commercial society, as represented in this image, is composed of social atoms—man alienated from man. Capitalism is a rat race in which "greed is good" and each man's hand is at war against every other's. Yet the history of European states in the past few centuries has been virtually the opposite of this representation. These states have exhibited a social cohesion so remarkable that nothing has matched them. Perhaps the most dramatic instance of this cohesion occurred in 1914 when an outburst of patriotic feeling effortlessly mobilized Europeans in support of their national states. We may perhaps regret that it was the alarms of war that dramatized this togetherness, but the fact itself leaves for dead any idea that freedom divides people from each other. Far from falling apart in a crisis, each of these states exhibited a cohesion seldom seen previously. In fact, "capitalism" and community go well together, even if that community is not the abstract kind that Communist ideologists so fatally tried to institute.

The hostile image of Western societies is thus false. But what makes this paradoxical? The answer is to be found in the character of contemporary Western societies. They are marked, as we have seen, by a notable collapse of commitment. Men and women do of course follow their instincts and often set up house together; much less frequently they marry each other. A similar lack of commitment relates individuals to the states in which they live. On the contrary, many Westerners, in their detachment from their own "natural allegiances," often reject their governments' foreign policies, as some remarkable Americans did in believing after September 11, 2001, that "we had it coming." Here, then, is a posture of abstract virtue that congratulates itself on being a rational transcendence of supposedly "uncritical" allegiances.

One notable consequence of this Western collapse of commitment in personal areas is that increasing numbers of individuals live alone. They are sometimes called, I believe, "singletons." And the reason for this atomized condition is not the commercial force of capitalism, but the eroding effect of state welfare benefits on the material conditions that sustained family loyalty in earlier generations. The paradox is, then, that the capitalism of commercial societies exhibited a remarkable social cohesion and that the growth of the welfare state itself has caused a collapse into atomism. No less remarkable is that democratic politicians who "shower welfare" on their citizens are despised as bribing pygmies, whereas the politicians of earlier times (when governments supplied nothing of this sort) had no trouble in commanding popular respect.

Another point seldom recognized in the hostile images of European individualism is that the liberating character of Western freedom results from its recognition of the legitimacy both of autonomous individuals and of independent institutions, and the result has been a remarkable explosion of disinterested pursuits.

A "disinterested pursuit" springs not from self-interest, but from a detached concern with some activity done for its own sake. The classic example of this passion for the disinterested was the emergence of universities from the twelfth century onward, but the same disinterested passion appears in the development and institutionalization of sport and games in the West, in the charitable endeavors of the rich in creating everything from homes for the poor to the grand collections of art galleries and museums, in the efflorescence of hobbies and inventiveness that has marked our civilization, in the integrity of our legal arrangements, and in much else.

From this point of view, the most alarming feature of our times is that the very concept of "disinterestedness" has almost disappeared from the language. Our world wants a bang from every buck. The point of anything valuable is to exploit it for some contemporary benefit, a kind of greed for advantage that is remarkably destructive of the free and disinterested creativity that made European modernity the exemplar of what it is to be civilized. In a world of creeping utilitarianism, everything we do must have some practical point. Indeed, such is the practical bias in our thought that in asking the question, "Why did people do X?" the clinching answer always takes the form of revealing that some practical interest was being pursued. The result is that every time disinterestedness creates something great—from the rules of cricket to the cultivation of mathematics—states (and sometimes corporations) step in to try to control and direct it. "Interests" have a positive lust to control "the disinterested," but even worse is that they even deny its reality. As F. A. Hayek and his comrades responded to "the crisis of their time," so we must respond to the special circumstances of ours. And among the many candidates for being thus described—collectivism, out-of-control compassion, quantitative easing, and so much else—I would specify the destruction of disinterestedness as the heart of the matter.

What, in so complex a world, has become of Robinson Crusoe, the archetypal individualist whose whole life was an exploration of what could be made of nature and of his own sentiments? Crusoe figures still exist, of course, but our conception of society has changed radically. Eighteenth-century Europe consisted of states understood as associations of independent individuals. Twenty-first-century Europe can be recognized only as an association of vulnerable people in need of help and guidance. But in order to manage their own vulnerability, these people have been equipped with a set of unconditional entitlements or rights. In *Ancient Law*,[3]

Sir Henry Sumner Maine famously characterized the emergence of the modern world as a move away from status toward contract.[4] Contract is essentially conditional; status is not. An association of people equipped with rights or entitlements is therefore a society in which individuals are increasingly assigned a status. In welfare theory, entitlements are things owed to those who cannot help themselves—the disabled, for example. A status that brings an entitlement to assistance—to unconditional medical help, for example, or to support for unemployment—is a release from the ordinary obligations individuals have always had to manage on their own account. It is no doubt a benefit for rather passive people to be relieved of these strivings, but these individuals have no control over their substance. They are at the mercy of their governmental masters. And dependence beyond the protection all governments should provide is, of course, an erosion of freedom.

We therefore arrive at a last paradox: that the conditional and contractual relations associated with capitalism directly stimulate social association, whereas the unconditional status of entitlements does precisely the opposite. We are wary of others, including families, because they make claims on us. Needing others less, we spend our lives attending to our own feelings. It might seem as if this new welfarist world of entitlements is a triumph of individualism. People, relieved at last of some of the need for thrift and prudence by the provision of general welfare, can use their resources (or rather the pocket money left to them after taxes) in doing whatever they might choose. An explosion of free choice at last? Alas, it is not, because here we encounter the ultimate confusion in understanding individualism. In our contemporary world, choice certainly abounds, but it is a choice of the trivia, disconnected from the moral commitments of earlier times, the commitments that alone made individual choice the essence of freedom. Instead of responding to rational desires about the management of life, contemporary choice degenerates into a twitch responding to the hedonistic beckonings of impulse.

The glamour of individualism to outsiders came from its prosperity and its freedom from external controls—its autonomy. This
was, however, a surface sustained by subterranean virtues such
as courage, integrity, and commitment. A moral agent's autonomy now seems to be shaded by a relentless concern with mere
life, honor shaded by a willingness to fall in with guidance about
"lifestyle," and responsibility shaded by a disposition to interpret
human beings as creatures of social circumstance. Virtues, by re-
description, can turn into vices, and vices into virtues. People always vary greatly, and there is, of course, a great deal of ruin in a
nation. In the eighteenth century, however, there was also a power
of regeneration. Is there still?

NOTES

1. Michel de Montaigne, *Essays* (New York: Penguin, 1958), p. 119.

2. Adam Smith, *An Inquiry into the Nature and Causes of the Wealth of Nations*
[1776], edited by Kathryn Sutherland (Oxford: World's Classics, 1993), pp. 291–
293.

3. Maine, Sir Henry Sumner, *Ancient Law*, Ch. IX (London: John Murray,
1861).

4. The growth of the idea of entitlements is a large subject in itself. British
members of Parliament in recent times notoriously thought themselves "entitled"
to every kind of "expense" arising from their being in London. Several generations
back, however, members of Parliament were not paid at all. The point about rights
and entitlements is that they are essentially consumerist, and therefore integrity
and other essentials of the moral life disappear because rights constitute an
unconditionally beneficial rule. Similar problems with malefactors claiming
"I never broke the rules" have arisen in Canada, which had the interesting problem
of translating the term *entitlement* into French. The Gomery Commission came up
with *la culture du tout m'est du* or "the culture of everything is mine by right" or
"everything is owed to me." See Barry Cooper, "Political Order and the 'Culture
of Entitlement': Some Theoretical Reflections on the Gomery Commission."
In *Political Cultures and the Culture of Politics*, edited by Jurgen Gebhardt
(Heidelberg: Universiteitsverlag, 2010).

The Self-Interested Society

SEPTEMBER 2013

Societies are all imperfect, but self-interested societies
fare far better than any of their counterparts.

Here in the Galápagos, the abstraction that must haunt our imagin-
ings is evolution. But the term has two distinct meanings. Here is
one genealogy, from Hayek:

> Modern biology has borrowed the concept of evolution
> from studies of culture of older lineage. If this is in a sense
> well known, it is almost always forgotten. Of course the
> theory of cultural evolution [sometimes also described as
> psycho-social, super-organic, or exsomatic evolution] and
> the theory of biological evolution are hardly identical.

Here is another, from Matt Ridley:

> Thomas Hobbes was Charles Darwin's direct intellectual
> ancestor. Hobbes (1651) begat David Hume (1739), who be-

Kenneth Minogue, "The Self-Interested Society." This article is reprinted
with permission from the publisher of *New Criterion* 32 (September 2013): 4.
© 2014, *The New Criterion*, www.newcriterion.com.

   Editor's note: Kenneth Minogue (1930–2013), a valued friend and contributor
to *The New Criterion*, delivered a version of these remarks to the Mont Pelerin
Society in the Galápagos Islands in June. He died suddenly on his return trip.

gat Adam Smith (1776), who begat Thomas Robert Malthus (1798), who begat Charles Darwin (1859).

Evolution is clearly a powerful word. The problem is that neither of these meanings has much to do with Darwinian natural selection which, by contrast with these meanings, is a blind process in which random mutations constantly generate new versions of a species that deals more successfully with the environment than its fellows. My concern by contrast is with the emergence of our free civilization, which has no blind random processes in it, though it may well be that Adam Smith's "invisible hand" might be taken to function in the same way.

I am concerned with the evolution of that grand thing called a "free society"—specifically, the only society or civilization that has ever evolved into freedom: our own.

What I mean by this is that our society—namely modern Western Europe and its offshoots in the rest of the world—has evolved into a set of national states, each of which is an association of individualists, managing their own lives and pursuing their own individual projects. That might sound like a description of any kind of human life, so why am I suggesting that it is unique?

The contrast I want to make here is with every other society and civilization because all of them rest, at some level, on legitimation in terms of a comprehensive system of justice. Most such societies are of course largely agricultural, and in them each individual notionally occupies a social status valued according to its supposed contribution to the common good. Human beings living in these just societies live—in principle—the way all human beings ought to live: in castes, or under Sharia, or the Mandate of Heaven, or whatever the hierarchy of belief locally may be, down to and including small tribal groups.

We in Western Europe, however, have taken a different path in which individualists, often identified as town-dwellers or "bourgeoisie," associate together generally according to their own inclinations rather than in terms of some determinate social status designed to contribute to the good of the community. Individualists (in their very role as individualists) merely associate rather than form a community, though as subjects of a state they may participate in various communities built around specific interests or passions—clubs, religions, industrial enterprises, and so on. But this is incidental to the free lives they lead.

Those who live in just societies have clear functions, and up to a point enjoy the respect appropriate to such a function. Some of these functions are precisely defined: ruler, wife, warrior, priest, etc. But in all cases there will be a well-understood hierarchy governing social life, and its purpose is to preserve the basic aspiration of such comprehensively just societies—namely, social harmony. Thus the Forbidden City in Beijing had a Gate of Supreme Harmony leading to the Hall of Supreme Harmony, passing on to the Hall of Central Harmony and the Hall of Preserving Harmony, all of them clearly issuing from the idea of individual imperial authority.

Individualists in free societies, by contrast, merely have a duty to conform to the laws of their state, which ideally do not distinguish specific functions. In advancing this distinction, I am obviously perilously engaged in an abstract sociological sketch, one at a level comparable to David Riesman's famous distinction between people living in traditional and modern societies in *The Lonely Crowd*. In these terms, free individualists are notionally equal under the law, including the ruler himself or herself. But what is it, we may ask, that guides and motivates the lives of these free individualists? The common answer is: self-interest. And my central concern in this paper will be with making sense of this remarkable —and troublesome—term.

In an obvious sense, we all know what "self-interest" means. If a car comes careering towards me, I jump out of the way; it is the basic instinct of self-preservation, and hardly distinguishes an individualist from any other human being. More specifically, as self-interested, I prefer to get a higher rather than a lower wage for the same work. Again, I want my family to prosper and my children to do well at school. Obvious, in fact.

It should be clear that the meaning of self-interest must be understood as responding to the situation of individuals moving from a traditional to a modern society. In a traditional society, politics (to the extent that such a thing may be recognized amid absolutist justice) is not about interests but about ideals, and most notably about justice itself. People may be nice or nasty, selfish or generous, but the sphere of their actions is largely determined by the role or status they have. But as we move into an urbanized modern society, increasing numbers of individuals must find some niche or enterprise of their own within which to live. They must become, as it were, self-reliant so as not, if possible, to become a burden on others, and in order to respond to their own responsibilities. This virtue of self-reliance, more exactly than the idea of self-interest, recognizes the situation of the individualist as modernity spreads and people move from the countryside to the towns.

In spite of its necessary place in responding to modernity, there is a great deal of hostility towards the idea of self-interest. It is associated with ruthless self-promotion, taking no account of the good of others. It is sometimes thought to be at war with common decency, and even a form of exploitative attitudes to others. We sometimes think that La Rochefoucauld got it right in remarking, "We all have courage enough to bear the troubles of others," in addition to his many other cynical remarks. Or we may take our bearings from Gore Vidal: "It's not enough to succeed. Others must fail." Or even the fictional Gordon Gecko: "Greed is good." And at that point, self-interest has become quite explicitly identified with the vice of selfishness.

It is common ground, of course, that human beings are fallible and sinful creatures, much given to what Hobbes recognized as vainglory. Hobbes was particularly impressed by the pleasure humans take in thinking they are superior to others—being "foremost" as Hobbes put it. Hobbes thought he was talking of all men, and his account of human nature was certainly always true of prominent men and women, but it is plausible to think that Hobbes was particularly generalizing the individualists of his own time. Christianity of course emphasizes the place of foolish vanities in human lives. But there is nothing essentially individualistic about such human imperfections. They are universal. All human beings exhibit such weaknesses.

It is also noticeable, however, that free individualists are remarkably generous and public spirited, and not only because they belong to richer societies. They are generous in helping the poor all over the world, in responding to remote catastrophes, and in endowing museums and other cultural institutions. Individualists can also exhibit the most remarkable solidarity in helping each other in difficult situations. In spite of their supposedly isolating and selfish individualism, their capacity for spontaneous fruitful cooperation if a crisis occurs is striking. They have succeeded in creating societies in which the vulnerable are helped, and in which women may live on equal terms with men in ways hardly to be imagined in some "superior" just societies. The test of these judgments lies not in any "Eurocentric" vanity, but in the fact that millions from supposedly just and perfect societies will do almost anything to migrate into our vile, self-interested, capitalist world.

In spite of these facts, two remarkable beliefs have come to be widely held about free, Western societies.

The first is that human beings are naturally selfish creatures, and that they can only become virtuous by overcoming their natural self-partiality. This moral opinion descends from some versions of Christianity, was powerfully taken up by French moralists in the seventeenth century, contributed to satirical views of commerce in the early eighteenth century, was influentially refuted by Adam Smith, and was revived to plague us once more by the Marxists (and other ideologists) in the nineteenth century. But the individualist, in pursuing self-interest, is not, according to our critics, overcoming self-partiality.

The second and related view is that Western Civilization is technically prodigious but has basically failed to overcome prejudice, superstition (e.g. religion), bigotry, racism, imperialism, national selfishness, and other such evils from which only the wisdom of international organizations can save us. This curious form of civilizational self-hatred results not from judging that we are worse than others but from the belief that since we have more control over our nature, we ought to have been able to do better.

We have, then, a problem and a solution. The problem is how to give a more or less neutral account of the broad motive that animates our free societies, and the common solution is to say that it is "self-interest." But then we discover that the expression "self-interest" loses its neutrality, and thus cannot function without becoming pejorative. We might, I have suggested, replace self-interest with self-reliance, but that would be to identify free societies with a virtue. What to do? We must, I think, look again at the character of the free societies we inhabit.

How did our free society emerge, evolve, develop . . . get off the ground? The answer is that it has emerged from an immensely complex set of social and moral contingencies, and even to ask about its "causes" is hopelessly to simplify the remarkable thing that has emerged. Some signs of it may be found in the peoples to whom we look back with admiration—the Greeks and Romans, most notably, but also the Jews and, later, the various barbarian peoples who moved into the western Empire. The form that Greek philosophy took, and its flourishing from Thales to Aristotle and beyond, clearly became one of the central resources of our freedom. The Romans valued this feature of classical Greek culture, and passed it on to those working to turn the Christian revelation into a faith that could animate new ways of life. But there were many other elements of social life that adumbrated the possibility of free relations between individuals—for example the consultative practices of feudal monarchies that came to be generalized in England by Magna Carta. And the common account of our civilizational past, the story that takes us from the Greeks to the present over a period of several millennia, amounts to a sketch of how this new thing emerged.

The obvious move would be to consider the "causes" of this new thing, but "cause" is too crude an idea for this task. Instead, we must imagine a vast range of face-to-face encounters between Europeans, over a long period under many varied circumstances, changes of demeanor which sometimes evolved into doctrines or explicit practices—such as chivalry—but which were more commonly slight variations in manners and moral assumptions, feeding slowly into institutional practices (in universities as they emerged, for example) that, towards the end of what we call "the Middle Ages" began to make it clear that something quite new was coming into existence. For institutional change emerges spontaneously from personal responses.

The growth of modern natural science is one example of how a tradition—in this case, of philosophical questioning—became the route into a quite new intellectual adventure as it came to involve enterprising thinkers in countries ranging from Poland to France and Britain. But perhaps the most notable verbal sign of something new happening was the rising currency, from the seventeenth century onwards, of words hyphenated with "self-"—as in my central example of "self-interest." In this idiom, human experience was being bifurcated into two elements—a subjective and an objective part—and it was registered in language by the recognition of "self," often as a kind of managing agent in how human beings respond to the world.

My concern is with "self-interest," but there is an endless sequence of such hyphenated terms emerging from the seventeenth century onward. Such terms might be used by individuals explaining themselves, or they might be used analytically, or critically, by outsiders. "Self-expression" might be a good thing, but being "self-opinionated" was generally not. In moral discourse, the distinction between "self" and "others" came to be prominent, and approval was likely to focus on how any particular "self" responded to "others." In traditional societies, a focus on "others" obviously had been possible, but in that context the "others" were more commonly specified in terms of their relative social status. They were less likely to be merely abstract "others." Thinking in these terms led many to the cynical view that underneath most, indeed perhaps all, social life would be found a destructive selfishness. A common thought was that the men of this period were living through a period of decline.

The real significance of the "self-interest" formula is that it reveals to us some elements of the basic conflict in our society between freedom on the one hand and justice on the other. Here is an expression that might merely mean a rational response to circumstances, or could signify the moral fault of selfishness (and it was often assumed to do just that), but there can be little doubt that its usage has generally been pejorative. It thus constitutes the basic premise that slides to, rather than actually entails, the idea that a free society is essentially unjust because the strong, in pursuing their interests, oppress the vulnerable, and hence that justice requires that the state should take steps to restore, by political action, the fairness that has been lost in the very operation of the economic process. The "strong" in these cases might turn out to be the rich, or the enterprising, or those who have better "social capital" because of more fortunate family life, or such further variations of the idea of "privilege" as may respond to the discovery of relative (rather than merely absolute) deprivation. On such a view, a free market economy is essentially unfair because the basic drive animating it has no moral content. Individualists in pursuit of self-interest are merely seeking benefits for themselves. And yet, in the real world, morally valuable and cooperative behavior is evidently a feature of our modern societies. The question thus becomes: How might we describe such virtue in our real world, and how account for it?

The answer, of course, has generally been in terms of the virtue of altruism or benevolence, which, as distinct from self-interest, is recognized as the model of goodness when it occurs between "self" and "others." It is this contrast that is at the heart of a good deal of moral theorizing. Our world is full of benevolent people performing prodigies in order to raise money for charities. This is one way of showing that they are not spending their lives merely pursuing their own interests. Such activities are clearly admirable. But as exhibitions of virtuous conduct, they raise problems.

The first problem is that the virtue of benevolence can attach itself, like a parasite, merely to the having of good intentions. The crimes of communist regimes often avoided censure by virtue of the supposed good intentions of those committing them. Again, people lacking integrity (in, for example, exploiting claims for expenses) commonly defend themselves by the claim that they had broken no rules. Further, the term "interest," even in the moral context of "self-interest," invokes politics, understood as an arena in which interests conflict with each other. Hence at its least sophisticated, one form of self-ascribed good intentions may be the mere fact of supporting welfarist political policies. Such a view, not uncommon in leftish parties, takes the illusion of costless good intentions to its limit.

And this leads us to a second defect of this version of the moral life: That altruism and benevolence, as the essence of goodness, cast into the shade such more elusive and subtle virtues as integrity and courage. One notable collapse of integrity consists in the happy belief that the costs of one's policies will be borne by others, and particularly in politics, by the more heavily taxed rich. Just such a belief is a popular recourse in the more demagogic versions of current politics. Such a view corresponds precisely to the corruption that Greek philosophers diagnosed in democracy as a political system, understanding it as an instrument by which the poor might plunder the rich.

Even the device of off-loading the costs of one's public altruism on the taxable rich, however, is merely a political solution to the problem, and what politics gives, politics can also take away. The ideal solution to such a problem is—an ideal! The public altruism of welfare must be entrenched in the ideals of justice and of rights. A real solution to the conflict between self and others must transcend this distinction itself, for in a real community, cooperation transcends conflicts of interest between individuals. Such, I think, is the logic behind our admiration for "social justice," however difficult we may find it to define. And it seems to me that in the concept of justice, in its contrast with self-interest, we have one clue to the destiny of our free society: That we shall never quite be free of the illusion that our psychological foundation in self-interest is the imperfection, the vice, that stands in the way of the social and human perfections that would create a better world.

And it is in terms of this move to social justice that we leave our free societies behind and find ourselves entertaining a comprehensive system of justice understood as the right and fair and just outcome of economic enterprise. Our Western understanding of merely civil justice in a free society cannot lead to any precise conception of a right order of things (as entertained in other civilizations), because no free process can be relied upon to guarantee any particular outcome. It is further important that no particular outcome, if it did occur, could then be protected against later change. Freedom is thus incompatible with any version of comprehensive justice.

The point is that justice in our Western understanding is thought to be (in principle) a freely accepted rule that mitigates some problem arising from a pre-political condition, often theorized as a "state of nature." This understanding of civil law in no way depends on whether we take the story of the state of nature seriously. What is fundamentally involved is a recognition that justice in a free society comes from the needs of the ruled, and that it consists in a process of rules that could not generate any particular desired outcome. Historically generated rules of law based upon this basically contractual order of social relationships were early professionalized in Europe and embedded in our governing practices as a limitation upon the caprice of executive action.

What we may call "the moral life" as it exists among Western Europeans emerges directly from these conditions. Practical moral judgments result from asking, in a moral sense, "what ought I to do in this situation?" and in most societies, the appropriate answer is given by religion, or by custom, or by the realities of situational power.

Both religion and custom will also be found in European states, of course, but the moral life as we experience it may be distinguished from these concerns. It consists in judgments balancing reasons about the consequences of alternative actions for the interests of both the actor and those his act will affect. It is, in principle, no less independent of custom and religion than the Socratic model of living the right kind of life which our moral practices (very distantly) echo. Custom and religion may become influences, but only as elements in a process of moral calculation. That is one element of what is individualistic about such a moral practice, and it may affect both actions that come within the ambit either of the distinction between good and evil or of right and wrong. An important element in the moral life as Max Weber analyzed it resulted from the Protestant judgment that a holy life could be lived in the world, rather than requiring immersion in a specialized religious institution. And as the modern world developed, the aristocratic concern with honor became generalized into various criteria of identity such as conscience and reputation. In other words, the competitive character of every other feature of free modern societies became a feature more in our moral life than in the economy. The outcome has been that in this area, as in most others, Europeans found themselves living within a world of conflicting understandings about what ought to be done. And it was precisely in embracing this and other forms of conflict that Europeans recognized themselves as free.

Some people take the view that we in the West are fortunate to enjoy freedom, because it is a universal human aspiration that has been commonly frustrated in most societies. This is one of the more pernicious illusions we entertain about human kind. Most people have never lived in free societies, nor exhibited any desire or capacity for freedom. Totalitarian movements reveal even the danger that many who have enjoyed freedom can be happy to abandon it in the name of some passionate cause. The illusion that everyone wants to be free means only, perhaps, that people don't much like being frustrated, but that is quite different from the self-discipline involved in an association of individualists managing their own lives. This illusion has been happily indulged by many commentators on the "Arab Spring" of recent times, in which the instability of authoritarian regimes might suggest a whiff of libertarian feeling. What most people seem to want, however, is to know exactly where they stand and to be secure in their understanding of their situation.

Rules and processes are risky because they will produce unexpected and sometimes unwelcome outcomes, and it is this contrast which makes freedom constantly vulnerable to those who try to seduce us with dreams of perfection. My argument has been that even perfectly valid ways of explaining ourselves can easily slide into pejorative accounts of freedom. When that happens, it can seem obvious that governments should not merely regulate the economy (as they must as part of the rule of law in modern societies) but that they should also intervene to manage its outcomes by the use of subsidy redistribution and welfarism. These policies are suggested by the slide from a descriptive account of human psychology (the pursuit of self-interest) to a corrupt identification of the description with the vice of selfishness, ruthlessness, greed, and similar evils. The reality of pursuing self-interest in a free modern society is no doubt better described by invoking some such virtue as self-reliance, but that is the demand which a free society makes on everyone, and it is that demand which is often found burdensome by those who find security in a structure of welfare from which they may benefit.

Much of this corruption may be regarded as political sentimentalism. I am not, of course, suggesting that individuals do not suffer in many ways from the ups and downs of economies and the many other conditions that invoke the concept of vulnerability. But politics can, of course, only respond to abstract classes of suffering—such as that of unemployed people, or drug addicts, or pregnant teenagers. The real situation of individuals in these classes is immensely variable. In political discussion it can only be grasped in terms of some image or archetype. Democratic politics extensively consists of the conversion of abstract classes of vulnerability or hardship into images of a persuasive kind. And politically, there is no doubt which way expenditure on these imaged policies will go. It rises relentlessly upwards. The classes of the vulnerable multiply, and the demands on the public purse rise in order to deal with problems that in earlier generations were accommodated within the exigencies of family life.

In politics, every policy has some advantages and also some disadvantages. But notable about the disadvantages of this range of welfarist reforms is that they have led most rich Western states into a condition of chronic bankruptcy. The crisis of the early twenty-first century is no doubt attributable to bankers and to other public actors, but unmistakably central to the problem is a level of both personal and public debt, which is unsustainable, and will get worse for more than demographic reasons. And when governments become indebted, they have virtually no solutions to the problem except to deceive their populations with inflation and other monetary forms of smoke and mirrors.

It is not merely governments that act corruptly. It is also the democratic voter. As we have seen, the demos is also corrupted. A great deal of political sentimentalism floats on the illusion that rising public expenditure would not affect most of the population because the rich can be taxed more heavily. Much indignation is often expended about large firms that "avoid" taxation, as if taxation were a form of charity one should offer to governments, rather than known rates to be paid by specific and well-defined classes of taxpayer. The problem is in part that the rules of taxation have become so complicated that skilled professionals are needed to reveal what must be paid and what may be kept. Politicians however are keen to talk of the rich "paying their share" of taxation; it is a cry advanced under the popular rubric of "fairness." It is only as it dawns upon voters that the costs of welfare cannot forever be loaded onto the rich without serious economic consequences that public opinion turns against welfare spending.

My argument is, then, that societies are necessarily imperfect, and making them perfect is not an option for creatures such as humans. We can, however—up to a point—choose where imperfection may least harmfully find an outlet in our complicated societies. And in making this judgment, we need to remember the practice of freedom on which our wealth seems to have depended. Solutions that reduce our freedom put modernity itself at risk.

The experience of twentieth-century politics presents us with an obvious alternative. We can accept the inequalities of economic life as necessary imperfections, or we may try to correct them by taking decisive political action, which means greatly expanding the power of states so that they may use their power to make economic outcomes more just. It will hardly be news that expanding the power of states has seldom been anything but a risky option. In the twentieth century, states taking over the economy generated totalitarianism. Merely to refer to the body count of those bold experiments is enough to rule that option out of contention. Here today, we are well into the twenty-first century, with a history of increasing welfarist policies long established, and they have led us to unsustainable levels of debt.

The unavoidable conclusion seems to me to be that letting economies rip, however much we may disapprove of the consequences, is much the better option. For one thing, it leaves open the possibility that the more vigorous members of society will take some action themselves to mitigate, at least in part, the sufferings of those genuinely in need of help. The balance in our tradition between the rules we must respect because they are backed by the authority of law, and the free choice in the other elements of our life is one that free agents rightly will not wish to see disturbed.

It seems to me that our preoccupation with the defects of our civilization is a standing temptation, and a dangerous one, to have recourse to civil authority in order to deal with what we may be persuaded to understand as social imperfections. And that preoccupation with our imperfections is most commonly grounded in the corrupt sense of explaining freedom in terms of self-interest. To recap, such an assumption about the motivation of moderns invokes the moral criterion of justice or fairness as condemning many of the consequences of our economic life (in terms of the supposed distribution of benefits). Such a view in turn generates a succession of vulnerable classes of people each with claims on the state for redress. Welfare programs responding to this process have no determinate end in sight. There is no viable conception of a society without vulnerable classes demanding special treatment as victims of one or other kind of injustice or unfairness. We begin to conceive of modern societies as associations of incompetents and cripples, which is absurd. The human condition is not like that. We entertain many foolish ideas, and no doubt will continue to do so. But this is a piece of nonsense that we can no longer afford.

ACKNOWLEDGMENTS

I am grateful to Roger Kimball for encouraging this project. I owe special thanks to Noonie Minogue, who approved the project at the outset and provided essential bibliographical resources, to Jackson Porreca, who undertook initial bibliographical searches, and to Jessica Pauls, who assisted in research and prepared the manuscript.

BIBLIOGRAPHY

.

BOOKS

The Liberal Mind (New York: Vintage Books, 1963), (Indianapolis: Liberty Fund, 2001).

Nationalism (New York: Basic Books, 1967), (London: Penguin, 1970).

The Concept of a University (Berkeley: University of California Press, 1973), (Piscataway, NJ: Transaction Publishers, 2004).

Contemporary Political Philosophers, edited by Kenneth Minogue and Anthony de Crespigny (New York: Dodd, Mead, 1975).

Thatcherism: Personality and Politics (Basingstoke: Palgrave Macmillan, 1987).

The Egalitarian Conceit: False and True Equalities (London: Centre for Policy Studies, 1989).

Does Socialism Mean Never Having to Say You're Sorry? (London: Adam Smith Institute, 1990).

Politics: A Very Short Introduction (Oxford: Oxford University Press, 1995, 2000).

Conservative Realism: New Essays in Conservatism (New York: HarperCollins, 1996).

The Silencing of Society: True Cost of the Lust for News (London: Social Affairs Unit, 1997).

Democracy and the Welfare State (St. Leonards, NSW: Centre for Independent Studies, 1997).

Waitangi: Morality and Reality (Willington: New Zealand Business Roundtable, 1998).

Civil Society and David Blunkett: Lawyers vs Politicians (London: Civitas, Institute for the Study of Civil Society, 2002).

Alien Powers: The Pure Theory of Ideology (New Brunswick, NJ: Transaction

Publishers, 2007), (Wilmington, DE: Intercollegiate Studies Institute, 2008).

The Servile Mind: How Democracy Erodes the Moral Life (New York: Encounter Books, 2010).

BOOK CHAPTERS

"Thomas Hobbes and the Philosophy of Absolutism," in *The New Thinkers Library of Political Ideas*, ed. David Thomson (London: Watts, 1966).

"Conservatism," in *The Encyclopedia of Philosophy*, ed. Paul Edwards (New York: Macmillan, 1967).

"Revolution, Tradition and Political Continuity," in *Politics and Experience: Essays Presented to Professor Michael Oakeshott on the Occasion of His Retirement* (Cambridge: Cambridge University Press, 1968).

"Hobbes and the Just Man," in *Hobbes-Forschungen*, ed. Reinhart Koselleck and Roman Schnur (Berlin: Duncker and Humblot, 1969).

"Che Guevara," in *The New Left: Six Critical Essays*, ed. Maurice Cranston (London: Bodley Head, 1970).

"Theatricality and Politics: Machiavelli's Concept of *Fantasia*," in *The Morality of Politics*, ed. Bhikhu Parekh (London: Allen and Unwin, 1972).

"An Introduction" to *Leviathan*, Thomas Hobbes (London: JM Dent, 1973).

"Universities: What They Are and the Many Ways They Are Currently Misunderstood," in *Purposes in Education* (London: Institute for Cultural Research, 1974), 14–29.

"Michael Oakeshott: The Boundless Ocean of Politics," in *Contemporary Political Philosophers*, ed. Antony De Crespigny (London: Methuen, 1976).

"Nationalism and the Patriotism of City-States," in *Nationalist Movements*, ed. Anthony D. Smith (London: Macmillan, 1976).

"Natural Rights, Ideology and the Game of Life," in *Ideas and Ideologies: Human Rights*, ed. Eugene Kamenka (London: E. Arnold, 1978).

"On Hyperactivism in Modern British Politics," in *Conservative Essays*, ed. Maurice Cowling (London: Cassell, 1978).

"Social Contract and Social Breakdown," in *Democracy, Consensus and Social Contract*, ed. Pierre Birnbaum, Sage Modern Political Series vol. 2 (London: Sage, 1978).

"The Concept of Property and Its Contemporary Significance," in *Nomos* XXII (New York: NYU Press, 1980).

"Identifying Ideology," in *Ideology and Politics*, ed. Maurice Cranston and Peter Mair (Alphen aan den Rijn, Netherlands: Sijthoff, 1980).

"The Thatcher Experiment," in *The New Liberalism: The Future of Non-Collectivist Institutions in Europe and the US* (Symposium) (Centre for Political Research and Information, Athens, 1981), 99–119.

"The Place of Metaphor in the Construction of Political Reality," in *Language and Politics*, ed. Maurice Cranston and Peter Mair (Brussels: Bruyland, 1982).

"What If Karl Marx Had Drowned in a Cross-Channel Ferry Accident" [1847], in *What If? Explorations in Social-Science Fiction*, ed. Nelson Polsby (Lexington, MA: Lewis Publishing, 1982).

"Bacon and Locke: Or Ideology as Mental Hygiene," in *Ideology, Philosophy and Politics*, ed. Anthony Parel and Frederick C. Copleston (Waterloo, ON: Calgary Institute for the Humanities, 1983).

"Freedom as a Skill," in *Of Liberty*, Supplement to "Philosophy," ed. A. Phillips Griffiths, Royal Institute of Philosophy Lecture Series 15 (Cambridge: Cambridge University Press, 1983).

"The Conditions of Freedom and the Condition of Freedom," in *The Prospects of Liberalism*, ed. Timothy Fuller, Colorado College Studies no. 20 (Colorado Springs: Colorado College, 1984).

"A Realist View of the Welfare State," in *L'etat Providence: The Welfare State*, ed. François Ewald (Paris: B. Grasset, 1986).

"Treason and the Early Modern State: Scenes from a Mésalliance," in *Die Rolle der Juristen bei der Entstehung des modernen Staates*, ed. Roman Schnur (Berlin: Duncker and Humblot, 1986).

"What Is Wrong with Rights," in *Public Law and Politics*, ed. Carol Harlow (London: Sweet and Maxwell, 1986).

"An Introduction: The Context of Thatcherism," in *Thatcherism: Personality and Politics*, ed. Kenneth R. Minogue and Michael Biddiss (Basingstoke: Macmillan, 1987).

"Loquocentricity and Democracy: The Communicative Theory of Modern Civil Unity," in *Political Discourse: Explorations in Indian and Western Political Thought*, ed. Bhikhu Parekh and Thomas Pantham (London: Sage, 1987).

"Loyalty, Liberalism and the State," in *Lives, Liberties and the Public Good: New Essays in Political Theory*, ed. George Beaver and Frederick Rosen (Basingstoke: Macmillan, 1987).

"The Emergence of the New Right," in *Thatcherism* by Robert Skidelsky (Oxford: Basil Blackwell, 1988).

"On Market Economies," in *Thatcherism* by Robert Skidelsky (Oxford: Basil Blackwell, 1988).

"Theorising Liberalism and Liberalising Theory," in *Traditions of Liberalism: Essays on John Locke, Adam Smith, and John Stuart Mill*, ed. Knud Haakonssen (St. Leonards, NSW: Centre for Independent Studies, 1988).

"Nietzsche and the Ideological Project," in *The Structure of Modern Ideology: Critical Perspectives on Social and Political Theory*, ed. Nöel O'Sullivan (Aldershot: E. Elgar, 1989).

"The Concept of Policy in the Modern State," in *Philosophy of Social Choice*, ed. Piotr Ploszajski (Warsaw: IFiS, 1990).

"Equality: A Response," in *Philosophy and Politics*, ed. G.M.K. Hunt (Cambridge: Cambridge University Press, 1990).

"The History of the Idea of Human Rights," in *The Human Rights Reader*, ed. Walter Laqeur and Barry Rubin (New York: Plume, 1990).

"Locke, Kant and the Foundations of Liberalism," in *John Locke und Immanual Kant Historische Rezeption und gegenwärtige Relevanz*, ed. Martyn Thompson (Berlin: Duncker and Humblot, 1991).

"Does the Social Gospel Involve the Collapse of Christianity?" in *Religion: Contemporary Issues*, The All Souls Seminars in the Sociology of Religion, ed. Bryan R. Wilson (London: Bellew, 1992).

"Europe: Limits to Integration," in *Hubris: The Tempting of Modern Conservatives*, ed. Digby C. Anderson and Gerald Frost (London: Centre for Policy Studies, 1992).

"Transcending the European State," in *Reshaping Europe in the Twenty-first Century*, ed. Patrick Robinson (Basingstoke: Macmillan in association with Bruges Group, 1992).

"Ideal Communities and the Problem of Moral Identity," in *Democratic Community*, ed. John W. Chapman and Ian Shapiro, *Nomos XXXV* (New York: NYU Press, 1993).

"Modes and Modesty" and "History of Political Thought Seminar," in *The Achievement of Michael Oakeshott*, ed. Jesse Norman (London: Duckworth, 1993).

"Olympianism and the Denigration of Nationality," in *The Worth of Nations: The Boston, Melbourne, Oxford Conversations on Culture and Society*, by Bernard Levin, ed. Claudio Véliz (Boston: Boston University, The University Professors, 1993).

"Identity, Self and Nation," in *Integration and Fragmentation: The Paradox of the Late Twentieth Century*, ed. Institute of Inter-Governmental Relations (Kingston, ON: Queens University, 1994).

"Ideology and the Collapse after Communism," in *The End of "Isms"? Reflections on the Fate of Ideological Politics after Communism's Collapse*, ed. Alexander Shtromas (Oxford: Blackwell, 1994), 5–21.

"Nationalism, Nationality and the European Community," in *Politisches Denken Jahrbuch* (1994).

"The End of Authority and Formality: And Their Replacement by Intrusive Regulation," in *This Will Hurt: The Restoration of Virtue in Civic Order*, ed. Digby Anderson (London: The Social Affairs Unit, A National Review Book, 1995).

"The Positive Side of Freedom," in *LSE on Freedom*, ed. Eileen Barker (London: LSE Books, 1995).

"Two Concepts of Citizenship," in *Citizenship East and West* (Geneva: Graduate Institute of International Studies, 1995).

"Ernest Gellner and the Dangers of Theorising Nationalism," in *The Social Philosophy of Ernest Gellner* by John Hall and Ian Jarvie (Leiden: Brill, 1996).

"Introduction" and "Three Conservative Realists," in *Conservative Realism*, ed. Kenneth Minogue, Centre for Policy Studies (New York: HarperCollins, 1996).

"Machiavelli and the Duck-Rabbit Problem of Political Perception," in *LSE on Social Science: A Centenary Anthology*, ed. Helen Sasson and Derek Diamond (New Brunswick, NJ: Transaction Publishers, 1996).

"National Self-Hatred and EC," in *The Eurosceptical Reader*, ed. Martin Holmes (Basingstoke: Macmillan, 1996).

"Celebrity and Style: The Twin Idols of Magazine Woman," in *The British Woman Today*, ed. Digby Anderson and Michael Mosbacher (London: Social Affairs Unit, 1997).

"Social Justice in Theory and Practice," in *Social Justice from Hume to Walzer* (New York: Routledge, 1998).

"Theory of the Welfare State: An Exposition," in *Political Science Annual* (Focus on Political Theory), ed. S. Mukherjee, S. Ramaswamy, and M.M. Sankhdher (1998–1999).

"Discussion: Social Implications of a Global Economy," in *Cultures in the Twenty-first Century: Conflicts and Convergences*, a selection of papers presented at a symposium celebrating the 125th anniversary of Colorado College, ed. Timothy Fuller, Colorado College Studies no. 32 (Colorado Springs: Colorado College, 1999), 71–83.

"Freedom and Its Many Facets," in *The Risk of Freedom: Individual Liberty in the Modern World* (London: Institute of United States Studies, University of London, 1999).

"The Collapse of the Academic in Britain," in *Buckingham at 25: Freeing the Universities from State Control*, ed. James Tooley (London: Institute of Economic Affairs, 2001).

"Oakeshott and Political Science," in *Annual Review of Political Science*, vol. 7 (2004).

"Conservatism in a Rationalist Age," in *Ronald Reagand A Wyzwania Epoki*, ed. Andrzej Bryk and Andrzej Kapiszewski (Krakow: Krakowska Szkoła Wyższa im. Andrzeja Frycza Modrzewskiego, 2005).

"Multiculturalism, A Dictatorship of Virtue," introduction to *The Poverty of Multiculturalism* by Patrick West (London: Civitas, 2005).

"Oakeshott's Rationalism Revisited," in *The Intellectual Legacy of Michael Oakeshott*, ed. Corey Abel and Timothy Fuller (Exeter, UK: Imprint Academic, 2005).

"Universities as Ideological Training Institutions," in *Can the Prizes Still Glitter? The Future of British Universities in a Changing World*, ed. Hugo De Burgh et al. (Buckingham: University of Buckingham Press, 2007).

"Social Justice and the Metaphor of Gaps," in *The United States, the European Union and Modernity*, ed. Andzej Bryk, Krakowskie Studia Międzynarodowe 5 (Krakow: Księgarnia Akademicka, 2008).

Introduction to *The Servile State* by John Anderson (St. Leonards, NSW: Centre for Independent Studies, 2009).

"Liberalism, Conservatism and Oakeshott in Cowling's Account of Public Doctrine," in *The Philosophy, Politics and Religion of British Democracy: Maurice Cowling and Conservatism*, ed. Robert Crowcroft, SJD Green, and Richard Whiting (London: IBTauris, 2010).

"Are Ideologies Political?" in *Politics and Ideology*, the Engelsberg Seminar (2011).

ARTICLES, REVIEWS, AND PAPERS

American Outlook

"Transnational Interest," *American Outlook* (Spring 2000).

"Moral Evolution and the Future of the Anglosphere: The Decline of Traditional, Informal Systems of Restraint and the Rise of Political Correctness Suggest a New Moral Order That Bodes Ill for Western Civilization," *American Outlook* (March 2001).

American Scholar

"A Fable of Time and Class," *American Scholar* (Spring 1961).

"How to Make Trends and Influence People," *American Scholar* (Summer 1961).

"The Modern Liberal's Casebook," *American Scholar* (Summer 1962).

"On the Fashionable Idea of National Guilt," *American Scholar* (Autumn 1970).

American Spectator

Review of *History and the Idea of Progress*, by Robert Nisbett, *American Spectator* (August 1980).

Review of *On History and Other Essays* by Michael Oakeshott, *American Spectator* (September 1983).

Review of *Finest Hour: Winston Churchill 1939–1941* by Martin Gilbert, *American Spectator* (April 1984).

Comment in *American Spectator* (April 1985).

Review of "In Pursuit of Happiness and Good Government" by Charles Murray, *American Spectator* (February 1989).

"A Letter-Perfect Jean-Jacques Rousseau," review of *The Solitary Self: Jean-Jacques Rousseau in Exile and Adversity* by Maurice Cranston, *American Spectator* (June 1997): 73–74.

"Modernizing the Brits: Letter from London," *American Spectator* (January 1999).

Cambridge Review

"Habermas on Legitimation," *Cambridge Review* (December 1979).

"Michael Oakeshott and the History of Political Thought Seminar: Symposium," *Cambridge Review* (October 1991).

Claremont Review of Books

"The Iron Lady," review of *"There Is No Alternative": Why Margaret Thatcher Matters* by Claire Berlinski, *Claremont Review of Books* 9, no. 2 (Spring 2009).

"Opiate of the Intellectuals," review of *Why Marx Was Right* by Terry Eagleton and *How to Change the World: Reflections on Marx and Marxism* by Eric Hobsbawm, *Claremont Review of Books* 12, no. 2 (Spring 2012).

Encounter

"Two Hisses for Democracy: Politics and Theory," *Encounter* (December 1973): 61.

"Ideas, on the Stage and Off: From Rousseau to Marx," review of *Economic Materialism and Social Moralism* by Shirley M. Gruner, *Encounter* (April 1974).

"Doctor Fromm's Attempt at a Cure," *Encounter* (July 1974).
"Defending the Single Realm: On Ernest Gellner," a review of *Cause and Meaning in the Social Sciences: Contemporary Thought and Politics, the Devil in Modern Philosophy* by Ernest Gellner, *Encounter* (October 1974).
"Dr Spock Thinks Again," *Encounter* (July 1975).
"The Guru: Carlos Castaneda," *Encounter* (August 1976).
"On the Illusions of Party Participation and Social Contracts," *Encounter* (August 1977).
"Galbraith's Wit and Wisdom," response to *The Age of Uncertainty* by John Kenneth Galbraith, *Encounter* (December 1977).
"Galbraith on Minogue and Vice Versa," *Encounter* (April 1978).
"Can One Teach 'Political Literacy,'" *Encounter* (June 1979).
"The Prison Cell of Political Theory," review of "Captive Mind" by John Dunne, *Encounter* (September 1979).
"Between Rhetoric and Fantasy," *Encounter* (December 1980).
Discussion [About the Brant Report], *Encounter* (April 1981): 78.
Discussion: "Towards a New Disorder," *Encounter* (October 1981).
"How Critical Is the 'Crisis' in Liberalism?" *Encounter* (June 1984).
"The Hucksters of Happiness: From Ideas to Slogans," review of *Politics and the Pursuit of Happiness* by Ghita Ionescu, *Encounter* (April 1985).
"Marx and Vico," *Encounter* (March 1986).
"The Idea of Liberty and the Dream of Liberation: Two Themes in the Western Political Tradition," *Encounter* (July/August 1987).
"The Preoccupation with Equality: Drabble's Rabble," review of *A Case for Equality* by Margaret Drabble, *Encounter* (November 1988).
"Practitioner of Politics: The Younger Harold," *Encounter* (April 1989).
"Societies Collapse, Faiths Linger On: Christians in Communists in Confusion," *Encounter* (March 1990).

Government and Opposition

"Less Darkness at Noon," review of *Key Concepts in Political Science: Totalitarianism* by Leonard Schapiro, *Government and Opposition* 8, no. 1 (1973).
"Marx and the Unpredictability of Human Folly," review of *Marx and the Disillusionment of Marxism* by Walter L. Adamson, *Government and Opposition* 21, no. 1 (1986).
"Loquocentric Society and Its Critics: The Case of Habermas," *Government and Opposition* 21, no. 3 (1986): 338–361.
"Political Science and the Gross Intellectual Product," *Government and Opposition* 21, no. 4 (1986): 396–405.
"Journalism and the Public Mind," *Government and Opposition* 24, no. 4 (1989).
"Hobsbawmian Mythology," review of *Nations and Nationalism Since 1780: Programme, Myth, Reality* by Eric Hobsbawm, *Government and Opposition* 26, no. 3 (Summer 1991).
"Language and Domination in Some Latter Day Marxists," review of *Language*

and Symbolic Power by Pierre Bourdieu, *Government and Opposition* 27, no. 3 (Summer 1992).

"Two Crusaders in a Political Landscape," review of *A Conservative Revolution? The Thatcher-Reagan Decade in Perspective*, ed. Andrew Adonis and Tim Hames, *Government and Opposition* 29, no. 4 (1994).

"Politics and Morality in the Thought of Karl Popper," *Government and Opposition* 30, no. 1 (Winter 1995).

"Hard Choices," review of *The New Reckoning: Capitalism, States and Citizens* by David Marquand, *Government and Opposition* 33, no. 2 (Spring 1998).

"Religion and Politics," review of *Does Christianity Cause War?* by David Martin, *Government and Opposition* 33, no. 4 (Autumn 1998).

"Casting Bread Upon the Waters," review of *Classical Liberalism and International Economic Order: Studies in Theory and Intellectual History* by Razeen Sally, *Government and Opposition* 34, no. 2 (Spring 1999).

"A Sceptical View of Public Management," review of Christopher Hood's *The Art of the State: Culture, Rhetoric and Public Management* , *Government and Opposition* 34, no. 3 (1999).

"Cowling on Morality and Religion," review of *Religion and Public Doctrine in Modern England*, vol. 3 by Maurice Cowlings, *Government and Opposition* 37, no. 1 (Winter 2002).

National Interest

"Classy but Shaky," review of *The End of History and the Last Man* by Francis Fukuyama, *National Interest* 26 (Winter 1991).

"Uneasy Triumph," *National Interest* 30 (Winter 1992).

"Necessary Imperfections," review of *Conditions of Liberty* by Ernest Gellmer, *National Interest* 38 (Winter 1994).

"The Appeal of Decline," review of *The Idea of Decline in Western History* by Arthur Herman, *National Interest* (Summer 1997).

"ID Control: As Quickly As Social Restraints Are Toppled, Governments Erect New Ones in the Form of Regulations," *National Interest* (November 1997).

"Totalitarianism: Have We Seen the Last of It?" *National Interest* 57 (Fall 1999).

"The Vanity of Reason," review of *The Crisis of Reason: European Thought* by J.W. Burrow and *The Cunning of Unreason: Making Sense of Politics* by John Dunn, *National Interest* (Winter 2000/2001).

"Religion, Reason and Conflict in the 21st Century," review of *The Next Christendom: The Coming of Global Christianity* by Philip Jenkins, *National Interest* (Summer 2003).

National Review

"A Politics of Homosexuality," *National Review* (November 1954).

"The Third Earl Versus the Thirty Million," review of *Bertrand Russell: A Political Life* by Alan Ryan, *National Review* (October 14, 1988): 46.

"Pisher's Progress," review of *The Examined Life* by Robert Nozick, *National Review* (December 31, 1989): 38–39.

"The Moral Passion of Mrs. Thatcher," *National Review* (May 1989).

"Not Quite Forever," review of *Reflections on the Revolution in Europe* by Ralph Dahrendorf, *National Review* (October 1990).

"The Goddess that Failed: Like Other Ideologies, Feminism Asks Not, What Is Right? But, What's In It for Me?" *National Review* (November 1991).

"Conservatism and the Future?" review of *The Anatomy of Thatcherism* by Shirley Letwin, *National Review* 45 (May 10, 1993): 46.

"The Statist Temptation," review of *Democracy Against Itself* by Jean Francois Revel, *National Review* (March 7, 1994): 67.

"Does National Sovereignty Have a Future?" *National Review* (December 1996).

"The Anti-Rationalist," review of *Rationalism in Politics and Other Essays* by Michael Oakeshott, *National Review* (December 19, 2005).

"Leading with Luck: Thatcher Had Virtue and Good Fortune," *National Review* (May 2013).

New Criterion

"How Civilizations Fall," *New Criterion* (April 2001).

"The Survival of Culture, I: The New Epicureans," *New Criterion* (September 2001).

"Hayek's Prophetic Scepticism," *New Criterion* (May 2002).

"Laughing Matters," review of *The Mirth of Nations* by Christie Davis, *New Criterion* (March 2003).

"'Christophobia' and the West," *New Criterion* (June 2003).

"Fundamentalism Isn't the Problem," *New Criterion* (June 2004).

"Journalism: Power Without Responsibility," *New Criterion* (February 2005).

"Power and Responsibility," *New Criterion* (February 2005).

"Notebook: Maurice Cowling 1926–2005," *New Criterion* (November 2005).

"Democracy and Political Naivety," *New Criterion* (March 2006).

"Seduction and Politics in '"Christophobia" and the West,'" *New Criterion* (November 2006).

"A Triumvirate for Our Time," review of *The President, the Pope and the Prime Minister: Three Who Changed the World* by John O'Sullivan, *New Criterion* (February 2007).

"Conservatism & the Morality of Impulse," *New Criterion* (January 2008).

"Marriage in Our Time," *New Criterion* (June 2009).

"Morals & the Servile Mind," *New Criterion* (June 2010).

"A Dislocated Society?" review of *The New Few* by Ferdinand Mount, *New Criterion* (September 2012).

"A March of Folly," *New Criterion* (October 2012).

"A Grand Old Party," review of *The Conservatives* by Robin Harris, *New Criterion* (March 2012).

"Swimming with 'Leviathan,'" *New Criterion* (March 2013).

Philosophy

Review of *The Nature and Limits of Political Science* and *Mill and Liberalism* by
Maurice Cowling, *Philosophy* 39, no. 150 (October 1964).
Review of *Social Ends and Political Means* by Ted Honderich, *Philosophy* 52,
no. 200 (April 1977).
"Method in Intellectual History," *Philosophy* 56, no. 218 (October 1981).

Policy

"Universal Reason Covers All: Hiram Caton's *The Politics of Progress*," *Policy*
(Spring 1991): 34.
"Can Individualism Survive in a Collectivist Age? Kenneth Minogue Speaks to
Andrew Norton," *Policy* (Summer 1995): 52.
Review of *The Minimal Monarchy and Why It Still Makes Sense for Australia* by
Tony Abbott, *Policy* (Summer 1995).

Policy Review

"The Myth of Social Conditioning," *Policy Review* (Fall 1981).
"Marxism: The Apologetics of Power," *Policy Review* (Winter 1981).
"Fellow Travellers Tails," review of *Political Pilgrims: Travels of Western Intellec-
tuals to Soviet Union, China and Cuba* by Paul Hollander, *Policy Review* (1982).
"Madness and Guilt," *Policy Review* 25 (Summer 1983): 12–21.

Political Studies

"The Language of Comparative Politics," *Political Studies* (October 1958).
"Power in Politics," *Political Studies* (October 1959).
"Epiphenomenalism in Politics: The Quest for Political Reality," *Political Studies*
(December 1972).
"Recent Discussions from Machiavelli to Althusser," *Political Studies* (March 1975).
"A Memoir: Michael Oakeshott 1901–1990," *Political Studies* 2, no. 39 (June 1991).
"Obituary: Shirley Letwin (1924–93)," *Political Studies* 4, no. 41 (1993): 11–17.

Quadrant

"Oakeshott and the Idea of Freedom," *Quadrant* (October 1975).
"A Tragic Pragmatism," review of *Pragmatism and the Tragic Sense of Life* by
Sidney Hook, *Quadrant* (May 1976).
"The Road to Damascus: An Intellectual History of the Left in Australia,"
Quadrant (April 1978).
"A Simple History," *Quadrant* (April 1982).
"Underemployed Titans," *Quadrant* (May 1982).
"Australia 2000," *Quadrant* (October 1982).
"The Roots of Modern Dogmatism," *Quadrant* (June 1983).
"The Thatcher Reign and the Westminster System," *Quadrant* (November 1987).
"Not Guilty! The Moral Premises of Modern British Conservatism," *Quadrant*
(December 1988).

"What Has Happened to Robert Nozick?" *Quadrant* (May 1990).
"The Great Thatcher Mystery," *Quadrant* (February 1991).
"Aborigines and Australian Apologetics," *Quadrant* (September 1998).
"Does Australia Have an Identity Problem?" *Quadrant* (November 2003).
"The Intellectual Left's Treason of the Heart," *Quadrant* (September 2011).

Spectator

"A Christian Hobbes," review of *The Divine Politics of Thomas Hobbes* by F.C.
    Hood, *Spectator* (April 1964).
"The Collection Cult," review of *Sociological Theory and Philosophical Analysis* by
    Dorothy Emmet and Alasdair MacIntyre, *Spectator* (October 1970).
"Guide to Galbraith," review of *A Contemporary Guide to Economics, Peace and
    Laughter* by Kenneth Galbraith, *Spectator* (November 1971).
"Grasping Nettles," review of *Imagination and Precision in the Social Science*, ed.
    T.J. Nossiter, A.H. Hanson, and Stein Rokkan, *Spectator* (July 1972).
"Erotics in Wonderland," review of *The Party of Eros Spectator* by Richard King,
    Spectator (October 1972).
"Politics Without Pain," review of *Political Theory and Practice* by Bernard Crick,
    Spectator (December 1972).
"Hard Shell and Soft Head," review of *Reflections in the Causes of Human Misery*
    by Barrington Moore, *Spectator* (March 1973).
"Bags of Tricks," review of *Nationalism and the International System* by F.H. Hin-
    sley, *Spectator* (April 1973).
"Philosophy and Fashion," review of *Tools for Conviviality* by Ivan Illich, *Specta-
    tor* (October 1973).
"Political Science," review of *The Limits of Human Nature* by Jonathan Benthall,
    Spectator (December 1973).
"Who Are the Masters Now?" *Spectator* (February 1974).
"Wrong Terms," review of *Karl Marx's Philosophy of Man* by John Plamenatz,
    Spectator (December 1975).

Standpoint

"To Hell With Niceness: The Spread of 'Political Compassion' Has Led to the
    Breakdown of Family and School Discipline. The Results Have Been Cata-
    strophic," *Standpoint* (March 2009).
"Slaves of the Bonus Culture: The Demise of the Professions Is Having a Profound
    Impact, Starting with the Disappearance of Integrity in Public Life," *Stand-
    point* (July/August 2009).
"The Rise of Rights and the Fall of Man: Healthy Societies Have an Inbuilt Sense
    of How Things Are and How They Ought to Be, But We Have Abandoned
    Common Sense, Integrity and Virtue," *Standpoint* (May 2011).
"Why Shouldn't I Cheat, Everyone Else Does?" *Standpoint* (March 2012).

Wall Street Journal

"American Virtue Gives Root to Vice," review of *The Present Age: Progress and Anarchy in Modern America* by Robert Nisbett, *Wall Street Journal* (August 1, 1988).

"Hollywood vs. Britannia: In Their Search for Political Correctness, Hollywood Producers Have Found Their Target: Englishmen," *Wall Street Journal* (November 2000).

"A Guide to Right-Thinking," review of *American Conservatism: An Encyclopedia*, ed. Burce Frohnen, Jeremy Beer, and Jeffrey O. Nelson, *Wall Street Journal* (August 12, 2006).

"Modern Love," review of *The Paradox of Love* by Pascal Bruckner, *Wall Street Journal* (March 10, 2012).

"When the Lamps Went On," review of "The Enlightenment" by Anthony Pagden, *Wall Street Journal* (June 8, 2013).

Other Publications

"Can Politics Survive the Twenty-first Century?" academic chapter (date/publisher unknown).

"Civil Identity and the Anglosphere in Australia" (Appendix II) (date/publisher unknown).

"Concrete Individualism and the Classical Model: A Tension in Modern Politics," academic chapter (date/publisher unknown).

"Creeping Regulation: Smoking and the Citizen" (date/publisher unknown).

"Der Konflikt Zwischen Ideal und Interesse," *Merkur: Deutsche Zeitschrift für Europäisches Denken* (Stuttgart: Klett-Cotta, n.d.).

"Gellner's Theory of Nationalism: A Critical Assessment" (date/publisher unknown).

"Health and Justice (1)," in *Medicine and Humanity* (date/publisher unknown).

"Keeping Out the New Barbarians"; comment piece (date/publisher unknown).

"La teoria politica del successo economico," academic chapter (date/publisher unknown).

"The Lust for News—Our Greatest Sin"; comment piece possibly in *The Express* (date unknown).

"National Sovereignty versus Internationalism: The Importance of Repealability" (Appendix III) (date/publisher unknown).

"Socialism Is a Type of Perpetual Virgin," Socialists Answer the New Right [seminar], in *An Alliance for Workers Liberty* [pamphlet] (n.d.), pp. 6–10.

"The British Left: Innocent Part of the Guilty Whole," *Twentieth Century* 167, no. 998 (April 1960).

Review of *The Life and Opinions of Thomas Ernest Hulme* by Alan R. Jones, *London Magazine* 7, no. 10 (October 1960): 67.

"De Gaulle Pense Donc Je Suis," *Journal of the Franco-British Society* (Spring 1964).

"How Has Liberalism Affected Religion?" *Aryan Path* 36, no. 12 (December 1965): 535.

"Nationalism: The Poverty of a Concept," *European Journal of Sociology* 8, no. 2 (1967): 332–344.

Review of F.S. McNeilly's "The Anatomy of Leviathan" (Macmillan, 1968).

"How Strong a Force?" *Insight 3* (Autumn 1968).

Review of *The Idea of Progress* by Sidney Pollard, *History* 54, no. 182 (October 1969).

"The Modern State," a review of *The Origins of the Modern European State* by J.H. Shennan, *European Studies Review* 5, no. 2 (April 1975).

"The Department of Government," *LSE: The Magazine of the London School of Economics and Political Science* 49 (June 1975): 1–2.

Review of *The Aryan Myth: A History of Racist and Nationalist Ideas in Europe* by Leon Poliakov (1975).

"Humanist Democracy: The Political Thought of C.B. Macpherson," *Canadian Journal of Political Science* (September 1976) (a revised paper from a 1975 conference in Edmonton, Alberta).

"The Political Climate for Universities," *International Council on the Future of the University* 4, no. 1 (November 1977).

"Abstractions and Political Theory," *Canadian Journal of Political and Social Theory* 3, no. 2 (Spring/Summer 1979).

"The Metaphors of Politics," *New Lugano Review* 1 (1979).

"Tendencies to Transformation in the Modern European State," *Survey: A Journal in East and West Studies* 25, no. 4 (Autumn 1980).

"Bureaucracy," review of *Bureaucracy: The Career of a Concept*, ed. Eugene Kamenka and Martin Krygier, *ASLP Bulletin* (1980).

"Philosophy and the State in France: The Renaissance to the Enlightenment (Book Review)," *American Political Science Review* 75, no. 2 (1981): 479–480.

"Choice, Consciousness and Ideological Language," in *Metamedicine: An International Journal for Philosophy and Methodology of Medicine* 3, no. 3 (October 1982): 351–367.

"Two Worlds of Liberalism: Religion and Politics in Hobbes, Locke and Mill (Book Review)," *Journal of Modern History* 55, no. 2 (1983): 303–304.

"The Culture of the Gentleman," review of *The Gentleman in Trollope: Individuality and Moral Conduct* by Shirley Letwin, *Public Interest* 71 (Spring 1983).

"UNCTAD and the North-South Dialogue," Centre for Independent Studies Occasional Papers 9 (1984).

"Hegel Contra Sociology (Book Review)," *British Journal of Sociology* 36, no. 3 (1985): 477–478.

"Freedom as a Skill," in *Culture and Politics*, European University Institute Series C, *Political and Social Sciences* 12 (1988).

"The Life and Ideas of Niccolo Machiavelli," *Social Studies Review* (May 1988).

"The Case for Freedom of Speech," in *Racism and Freedom of Speech on the Campus* (The Commission for Racial Equality, June 1988), 12–19.

"Can Radicalism Survive Michael Foucault?" Review of *Foucault: A Critical Reader*, ed. David Couzens Hoy, and *Michel Foucault* by Mark Cousins and

Arthur Hussain, *Critical Review: A Journal of Books and Ideas* 3, no. 1 (Winter 1988): 138–155.

"Transcendence and the Ideological Significance of the Idea of God," *Dialogue and Alliance: A Journal of the International Religious Foundation Inc.* 1, no. 4 (Winter 1988): 74–83.

"The Egalitarian Conceit: False and True Equalities," spring address, Centre for Policy Studies (1989).

Review of David Berman's *A History of Atheism in Britain: From Hobbes to Russell*, International Hobbes Association newsletter (1989).

"Are Rights Under Threat in Britain?" (with Richard Holme), *Contemporary Record* 3, no. 1 (1989): 26–28.

"Political Theory versus the Philistines," *PSA News* (February 1989).

"From Precision to Peach; Hobbes and Political Language," *Hobbes Studies* 3, no. 1 (1990): 75–88.

"Is National Sovereignty a Big Bad Wolf," in *Is National Sovereignty a Big Bad Wolf* (Bruges Group Press, 1990), 19–25.

"Comments on 'The European Community in Change: Exit, Voice and Loyalty'" by J.H.H. Weiler, *Irish Studies in International Affairs* 3, no. 2 (January 1990): 27–31.

"Can Scholarship Survive the Scholars?" *Academic Questions* 4, no. 4 (Fall 1991): 62.

"Thinking Strategically about Reform," *IPA Review* 45, no. 1 (1992).

"The European Community: A New Political Paradigm?" *A PRI Breakfast Blurb Transcript, The Pacific Research Institute* (September 1992).

"Remarks on the Psychopathology of Euro-philia," in *The Erosion of Democracy: Bruges Group Occasional Paper No. 14* (Bruges Group Press, 1993), 11–17.

"The Constitutional Mania," *Policy Studies* 134 (1993).

"Anti-Americanism: Critiques at Home and Abroad, 1965–1990 (Book Review)," *International History Review* 15, no. 4 (November 1993): 851–852.

"Is the Academic World Essentially Critical?" *Australian Journal of Politics and History* 40 (1994).

"Does Popper Explain Historical Explanation?" *Royal Institute of Philosophy Supplement* 39 (1995): 225–240.

"LSE and the New Right," *LSE Centenary Review* (1995): 22–23.

"Hayek and Conservatism: Beatrice and Benedict?" in *Ideas About Freedom: A Discussion*, CIS Occasional Papers, Centre for Independent Studies (National Library of Australia, April 1996), 1–19.

"Citizenship and Monarchy: A Hidden Fault Line in Our Civilization," *The Institute of United States Studies, University of London* (1998).

"A View from Academe," *Middle Eastern Studies* 33, no. 5 (1998): 31–34.

"The Waitangi Process Cannot Go On For Ever," comment piece handed in March 31, 1998.

"Democracy as a Telos," *Social Philosophy and Policy* 17, no. 1 (2000): 203–224.

Review of Stephen May's *Language and Minority Rights: Ethnicity, Nationalism* and the Politics of Language, *Journal of Multilingual and Multicultural Development* 22 (2001).

"Oakeshott the Character," presidential address at Michael Oakeshott Association Inaugural Conference (2001).

"Some Doubts About Democracy: How the Modern State Is Evolving," in *Management Economics and Politics: Challenges, Opportunities and Discipline Perspectives in the 21st Century* (2002), 141–154 [translated into Turkish].

Review of *Language and Minority Rights: Ethnicity, Nationalism and the Politics of Language* by Stephen May, *Journal of Multilingual and Multicultural Development* 23, no. 4 (2002): 333.

"Understanding Nationalism" (vs. Brendon O'Leary), *New Left Review* 23 (September–October 2003): 95.

A Special Pamphlet: "Religion Manners and Morals in the US and Great Britain," Conference, Greenwich, CT (2004).

"Education and the Free Society," paper given at the conference "International Perspectives," organized by the Liberales Institut (*Fredrich Neumann-Stiftung, Potsdam,* September 2005).

"Rationalism Revisited," *Society* 43, no. 2 (2006): 81–87.

"Thatcher," *English Historical Review* 121, no. 494 (2006): 1569–1570.

"Education and the Free Society," *Critique and Humanism Journal* (сп. Критика и хуманизъм) 26 (2008): 199–206.

"Are the British a Servile People? Idealism and the EU," *Bruges Group Occasional Paper* (2008).

"Get Happy: The Secret to Happiness Is . . . Still Secret," *American Interest* 3, no. 6 (July/August 2008): 108–114.

"Portraits and the Reconstruction of Past Times," in *The Boston, Melbourne, Oxford, Vancouver, Conversazioni on Culture and Society* (2009).

"Is There Such a Thing as Wisdom? If So, Can It Be Taught?" (symposium presentation), *In Character: A Journal of Everyday Virtues* 5, no. 2 (2009): 59–75.

"The Elusive Michael Oakeshott," *American Conservative* 8, no. 13 (October 2009): 24–27.

"Individualism and Its Contemporary Fate," *Independent Review: A Journal of Political Economy* 17, no. 2 (Fall 2012): 257–269.

"Life and Soul of the Party," review of *Edmund Burke: Philosopher, Politician, Prophet* by Jesse Norman, *Literary Review* (May 2013): 5.

Transcripts

Interview with Michael Oakeshott (1988).

"Manners and Morals in Democracy," Lecture 1026 given to the *Heritage Foundation* (June 2007).

INDEX

Abelard, Peter, 145
abortion, 189–190
academics, as Democrats, 259
academic world: intellectual and, xii–xiii; role of, 148; universities and, xiii. *See also* teachers
action: apathy and, 47–48; autonomy of right, 227; free citizens and fully human, 109; freedom and, 228, 242; liberalism without, 44–45; original sin and forbidden courses of, 210; political, 178, 296, 303; seduction and course of, 200; selfishness and, 69n3; speculation and, 86; with thermodynamics, second law of, 5; Third World and political, 178
advertising, 92; commercial, 12; influence of, 16, 219; role of, 70, 179
Africa, 192, 258
After Virtue: A Study in Moral Theory (MacIntyre), 52–53
AIDS, 160, 189
Alexander the Great, 73–74
alternative reality, ideology with, xiv
altruism, self-interested society and, 297–300

ambivalence, individualism with modernity and, 271–275
ancien régime: Christianity as, 249, 250, 251; rights and overthrowing, 248–253; Rousseau and, 72
Ancient Law (Maine), 229
Anderson, John, 78, 79, 139
anxiety: in intellectual world, 10–11; modernity and, 79; with trend persuasion, 18
apathy: action and, 47–48; indoctrination and, 38; politics and, 46; as vice, 13
Areopagitica (Milton), 51
aristocracy: bourgeoisie and, 4; past and, 3. *See also* elite
Aristotle, 65, 72, 103–104, 105, 181; on courage and freedom, 107; on happiness, 69n1; influence of, 142; natural slave and, 107, 240
armed services. *See* military
Attaturk, Kemal, 177
Augustine, Saint, 174, 252
Augustus (Roman emperor), 247
Austen, Jane, 235
Australia, vii, 138, 260, 267; federal-